D0151056

Enterprise and Trade in Victorian Britain

Enterprise and Trade in Victorian Britain

Essays in Historical Economics

Donald N. McCloskey

Professor of Economics and of History, University of Iowa

London
GEORGE ALLEN & UNWIN
Boston Sydney

First published in 1981

GEORGE ALLEN & UNWIN LTD
40 Museum Street, London WC1A 1LU

British Library Cataloguing in Publication Data

McCloskey, Donald Nansen
Enterprise and trade in Victorian Britain.
1. Great Britain – Economic conditions – 19th century
I. Title
330.9'41'081 HC255 80-41654

ISBN 0-04-942170-0
ISBN 0-04-942171-9 Pbk

Cover illustration: Gustav Doré, *Steamers leaving Westminster Stairs* (courtesy of the Mansell Collection).

Set in 10 on 11 point Plantin by Typesetters (Birmingham) Ltd
and printed in Great Britain
by Billing and Sons Ltd, Guildford, London and Worcester

Contents

To my mother, Helen Stueland McCloskey,
a gemlike flame

Foreword

Like its author, any essay by McCloskey speaks forcefully for itself. And certainly the essays collected in this volume are sufficiently explicit in their methodological awareness not to need any elaborate exegesis. At the same time, however, since much of what follows was written in the heat of the day and at times in the heat of the battle, it may not be entirely redundant to offer a slightly more distanced introductory viewpoint. The overtones of scholarly polemics which can be detected in the following pages are based partly on the fact that proponents of the 'new economic history' have felt the need to proselytize, and partly on the fact that controversy *within* the field has been particularly violent as its members strive with fierce enthusiasm to satisfy two sets of scholarly standards – those of economic theory and of historical evidence. Moreover, in addition to its concern with fundamental questions of method, standpoint and theoretical assumptions, the 'cliometric' approach to the economic past has been distinguished by a choice of peculiarly controversial topics: the grand themes of economic evolution, innovation and enterprise, technology and welfare, the material implications of social institutions, and the national impact of international events.

McCloskey has made major contributions to these debates in a variety of fields, but the essays in this book reflect his critical role in only one area of discussion (albeit perhaps the most important): the controversies concerning Britain's economic performance between the mid-nineteenth century and the First World War.[1] Their appearance in this form has the advantage of enabling the reader to discover more easily the links between them and the continuity of perspective and argument which informs them. It will be seen that they illustrate a strong and distinctive view on the important elements in Britain's growth and economic maturity. And that view gets as near to a subjective approval as any scholar can allow himself to express. For its overriding theme is that Britain's own resources were consistently more productive, more resilient and more successful than is normally assumed. And if the economy's achievement was considerable, the influence on it of 'exogenous' factors (trade, international competition, policy) were much less significant than is normally supposed. In this sense, the book's publication has a powerful timeliness. For, even though its substantive themes are set firmly in British economic history before 1914, its concern with growth and productivity, enterprise and structural change, performance and disappointment, naturally bridges the years to our own preoccupations in the 1980s.

I

Before examining the explicit themes of the essays, however, it may be useful to indicate the academic framework from which they emerged. What we still think of as the 'new economic history' first saw the light some twenty-five years ago with the work of Conrad and Meyer on the nature of theoretical and statistical argument in history and on the profitability of American slavery.[2] Obviously, there were other budding 'new economic historians' working in other fields in the 1950s – notably those at Purdue, where a resoundingly successful annual seminar was held from December 1960.[3] And the pioneering work was in any case somewhat overshadowed by Robert Fogel's work – which not only debunked the popular conception of the economic importance of the railways in nineteenth-century America, but did so by that most provocative of devices, the 'counterfactual' – exploring a hypothetical late nineteenth-century America *without* railways.[4] Nevertheless, among the new economic historians themselves the critical nature of the Conrad–Meyer contribution to the field has always been recognized. Moreover, it embodied the two principal characteristics of the new approach: a concern with a very important empirical issue (the historical treatment of the economics of slavery has become virtually an academic discipline in its own right) and its defence of the use of economic theory and statistical analysis in tackling historical problems. The combination of ambitious questions, provocative methods and startling answers still seems, to other sorts of historians, the hallmark of the genre.

Thus, as McCloskey reminds us in Chapter 1, the origins of the new economic history were firmly American. From the standpoint of British historiography what was striking about the new school of economic history was not so much the reliance on quantitative data and theoretical concepts; rather, it was the rigorous, if critical, use of statistical and theoretical *argumentation*. Historians no longer merely transposed a few economic ideas to a historical setting; they defined and tested economic models. The compilation of quantitative tables for simple scanning was now to be augmented by complex statistical manipulation. Models and concepts were made ruthlessly explicit in an attempt to avoid indeterminate generalisations or exclusively intuitive modes of explanation. This last has been possibly the most important methodological feature of the new economic history: *all* historical explanation involves a set of assumptions about 'how things work'; the new school made those assumptions explicit so as to expose and examine the phenomena and relationships to be assessed or measured. Once this is done, historians have to be much more precise about the quantitative or analytical criteria in terms of which institutions or causal links are said to be 'significant'. It is therefore no accident that much of the new economic history is concerned to justify or disprove the importance of a particular 'factor' (exports, free trade, overseas investment, entrepreneurship – to take a few of McCloskey's favourites) in the process of economic change.

Indeed, the use of explicit models of economic relationships has naturally helped shape the subject matter of the new economic history, which lends itself more to the analysis of trends and basic causal links than to varied narrative. As a result, the contributions of its practitioners focus on particular problems or themes – productivity, growth, income distribution – rather than the simultaneous consideration of the varied relationship between social and economic institutions. At the same time, however, the techniques of the new economic history do not lend themselves more to the history of one country than another. Admittedly, there has been a vast preponderance of work on the economic history of the United States. But that is a function more of the institutional location of economic history in American universities than of the distinctive nature of America's economic past. Thus, professionally speaking, economic history in the United States has always been more closely identified with economics, and the research training of economic historians therefore involves a much more systematic acquaintance with statistical and theoretical analysis. There is, therefore, a much easier and more assured dialogue between economics and economic history than is the case in Britain.

Nevertheless, even though there is a sense in which the application of the new economic history to British subject matter has been handicapped, that handicap is being rapidly overcome – partly through the efforts of British economic historians and partly with the help of scholars like McCloskey himself, trained in other academic settings. Many of the British topics consequently explored by economic historians have had their parallels or analogues in work done on the other side of the Atlantic. This applies, for example, to systematic assessments of the course and pattern of economic growth, studies of the economic role of the railways, the impact of particular innovations such as the steam engine, the extent and determinants of productivity change in individual industries, or the assessment of a particular institution (for example, open-field farming) as an example of rational economic behaviour.[5] At the same time, however, British economic history has its own distinctive problem areas, which lend themselves to the newer approaches. Among these are questions relating to the origins of the industrial revolution or its effects upon living standards.[6] However, perhaps the central controversial issue of modern British economic history concerns the performance of the economy in the late nineteenth and early twentieth centuries. And it is this issue, in its various forms, which comprises the main subject matter of the essays collected in this book.

II

The question posed by McCloskey in Chapter 5 – did Victorian Britain fail? – dominates the economic historiography of the late nineteenth century. Yet 'failure', like 'success' has a special, and mutable, meaning in this sort of context. Indeed, whether the criteria of performance are to be found in earlier periods, later periods, other countries' achievements, or some hypothetical contemporary potential; whether success and failure are to be indicated in terms of growth rates or economic structures or the balance of economic activity; and whether attention is to be focused on the economy as a whole or on specific sectors within it, and if so which ones – all these issues are almost as much the subject of controversy as are the more substantive questions concerning the outcomes of economic activity.

In fact, the economic character of the forty years before the First World War have always had an ambiguous reputation. The central problem perhaps stems from the fact – the implications of which are widely disputed – that British manufacturing industry began to lose its industrial supremacy during the last quarter of the nineteenth century. To some contemporaries and observers this was no cause for anxiety; it reflected merely a relative shift, an inevitable concomitant of world economic change, just as Britain's economic maturity led inevitably to new patterns in the use of resources and a new role in the international economy. To others, it reflected an avoidable decline, a fall from an earlier pinnacle of achievement, while the structural changes which accompanied it were neither sufficiently radical nor sufficiently directed towards realistic national needs to provide the basis for future prosperity.

The emergence of industrial competition, or at least rivalry, most of all from the United States and Germany from the early 1870s, was accompanied by a deceleration in the rate of growth of exports, a faltering and down-turn in prices and profit margins, and the advent of widespread and prolonged (albeit not universal) agricultural depression. And it was this combination of circumstances which gave these years the unenviable reputation of being a 'Great Depression'. That particular concept was effectively undermined by later scholars[7] – and, indeed, given the fact that national income and living standards continued to grow, and that Britain's international position as a capital market and supplier of financial and commercial services boomed, it is difficult to see why the last years of the century got their original reputation in the first case.

Nevertheless, while the idea that the later decades of Victoria's reign were characterized by a prolonged depression in any normal sense of the word has long since been abandoned, alternative formulations of the pessimistic view swiftly replaced it. Broadly speaking, these have assumed two forms: on the one hand, a sense that in some rather general way British manufacturers and salesmen were not as enterprising and British industry not as technically and organisationally progressive as they might have been;[8] on the other, the hypothesis that at some point in the late nineteenth century there was a major discontinuity or 'climacteric' in the trend of output, and particularly of productivity, which can conceivably be explained in terms of the exhaustion of the potential of available technology or in deep-rooted problems of structural imbalance.[9] Analogous to these views, and sometimes linking them, are arguments to the effect that Britain's economic performance could have been improved (and in the long run critically improved) had less capital been invested overseas and more at home, had the structure of the British economy been 'modernised' more effectively, had exports been more concentrated in different products and directed more towards different markets.

These various gloomy interpretations of Britain's economic performance in the late nineteenth century have not, of course, gone unchallenged.[10] McCloskey's own contribution to the debate from the standpoint of the new economic history is largely reflected in the following pages, although as Part One suggests, the use of economic theory, explicit models and systematic argument does not necessarily lead to unanimity in such matters. Nevertheless, and precisely because of the methodology employed by the new economic history, the discussion of the presumed climacteric or deceleration of the British economy is now carried on in much more precise terms and its central issues identified with some confidence, even though the answers are not equally obvious.

The first, and oldest, question relates to the definition of the problem to be tackled: assuming (what is not the case) that comprehensive and adequate statistics were available, what *was* the performance of the economy in the period? Are we to be concerned with the rate of growth of total income or of manufacturing output? Above all, by what standards are we to assess 'failure' or 'success'?

There is, of course, no definitive set of answers to such questions since such answers would depend, in their turn, on the (debatable) importance to be attributed to manufacturing industry as against other sectors of the economy, to the survival of a nineteenth-century economic structure into the twentieth, and to the attainment of a maximum feasible growth rate in an arbitrarily circumscribed period. Nevertheless, it is now fairly clear that there was no very abrupt change in the trend of growth in the late nineteenth century, that there *was* something of a discontinuity in productivity with the opening of the twentieth century and that the critical issue of performance relates to the potential of the British economy itself: with the resources, skills and knowledge at its disposal could it have attained a faster growth rate and a sounder basis for future activity within an evolving world economy?

This is, indeed, the ultimate issue in much of the debate to which the following pages contribute. But since, expressed in this way, the question has an excessive generality, economic historians have necessarily isolated (that is, made explicit) the considerations most relevant to it. They concern, for example, the extent to which British productivity was lower than it might have been, or grew more slowly than it might have done; the 'rationality' of British entrepreneurs measured in terms of their use or neglect of the technology most appropriate to their circumstances; the consequences for Britain's economic development of the huge amount of capital invested overseas in this period; the possibility that the deceleration in the rate of growth of exports (whether through faults of salesmanship or production or choice of product) might have retarded the expansion of the economy; and the implications for relative economic performance of the structure of the British economy.

Each of these questions is touched on by McCloskey in the essays here collected together. Methodologically, his approach is characterized by the use of fairly straightforward economic models and, even though Chapter 1 is 'the first essay on cliometric method not to discuss counterfactuals', by a determined reliance on counterfactuals. By discussing 'alternative scenarios' – different patterns of trade, investment, output and entrepreneurial decisions – he sheds light on the economic performance that actually took place and on those arguments which express dissatisfaction with the achievement of the economy by assuming it could have been greatly improved by alternative decisions. Two of these essays also involve substantial comment on the international context of the British economy in the middle decades of the century, when the signs of prosperity and advance are more obvious, albeit not invariably unambiguous.[11] And here McCloskey, with no less provocation, challenges two of the most commonly accepted views (that export growth and free trade were vital components of British economic growth).

What emerges is a distinctive, important and controversial view of the performance of the British economy, and in particular of British manufacturing industry, at its meridian, launched in a far more independent manner, and sustained into its late Victorian and even Edwardian phase showing far fewer of the symptoms of impending decay, than most other economic historians have discovered in the decades before 1914. To McCloskey the nineteenth-century economy served its purpose well. No doubt, as some other commentators have observed, this line of argument is related to the neoclassical assumptions about market forces and the workings of an economy with which McCloskey begins his analysis. But both the logic and the empirical work which then sustain his argument demand (and often stimulate) direct responses rather than conceptual word play. Indeed, it is doubtful if there will ever again be a conventional wisdom concerning Britain's industrial maturity. But, whatever the nature of controversy concerning the economy's long-run performance, McCloskey's contribution will represent a force to be reckoned with.

BARRY SUPPLE

Nuffield College
Oxford

NOTES

1 Even in this context they should be supplemented by his extended case-study of the iron and steel industry: *Economic Maturity and Entrepreneurial Decline: British Iron and Steel, 1870–1913* (Cambridge, Mass., 1973).

2 See the two papers, first given publicly in September 1957 and reprinted as Chapters 1 ('Economic theory, statistical inference, and economic history') and 3 ('The economics of slavery in the antebellum South') in Alfred H. Conrad and John R. Meyer, *The Economics of Slavery and Other Studies in Econometric History* (Chicago, 1964). In their preface Conrad and Meyer quite properly draw attention to the critical role played by Professor Gerschenkron's seminar at Harvard in stimulating their work. The comment could be generalised to a very wide range of work in the new economic history – including that of Don McCloskey.

3 See *Purdue Faculty Papers in Economic History, 1956–1966* (Homewood, Ill., 1967).

4 See Robert W. Fogel 'A quantitative approach to the study of railroads in American economic growth', *Journal of Economic History*, XXII (1962); and idem, *Railroads and American Economic Growth: Essays in Econometric History* (Baltimore, Md., 1964).

5 See, for example, Donald N. McCloskey (ed.), *Essays on a Mature Economy: Britain after 1840* (1971); G. R. Hawke, *Railways and Economic Growth in England and Wales, 1840–1870* (Oxford, 1970); G. N. von Tunzelmann, *Steam Power and British Industrialization to 1860* (Oxford, 1978); Roderick Floud, *The British Machine Tool Industry, 1850–1914* (Cambridge, 1976); D. N. McCloskey, 'New perspectives on the old Poor Law', *Explorations in Economic History*, 2nd ser., XI (1973) and 'English open fields as behaviour towards risk', *Research in Economic History*, I (1976).

6 See N. F. R. Crafts, 'Industrial revolution in England and France: some thoughts on the question, "Why was England first?" ' *Economic History Review*, 2nd ser., XXX (1977), and discussion by W. W. Rostow and Crafts, in ibid., XXXI (1978); G. N. von Tunzelmann, 'Trends in real wages, 1750–1850, revisited', *Economic History Review*, 2nd ser., XXXII (1979).

7 H. L. Beales, 'The Great Depression in industry and trade', *Economic History Review*, V (1934); S. B. Saul, *The Myth of the Great Depression* (1969).

8 For example: D. H. Aldcroft, 'The entrepreneur and the British economy, 1870–1914', *Economic History Review*, 2nd ser., XVII (1964), and 'Technical progress and British enterprise, 1875–1914', *Business History*, VIII (London, 1966).

9 See E. H. Phelps Brown and S. J. Handfield-Jones, 'The climacteric of the 1890s: a study in the expanding economy', *Oxford Economic Papers* (1952); D. J. Coppock, 'The climacteric of the 1890s: a critical note', *Manchester School*, XXIV (1956) and 'The causes of the Great Depression, 1873–1896', *Manchester School*, XXIX (1961); the controversy between D. J. Coppock and A. E. Musson in *Economic History Review*, 2nd ser., XV (1963) and XVII (1964).

10 See the contributions of Professor Musson (note 9) and C. Wilson, 'Economy and society in late Victorian Britain', *Economic History Review*, 2nd ser., XVIII (1965).

11 See R. A. Church, *The Great Victorian Boom, 1850–1873* (London, 1975).

Preface

An eminent historian who published recently a *Selbstfestschrift* entitled *On Historians* admitted with disarming candor in the preface that the only unity was that all the pieces republished were about males writing in prose. The unity of the present collection is that all the pieces are about subjects with which I was concerned during the early 1970s, namely, the application of economics to history, particularly British history of the nineteenth century, and most particularly the three sections into which the collection is divided. The first section, on The Method of Historical Economics, expatiates on the theme of how very promising an intellectual movement it is that brings economic standards of logic to history and historical standards of fact to economics. The second, on Enterprise in Late Victorian Britain, begins to fulfill the promise, showing how economic thinking casts doubt on the common premise that late Victorian businessmen lost the vigor of their fathers. The third, on Britain in the World Economy, 1846–1913, fulfills it more, showing how historical thinking casts doubt on the common premise that foreign affairs dominate a nation's growth. The methodological theme is how important for finding the truth of the past or the present is the reunification of history and economics. The substantive theme is that Britain's only failing was its early success. Britain's domination of manufacturing trade in the 1840s (later given up), its technological leadership in the 1850s (later given up), its special position in world financial affairs in the 1860s (later given up), its leading role in the migration of men and capital in the 1870s (later given up) were all transitory, but naturally so. None was crucial to British prosperity. What made Britain rich then as now was not domination of others abroad but education, investment and peace at home.

The book, I say, represents my interests in the early 1970s, or rather the interests with which I was deluged by the flood of new ideas at the University of Chicago then: counterfactuals, the explanation of productivity change, the measurement of waste and the monetary approach to the balance of payments. The common element is a belief in the power of simple – some would say simple-minded – economics. 'Cliometrics' itself ('Clio', the muse of history, with 'metric', measurement) has consisted largely of simple economics applied to big historical questions. But the simplicity is a convenience arising from the absence of even the simplest economic arguments beforehand, not an epistemological principle. Be assured: most of the Chicago school and the cliometric school, like most economists, do not subscribe to the precepts of positive economics or its opposite (negative economics?), but to what might be called rhetorical economics, that is, an examination of the grounds for reasonable assent whether or not they fit someone's legislation for scientific progress. The economic arguments in the essays here reprinted are not the only grounds for reasonable assent, merely new grounds.

The contexts and audiences of the essays were various. Chapter 1 was one of three invited essays on the achievements of the cliometric, Marxist and *Annales* 'schools' of economic history for the September 1977 meetings of the American Economic History Association, and appeared in the March 1978 issue of the *Journal of Economic History.* Chapter 2, an epistle to the barbarians, appeared in June 1976 in the *Journal of Economic Literature* (the methodological and reviewing organ of the American Economic Association). Chapter 3 is a summary published in 1971 by the American journal, *Explorations in Economic History*, by Lars Sandberg and me of the first wave of economic work on Victorian entrepreneurship. As elsewhere, I have not attempted to bring the citations up to date: thus Sandberg's book on cotton textiles (Ohio State University Press, 1974) appears as an 'unpublished book-length manuscript', as does my own on iron and steel (Harvard University Press, 1973); and subsequent work by among others Robert Allen, Steven Webb and William Lazonick commenting on ours does not appear at all. The historiography of this and other matters will become plain with the publication in 1981 of *A Complete Bibliography of Historical Economics to 1980.* Chapter 4 is reprinted from McCloskey (ed.), *Essays on a Mature Economy: Britain after 1840* (Methuen and Princeton University Press, 1971), the outgrowth of the first of three Anglo-American conferences in the early 1970s on the applications of economics to British economic history sponsored by the American National Science Foundation and the British Social Science Research Council. Chapter 5, published in the *Economic History Review* in December 1970, was the opening shot in a battle still going on, as can be seen from the replies to critics gathered up as Chapter 6. The reply to Derek Aldcroft, appearing in the May 1974 issue of the *Review*, is typical of my responses to the historical proponents of entrepreneurial failure (compare the reply to David Landes reprinted as an appendix to Chapter 4). The replies to William Kennedy (previously unpublished) and to Nicholas F. R. Crafts (appearing in the November 1979 issue of the *Review*) are typical of my responses to the economic proponents. I thank Nicholas Crafts and Derek Aldcroft for agreeing to permit the reprinting of their penetrating comments. Chapter 7, previously unpublished, was to be the introduction to a book on the subject of Britain's foreign economic relations in the nineteenth century, and here introduces the microeconomic and macroeconomic portions completed. The book was stillborn, as I turned to the economic history of property rights, especially studies of English open fields and enclosures. Portions of the chapter were included in my chapter with C. K. Harley in the new *Economic History of Britain, 1700 to the Present*, edited by Roderick Floud and me, Cambridge University Press, 1980. Chapter 8, drafted in 1971, was finally published after many strange passages and contrived corridors in *Explorations in Economic History* in the spring of 1980. Chapter 9 appeared in *Explorations* ten years earlier (Winter 1970–1), but the two are linked in method and theme. Chapter 10, written with my colleague J. R. Zecher, appeared in Jacob A. Frenkel and Harry G. Johnson (eds), *The Monetary Approach to the Balance of Payments* (Allen & Unwin, 1976).

I thank all these journals and publishers for permission to reprint the essays here. In the opening footnote to each I have acknowledged help, often embarrassingly ample. Addicted readers of acknowledgments – and who among you is not? – will note that Stanley Engerman takes the prize hands down, as he would in any collection of cliometrics of the decade past.

I use Barry Supple's rewriting of Wordsworth later, but it belongs here as well. He composed it for the first Anglo-American conference, in 1970 ('Can the New Economic History Become an Import Substitute?'), describing the first meeting of cliometricians at Purdue in 1960:

> Bliss was it in that dawn to be alive,
> But to be young [and numerate] was very Heaven!

Iowa City
1980

Part One

The Method of Historical Economics

1

The Achievements of the Cliometric School

The members of the Association must be sick to death of 'The Achievements of the Cliometric School'. The health of a field, it is said, is inversely proportional to the percentage of essays on method, by which standard cliometrics itself was sick to death in childhood and is only just now recovering. The few essays on method appearing nowadays are usually commissioned, lack revolutionary fervor and have become as predictable as sportswriting: gee whiz, how extraordinary has been the growth of cliometrics; cliometrics, of course, is gravely limited by its attachment to neoclassical economics; do not be alarmed by counterfactuals.[1] Essays on method, like articles on the sportspage, irritate the players (nobody loves a critic), flatter the owners (in whose pay he sometimes labors), and hearten the loyal fan (with the written equivalent of the chant 'We're number one'). They foreshadow the post-season banquets and their awards: Most Valuable Scholar, Best Book Reviewer (Golden Glove), or, in another mode, Best Historian in a Supporting Role, and Farce of the Year.

The most important of their social roles is to enable busy people to speak wisely of the game without putting in the hours at the park. Sad to say, many historians and economists get their knowledge of cliometrics from the academic sportspage: articles in the 'Tasks' issue of this *Journal*, scholarly and not so scholarly book reviews, or, to descend to the ridiculous, the *New York Review of Books*. The fatuities that result are those of wholly theoretical sportsmen. A fine historian sympathetic towards counting and the social sciences, for example, felt competent after perusing his sportspage to deliver in 1975 the following judgment on cliometrics (described as 'coming out of the American Midwest'):

There are grave doubts whether counterfactual history . . . is of much

I have benefited here from the Workshop in Economic History at the University of Chicago and the wisdom of: Trevor Dick, Rolf Dumke, Stanley Engerman, Stefano Fenoaltea, Robert Fogel, David Galenson, Henry Gemery, Robert Higgs, Thomas Huertas, John Komlos, Robert Lucas, Michelle McAlpin, Jacob Metzer, Joel Mokyr, Joseph Reid, Richard Steckel, and Gary Walton. The acknowledgement does not imply, to put it mildly, that these people agree with what is said.

> practical use to historians, who are concerned with what happened, not with what might have happened but didn't. . . . There are even graver doubts whether the very shaky statistical data surviving even for periods as late as the nineteenth century are firm enough to form a solid foundation for the fragile and sophisticated superstructures which the 'cliometricians' . . . delight in building. . . . One of the difficulties with applying economic theory to history is that it works best on problems where the variables are small and therefore manageable; but these problems are often so narrow as to be trivial. Another is that it deals with a world where choice is always free and always rational and is never distorted by personal prejudice, class bias, or monopoly power; but no such world has ever existed.[2]

Such suspicions that cliometrics is impossible survive independent of the game itself, passing from one newspaper column to the next like rumors of a new salary for Reggie Jackson or a new club for Tom Seaver. That the suspicions have survived dozens of cliometric successes casts doubt, surely, on the pedagogic value of academic sportswriting.

What follows, then, assumes that historians and economists unfamiliar with cliometrics will better spend their time if they now close this *Journal* and visit instead one of the games being played at their local library. They will be astonished by the range and quality of actual play: in the twenty years or so that cliometrics has had an organized league the number of articles and books has expanded to several hundreds, growing exponentially. This essay, in the manner of *Sporting News*, speaks instead to economic historians of some experience, whether cliometricians or cliologicians, well-tanned from repeated sojourns on the field or in the bleachers. It selects a random few out of the hundreds of strike-outs, home-runs, routine grounders, shut-outs and world series to recall to these veterans, for their off-season amusement, how the game was played.

ECONOMIC THEORIES IN HISTORY

None of the three 'schools' under discussion here are schools of preselected conclusions. Bloch, Marx or Adam Smith could conclude that open fields were insurance, that the proletariat was becoming miserable or that tariffs were pernicious without their students following them in more than method. Economic theory, as Keynes said, 'Is a method rather than a doctrine'; it is the possession of this method that distinguishes the cliometrician from other economic historians. The misapprehension embodied in its name (and worse: 'econometric history') that cliometrics is merely quantitative has permitted two irrelevant responses from outsiders: sage doubts that old statistics are reliable; and astonishment at the lack of historical perspective in the claim to have given counting to history. Not counting but economic theory, especially the theory of price, is the defining skill of cliometricians, as of other economists. A cliometrician is an economist applying economic theory (usually simple) to historical facts (not always quantitative) in the interest of history (not economics).

The first and least creative accomplishment of the cliometric school follows nicely from the definition: rethinking bad economics and reshuffling misused numbers. Although it is not an accomplishment of the highest intellectual order to rethink the thoughts and reshuffle the numbers of others in the light of economic theory, it is an important preliminary to higher things. The opportunities have been great because the prevailing standard of economic thinking has been low. The man in the street, and too often the historian in the study, reckons that because he participates in an economy and has watched others do so, supplemented by a course on economics in 1949 and the ability to read a simple table, he knows enough economics to trust his own opinions. He views economics as mere mumbo-jumbo, consisting of a few pieces of jargon (such as 'micro/macro,' 'monopsony' or 'perfect competition' comically misunderstood) mixed with economic ideology. In common with journalists, politicians, lawyers and other educated men, he is master of Ersatz Economics: the supply of iron outruns its demand; wages chase prices in a vicious spiral; war creates jobs; larger demand for cotton textiles permits each firm to experience economies of scale; more machinery is more efficient. He cannot believe that genuine (Echt) is better than Ersatz Economics, that it is more reasoned and reasonable.

It has been childsplay to make such foolishness look foolish. Embarrassingly obvious as the points are, they are usually confined to instruction of the young or sharp comments at conferences; but sometimes they see print. Richard Ippolito's intervention in a debate on the significance of large harvests in eighteenth-century Britain is a good example.[3] One historian had argued that large harvests, by driving down the price, increased the real incomes of consumers and therefore caused industrial demand to rise; another had argued that large harvests, by driving down the price, reduced the real income of farmers (demand was inelastic) and therefore caused industrial demand to fall. Ippolito pointed out that as a first approximation the two effects cancel each other out, for the consumer's gain is in fact the farmer's loss; and that as a second approximation, contrary to both sides of the debate, the large harvests probably caused little change in industrial demand at all. Peter Temin's article on labor scarcity in America is a similar example of the unassisted exercise of economic reasoning, as is Robert Fogel's subsequent comment.[4] The unersatzlich premise on which this little debate took place was that, certainly, efficiency is not the same as mechanization. Likewise, whatever the disagreements among Fishlow, Fogel, their imitators and their economist reviewers may be on the significance of railways for economic growth, they all agree on what the layman does not – that the relocation of production (the growth of Chicago or Birmingham) is not necessarily new production. The agreed premise of cliometric analyses of trade and growth is that exports are not income, the hardy mercantilism of press and professors to the contrary.[5] The agreed premise of cliometric analyses of inflation is that relative and absolute prices are to some degree disjoint, vulgar Keynesianism to the contrary.[6] And so on.

The custom is to scorn such ordinary rethinking of arguments and reshuffling of numbers, as a doctor trained to transplant organs scorns general practice. The custom has the merit of encouraging loftier ambitions. Yet it is based on a faulty assumption, namely, that any fool can make a Marcus Welby, but only God can make a Christiaan Barnard. More cases of historical nonsense are cured by applying opportunity cost and common observation than by applying the more elaborate devices of economic medicine. The patients, alas, often do not believe their cure until treated by input-output, general equilibrium and instrumental variables; or, considering their usual background, by massed archives, footnotes and pellucid prose. The additional treatments are in many cases mere placebos: the cure is effected by a simple regimen of economic sense – an admirable achievement.

QUANTITATIVE FACTS IN HISTORY

The second and more difficult achievement has been the extension to history of modern economic counting:

Boswell: Sir Alexander Dick tells me, that he remembers having a thousand people in a year to dine at his house; that is, reckoning each person as one, each time that he dined there.

Johnson: That, Sir, is about three a day.

Boswell: How your statement lessens the idea.

Johnson: That, Sir, is the good of counting. It brings every thing to a certainty, which before floated in the mind indefinitely.

Boswell: But *Omne ignotum pro magnifico est:* one is sorry to have this diminished.

Johnson: Sir, you should not allow yourself to be delighted with errour.[7]

The cliometrician has not on the whole been delighted with errour. The phrase-turner in economic history, yearning for romance in the countinghouse and factory, delights in verbal play with big events and big machines – foreign trade was Britain's lifeline; the steam engine powered the industrial revolution; the Civil War nurtured industry; foreign investment dominated Russian growth in the 1890s. In their dismal way, cliometricians have introduced meters into the playground, measuring these metaphors and finding them misleading.[8] Scholarly chatter about 'vital factors' and 'it-is-difficult-to-exaggerate-the-importance-of' has ceased in American economic history and is quieting elsewhere. True, chatter hath charms to soothe the savage meternik. An economist eager to civilize himself is apt to decide that tautology, eclecticism and metaphor is fine stuff, after all; and he has his own profession's chatter to fall back on. One of the leaders in applying economics to history, W. W. Rostow, is a case in point, moving from metaphor-smashing in his *British Economy of the Nineteenth Century* (1948) to metaphor-making in *The Stages of Economic Growth* (1960) and beyond. Indeed, attacks on his aerodynamic metaphors were among the most popular amusements of early cliometrics. Deane and Habakkuk disagreed with his timing of the rise in the British savings ratio and in the course of disagreeing began to measure it.[9] Paul David disagreed with his timing of the 'take-off' in America, and measured it.[10] Robert Fogel and Albert Fishlow disagreed with his assessment (and Schumpeter's) of the importance of the railway, and measured it.[11] If the ruling metaphor in Rostow's non-communist manifesto was an errour, it was a fruitful one.

From the beginning of cliometrics – the countings (or, as it turns out, miscountings) of the first 1,945 British steamships by two young professors at Purdue and of the rate of return on slaves by two young professors at Harvard[12] – the cliometrician has had a passion for answering the questions that most other historians find dull beside the fine phrase and generous sentiment: 'how large? how long? how often? how representative?' Purdue and Harvard represented for some time different attitudes towards statistical facts, Purdue collecting new facts from archives but being bashful about exploring the more remote implications of its haul; Harvard taking the first number in a book in the nearest library but thinking about it with great subtlety.[13] The gap, first bridged by Johns Hopkins and Pennsylvania, is now closed. The notion that cliometrics is a mere parasite on real research historians is now as mistaken as the notion that cliometrics is mere numerology. The characteristic catalyst is, again, economic theory. Economic theory dominates the cliometric counting of the unknown as it dominates the cliometric rethinking of the erroneous. Even the simplest (and most useful) statistic of the economist – national income – embodies theoretical convictions about the consumers' equilibrium, non-market activities, depreciation and index numbers. It is therefore no accident that the best work bringing new quantitative facts to economic history has consisted of filling such empty economic boxes. Richard Easterlin,

Robert Gallman, William Parker, Franklee Whartenby and Terry Anderson, among others have pushed the measurement of American income and its composition back before the years considered by the incomparable Simon Kuznets and his many colleagues at the National Bureau of Economic Research.[14] Phyllis Deane, W. A. Cole and Charles Feinstein remeasured income and especially capital formation in the United Kingdom back to 1854, 1830 and, most recently, 1760.[15] And the measurement of past income is not an exclusively Anglo-American accomplishment: Australia, Austria-Hungary, Canada, Denmark, France, Germany, Italy, Japan, The Netherlands, Norway, and Sweden have income estimates for the nineteenth century, and still more countries have estimates of the industrial or commodity share of income.[16] Nor is income the only object of measurement. The role of theory in the collection of statistics on prices and foreign trade is not as obvious, which may explain the comparative lack of interest cliometricians have had in their improvement – James Shepherd and his collaborators aside.[17] It is more obvious in the collection of statistics on money and on productivity, and these have flourished. Money lies at the center of an economic controversy about the causes of depressions. A study of its past is likely to have a present economic purpose.[18] Productivity lies at the center of several historical controversies – about economic growth generally, its causes and prevention. A study of its past is likely to have a historical, not economic, purpose. It is in pursuit of facts on productivity, usually from the perspective of a single industry, that cliometricians have been most likely to enter the historian's holy of holies – the unexplored archive. Charles Hyde and C. K. Harley, for example, explored the archives of British firms in iron in the eighteenth century and shipbuilding in the late nineteenth century in search of evidence of Britain's relative rise and decline.[19] Early on in the cliometric movement Douglass North and his students studied productivity in shipping from original sources.[20] The alternative to productivity change – the mobilization of capital – has long attracted cliometric work on firms in the United States, especially from Lance Davis and Paul McGouldrick.[21] And short of the dusty ledger and wage book is the manuscript census of American manufacturing and agriculture, a rich source ignored by earlier historians (the ones committed, you may recall, to examining *all* the sources) but now being mined by cliometricians. The Parker-Gallman sample from the 1860 agricultural census has been followed by Soltow's linking of statistics on wealth from 1850 to 1870, the post-bellum sample of southern farms taken by Ransom and Sutch, and a series of studies by Bateman, Foust, Weiss and others on samples from manufacturing and agriculture, north and south.[22] The largest fact-gathering mine in America has been Fogel and Engerman Inc., first working on the slavery lode and now on American mortality. The company's size and ambitions have irritated its rivals, but collaborative projects similar to it are in fact common in other histories, especially European. Hans Christian Johansen at the University of Odense, for example, is directing a project reducing the facts on 230,000 ships passing through the Sound between Denmark and Sweden, 1784–1807, to computer tape; likewise, a project is under way to index the fire insurance policies issued by the major British companies in the eighteenth century, and to reduce to tape the details of a large sample of them; and the Cambridge Group for the Study of Population and Social Change has nearly completed a massive reconstruction of the demographic history of dozens of English parishes from the sixteenth to the nineteenth century.

The limits on curiosity about the economic past set by the available facts are few, and cliometricians – bemused by production functions and demand curves and a lunatic belief that they can actually measure them – have led the way in pushing the limits further.

REINTERPRETATIONS OF ECONOMIC HISTORY

The third (and last) achievement is the accumulation of the rethinking and remeasurement around major historical issues; that is, the reinterpretation of American (and recently other) economic history. The breadth of the research confutes the view that cliometrics is narrow. Here again economic theory dominates the research, giving it coherence, not conclusions. True, the conclusions have often been variations on the theme, 'The Market, God Bless It, Works': that the settlement of the American frontier was not a matter of mere theft or speculation; that free banking called forth to tame the wildcats a market in information on the credit-worthiness of banks; or that the Navigation Acts affected colonial America like a small and ordinary tax.[23] But economic theory is varied in its premises: it treats monopoly as well as competition. The findings of Davis and Sylla on the convergence of western and eastern interest rates in the late nineteenth century, now heavily revised by Smiley and James, can be read as a tale of monopoly and barriers to entry; the findings of Kolko and MacAvoy on the origins of the Interstate Commerce Commission, now heavily revised by Haddock and Ulen, can be read as a tale of cartels and conspiracies.[24] Nor are the uses of economic theory confined to rationality. If lower returns cannot explain worse education and worse training for blacks in the late nineteenth century, then discrimination has been identified and measured.[25] If economic interests cannot explain Britain's enthusiasm for the abolition of slavery and of the slave trade, then some other interest – perhaps, after all, idealistic altruism – has been identified and measured.[26] Irrationality leaves footprints in the snow of informed selfishness. The cliometrician interpreting the footprints has revised the history of capitalism and slavery, of the strange career of Jim Crow, and of other irrationalities.

Furthermore, these reinterpretations are not dogmas but findings; not shell games with definitions but falsifiable assertions. The best proof that they are falsifiable is that they have on occasion been shown to be false, at least to the satisfaction of the falsifier. The finding by Fishlow and, especially, Fogel that the coming of the railway was no epoch-making event in American economic history provoked a minor industry of gainsaying, a case of intellectual linkages forward and back. The finding by Fogel and Engerman (extending earlier research) that slaves were capital goods has provoked more than an industry – it is a calling, a vocation. The debate on whether southern sharecropping was mutually advantageous exchange or a system of exploitation has yet to reveal fully its character, whether generous or mean-spirited. It will probably be as intense as the others, protecting the outsider from bad merchandise but also feeding his suspicion that economists cannot agree on what is good. Yet the correct moral to be drawn from the controversies is quite the opposite: in the debate on slavery, for example, Sutch could dispute Fogel and Engerman in detail because their case is built on factual and logical detail, not on unreproducible *verstehen*; Fogel and Engerman could then reply in kind. The debates go on (and on and on) because they are so fruitful in suggestions for new experiments, refining the first results. Debates between historians and economists, by contrast, are sterile. The deep agreement underlying the superficial disagreement in the fratricide of cliometrics is agreement on the methods of economics.

For the first decade and a half or so of its self-conscious life cliometrics pondered with this method the history of economic growth in nineteenth-century America. If the *Annales* school is characteristically French, and the Marxist school characteristically German, the cliometric school is characteristically American. The monument to the work (a monument, be assured, and not a tombstone; the work goes on) is *American Economic Growth: An Economist's History of the United States*.[27] Lately cliometrics has turned to subjects other than economic growth, during centuries other than the nineteenth, and in countries other than the United States. These novelties have not for the most part congealed into reinterpretations, although there are a number in the making. The most finished is the denial of entrepreneurial failure in Victorian Britain. The denial was accomplished by measuring what earlier writers had airily assumed, namely, slow productivity growth and tardy adoption of new techniques. Similar methods – obvious, but unavailable to the historian innocent of economics – are now revising the neat formula that around 1800 Britain had an industrial but not a political revolution and France a political but not an industrial revolution.[28] The Lemma of

Dispensability – if a sector is a small part of national income, then even large changes in it will have small national consequences – has had fruitful applications, first to railways in many places from England to Russia,[29] then to tariff policy in Central Europe.[30] It is no small matter to know that railways did not utterly dominate economic change in the nineteenth century; or that the tariff, however momentous its politics, was no magic key to economic change in German-speaking Europe.

What is known and unknown is less clear in other areas. The cliometric history of America has been pushed back to the origins of slavery and indentures (after Fogel and Engerman)[31] and forward to the Great Depression (after Friedman and Schwartz).[32] It has a broader range, moving away from a fascination with Rostow's vision and its flaws to historical questions unconnected with industrialization: political economy, the distribution of income, the microeconomics of population.[33] Just begun, these researches are necessarily tentative. So, too, in other countries. Tales of the adventures of *homo economicus* in unlikely places are beginning to accumulate, in nineteenth-century India,[34] for example, or medieval Europe[35] or declining Rome.[36] But it would be premature to announce his conquest of those places. Still, the frontier of cliometrics is the wide world beyond America, or indeed, beyond Europe. Cliometrics has at least begun in the histories of Canada, Mexico, Brazil, Australia, Japan, China, India, Russia, West Africa, Israel, Italy, France, Central Europe, the Low Countries, Scandinavia, Ireland, and England.[37] The opportunities are immense, because the facts are unknown but knowable, the historical questions are dominated by scarcity, and the existing understandings – except when they are the products of untutored geniuses of perspicacity like Maitland and Bloch – are models of Ersatz Economics. Barry Supple, with some assistance from W. Wordsworth, has put it this way:

> Bliss was it in that dawn to be alive,
> But to be young [and numerate] was very Heaven!

He was speaking of the first cliometrics conference at Purdue in 1960. In truth the dawn is just now breaking.

THE DUAL STANDARD

The dawn, however, has come up like thunder, especially on the American side of the bay. The violence surrounding *Time on the Cross* is only the latest and largest in a series of intellectual muggings. Cliometrics has been prone to controversy, especially on the disputed turf of black history: if monetary economics, say, is the Detroit and Houston of economics, cliometrics is its New York and the cliometrics of slavery its South Bronx (in several senses). The receptions of *Did Monetary Forces Cause the Great Depression?*,[38] itself an assault on Friedman and Schwartz, and of *One Kind of Freedom*[39] promise to be similarly violent, with some shifts of muggers to the ranks of muggees. In common with street crime, political purges and scholarly controversy in other fields, the violence is greatest among the closest neighbors. The study of the Indo-European language was obstructed for years in the late nineteenth century by an absurd quarrel between one Brugmann and his teacher, the comically misnamed Curtius. Similarly, the cliometrician reserves his foulest eye-gougings (for example, 'This is a term paper, not a professional paper') for his closest colleagues, not – as the non-cliometric victims sometimes mistakenly believe – for the non-cliometric historian or economist. The cliometrician embraces the nonsense of the fact-blinded historian and, still more commonly, of the theory-crazed economist the better to assail the mistaken footnotes or errors in notation of the cliometrician next door.

And even aside from its violence, American cliometrics has favored internal criticism worthy of the Red Guard over creation. The book review – whether the normal size or the review essay so inadvisedly encouraged by editors these days or, at the extreme, the review puffed up to a book in itself – has become common. A reviewer's job is to raise plausible doubts, which is trivially easy for any moderately intelligent reviewer assigned to any moderately complex subject. He needs only to suppose the biases to go the other way (it does not matter whether he has evidence that they do go that way) or to devise a set of market failures vitiating the argument (it does not matter whether he has evidence that the set assumed is a true one). Two results follow. First, there is proliferation of untested hypotheses. Second, there is an intrusion of high-brow doubts into low-brow controversies. The doubts are that neoclassical economics is able to explain economic growth; or that the application of economics to the study of property rights has been sufficiently subtle; or that anything can be proven, really. The reviewer's temptation to take the high road, which makes for a less tiring journey, may help explain the violence of the reviews, high-brow agnosticism about methods lending incongruous fervor to low-brow agnosticism about facts. The violence in other but related fields of the attacks on, say, Christopher Hill or Milton Friedman probably have such a source. Convictions about the unprovable distract the critic from his duty to offer proof.

Yet the passion for reviewing, even violent reviews, has its virtues. A reviewer of the achievements of the cliometric school cannot urge with much enthusiasm that all reviews be committed to the flames. The critic is always open to the malicious joke applied to Walter Pater's relationship with Botticelli: in our field, 'We are all very thankful to Fogel and North for having inspired those fine pages by Paul David,

Peter McClelland and Stefano Fenoaltea.' The joke is unfair. The critic is often sincere in his worrying about the present state of economics (say); even when he does not apply them to his own work, he maintains standards; and he enlivens the scene. Better to burn with a hard, gemlike flame than to slip into the somnolent habits of most historians or economists.

The explanation for the violence of the controversies in cliometrics, indeed, is at bottom this position the cliometrician takes up between two disciplines. The vices and the virtues have a common root. Like the fox who would rather be a hedgehog, the cliometrician is an economist who would rather be a historian – without sacrificing any of his foxy skills (or salary). The best cliometrics is both first-rate economics and first-rate history, publishable in either the *American Historical Review* or the *Journal of Political Economy*. That it is not easy to think of cases in point meeting this dual standard is simply a measure of how very difficult it is to meet the lofty professional standards that inspire scathing reviews of cliometric work. The acrobat meets with applause only when he not merely bicycles on a tightrope across Niagara Falls, but does it blindfold with an eel balanced on the end of his nose; the cliometrician gets unstinted praise for his accomplishment only when he satisfies to the full the historian's lust for fact and the economist's lust for logic. Small wonder the critics are ill-tempered, with such a standard before them.

But the dual standard has great advantages. It is a protection against the mediocrity that so often characterizes interdisciplinary work. And it is a protection against the more conventional mediocrity of too narrowly disciplined work. The *raison d'être* of cliometrics is avoiding the absurdities of economic history without economics. Set off in a discipline of his own the economic historian could once ignore the scholarly standards of economics. Now he cannot: such is the past achievement of cliometrics. The opposite achievement is also attainable: of persuading the economist that there are worthwhile scholarly standards other than the narrow discipline of the dull-normal science into which econometrics, mathematics and positive economics have led him. Cliometricians are among the most vigorous appliers of economics, but their balancing devotion to historical standards makes them careful of facts and mindful of milieu to an extent honored in economics only in presidential addresses.

The pressures of training and employment work against the balance. The reasonable-sounding requirement that the young economic historian be a 'real economist', for example, puts pressure on him to play the parlor games with the specification of error terms and the simulation of general equilibrium models that his colleagues in less serious fields think clever. And a cliometrician who complained (mistakenly) that cliometrics uses economic tools uncritically was nonetheless able to assert that '*theory tells us* [my italics] that population in the face of common property resources would have no tendency to develop a homeostatic relationship'.[40] 'Theory tells us' is as foolish in its own way as 'the facts say'. Yet he that is without sin among you, let him first cast a stone. The cliometrician should feel uncomfortable writing more than a page without a precise theory and a page without a particular fact (reviews and methodological essays excepted, of course), but this is a counsel of perfection. The opportunity of the cliometric school is to combine theory and fact. The best of its achievements have nearly matched its opportunity.

NOTES

1 This, by the way, will be the first essay on cliometric method not to discuss counterfactuals. The possible discussions lack point.

2 Lawrence Stone, 'History and the social sciences in the twentieth century', in Charles F. Delzell (ed.), *The Future of History: Essays in the Vanderbilt University Centennial Symposium* (Nashville, 1977), pp. 24–5. Compare p. 30, a summary of, among several, Haskell's (but not C. Vann Woodward's) review in the *New York Review of Books* of *Time on the Cross*; or p. 33. It is an irony of historiography that the same volume contains a witty and penetrating yet generous assessment of *Time on the Cross* by someone knowledgeable (most would agree) in the field, Woodward himself (pp. 144–7).

3 'The effect of the "Agricultural Depression" on industrial demand in England, 1730–1750', *Economica*, 1975, pp. 298–312. As will be the case elsewhere in the paper, Ippolito's is one hit chosen at random from many. The literature of cliometrics is by now so various and so large that the sportswriter is required to confine attention to a small sample. Even on the present narrow topic – models of general equilibrium applied to British growth in the eighteenth century – other cliometricians, Hueckel and Crafts in particular, have done important work. A complete bibliography of cliometrics is in preparation at the University of Chicago.

4 Temin, 'Labor scarcity and the problem of American industrial efficiency in the 1850s', *Journal of Economic History*, 26 (1966), pp. 277–98; Fogel, 'The specification problem in economic history', *Journal of Economic History*, 27 (1967), pp. 283–308.

5 For example, Joel Mokyr, 'Demand in the Industrial Revolution', *Journal of Economic History*, 37 (Dec. 1977); and R. E. Caves, 'Export-led growth and the new economic history', in J. N. Bhagwati (ed.), *Trade, Balance of Payments, and Growth* (Amsterdam, 1971).

6 D. L. Gadiel and M. Falkus, 'A comment on the "Price Revolution" ', *Australian Economic History Review*, 9 (1969), pp. 9–16; and R. A. Kessel and A. A. Alchian, 'Real wages in the North during the Civil War: Mitchell's data reinterpreted', *Journal of Law and Economics*, 2 (1959), pp. 95–113. On the latter, contrast (but by no vulgar route) Stephen DeCanio and Joel Mokyr, 'Inflation and the wage lag during the Civil War', *Explorations in Economic History*, 14 (1977), pp. 311–36.

7 Boswell's *Life* (Everyman edn, London, 1949), Vol. II, p. 456 (AD 1783, Aetat. 74).

8 S. L. Engerman, 'The economic impact of the Civil War', *Explorations in Entrepreneurial History*, 2nd ser., 3 (1966), pp. 176–99; F. V. Carstensen, 'American multinational corporations in Imperial Russia: chapters on foreign enterprise and Russian economic development', *Journal of Economic History*, 37 (1977), pp. 245–8.

9 H. J. Habakkuk and Phyllis Deane, 'The takeoff in Britain', pp. 63–82, in W. W.

Rostow (ed.), *The Economics of Take-off Into Sustained Growth* (London, 1964). Recent work by Charles H. Feinstein (forthcoming, *Deo volente*, in Volume VII of the *Cambridge Economic History of Europe*) puts the measurement on a much firmer base and, in fact, reinstates to some degree Rostow's conclusion ('Capital accumulation and economic growth in Great Britain, 1760–1860').

10 'The growth of real product in the United States before 1840: new evidence and controlled conjectures', *Journal of Economic History*, 27 (1967), pp. 151–97.

11 Fogel, *Railroads and American Economic Growth: Essays in Econometric History* (Baltimore, 1964) and Fishlow, *American Railroads and the Transformation of the Antebellum Economy* (Cambridge, Mass., 1965).

12 J. R. T. Hughes and Stanley Reiter, 'The first 1,945 British steamships', *Journal of the American Statistical Association*, 53 (1958), pp. 360–81; A. H. Conrad and J. R. Meyer, 'The economics of slavery in the antebellum South', *Journal of Political Economy*, 66 (1958), pp. 95–130.

13 Compare *Purdue Faculty Papers in Economic History* (Homewood, Ill., 1967) with, say, the first half of Henry Rosovsky (ed.), *Industrialization in Two Systems: Essays in Honor of Alexander Gerschenkron by a Group of His Students* (New York, 1966). It would not be wholly mischievous to suggest that the two approaches, still alive today, take these mottoes: for the one, 'Where speculation ends – in real life – there real, positive science begins . . . [O]ur difficulties begin only when we set about the observation and the arrangement – the real depiction – of our historical material' (Karl Marx and Friedrich Engels, *The German Ideology*, 1846, edn of NY, 1963, p. 15); for the other, '[I]n theoretical sciences like philosophy or economics . . . there is no empirical research; all must be achieved by the power to reflect, to meditate, and to reason' (Ludwig von Mises, *Human Action: A Treatise on Economics*, New Haven, 1949, p. 869). Method makes strange bedfellows.

14 Easterlin, 'Interregional differences in per capita income, population, and total income, 1840–1950', in W. N. Parker (ed.), *Trends in the American Economy in the Nineteenth Century*, Conference on Research in Income and Wealth, Studies in Income and Wealth, Vol. 24 (Princeton, 1960); Gallman, 'Gross national product in the United States, 1834–1906', in D. Brady (ed.), *Output, Employment, and Productivity in the United States after 1800*, Studies in Income and Wealth, Vol. 30 (New York, 1966); William Parker and Franklee Whartenby, 'The growth of output before 1840', in Parker (ed.), as cited; Terry Anderson, 'The economic growth of seventeenth century New England: a measurement of regional income' (unpubl. Ph.D. diss., Univ. of Washington, 1972; publ. now by the Arno Press); Simon Kuznets, *Capital in the American Economy, Its Formation and Financing*, NBER (Princeton, 1961).

15 Deane and Cole, *British Economic Growth 1688–1959* (Cambridge, England, 1964); Deane, 'New estimates of gross national product for the United Kingdom, 1830–1914', *Review of Income and Wealth*, 14 (1968), pp. 95–112; Feinstein, *National Income, Expenditure and Output of the United Kingdom, 1855–1965* (Cambridge, England, 1972); Feinstein, 'Capital accumulation, 1760–1860', as cited above.

16 Paul Bairoch, 'Europe's gross national product: 1800–1975', *Journal of European Economic History*, 5 (1976), pp. 273–340, attempts to collate some of these. His list on pp. 329–31 is one source for the assertion in the text. Others are: Simon Kuznets, *Modern Economic Growth: Rate, Structure, and Spread* (New Haven, 1966), esp. p. 64; J. D. Gould, *Economic Growth in History* (London, 1972), esp. p. 22; and works cited in these.

17 J. F. Shepherd and G. M. Walton, *Shipping, Maritime Trade, and the Economic Development of Colonial North America* (Cambridge, England, 1972); P. R. P. Coelho and J. F. Shepherd, 'Regional differences in real wages: the United States, 1851–1880', *Explorations in Economic History*, 13 (1976), pp. 203–30.

18 See the review article by Michael D. Bordo and Anna J. Schwartz, 'Issues in

monetary economics and their impact on research in economic history', in Robert Gallman (ed.), *Recent Developments in the Study of Economic and Business History: Essays in Memory of Herman E. Krooss*, supplement 1 to *Research in Economic History* (Greenwich, Conn., 1977).

19 Hyde, *Technological Change and the British Iron Industry, 1700–1870* (Princeton, 1977), and Harley, 'Shipping and shipbuilding in the late nineteenth century' (unpubl. Ph.D. diss., Harvard Univ., 1972), and related articles.

20 For example, North, 'Sources of productivity change in ocean shipping, 1600–1850', *Journal of Political Economy*, 76 (1968), pp. 953–70.

21 The most convenient collection of Davis' early work, as for other products of the Purdue School, is *Purdue Faculty Papers in Economic History*, as cited above. McGouldrick's book is *New England Textiles in the Nineteenth Century: Profits and Investment* (Cambridge, Mass., 1968).

22 Parker (ed.), *The Structure of the Cotton Economy of the Antebellum South* (Washington, DC, 1970) uses the Parker-Gallman sample; see also Lee Soltow, *Men and Wealth in the United States, 1850–1870* (New Haven, 1975) and (among many others by the same authors) F. Bateman, James Foust and Thomas Weiss, 'Profitability in southern manufacturing: estimates for 1860', *Explorations in Economic History*, 12 (1975), pp. 211–23. The study by Bateman and Jeremy Atack of the accuracy of the published relative to the manuscript census is a good example of high standards of historical veracity in cliometrics ('Northern agricultural profitability: some preliminary estimates', *Research in Economic History*, 4, 1978, forthcoming).

23 Stanley Engerman, 'Some economic issues relating to railroad subsidies and the evaluation of land grants', *Journal of Economic History*, 32 (1972), pp. 443–63, and works cited there; Hugh Rockoff, 'The free banking era: a reexamination', *Journal of Money, Credit and Banking*, 6 (1974), pp. 141–67; P. D. McClelland, 'The cost to America of British imperial policy', *American Economic Review*, 59 (Supplement, 1969), pp. 370–81.

24 Gene Smiley, 'Interest rate movements in the United States, 1888–1913', *Journal of Economic History*, 35 (1975), pp. 591–620; John A. James, 'The development of the national money market, 1893–1911', *Journal of Economic History*, 36 (1976), pp. 878–97. David D. Haddock, 'The advent of federal regulation of railroads' (unpubl. Ph.D. diss., Univ. of Chicago, 1978); Thomas Ulen, 'The ICC as a railroad cartel regulator: was it necessary?' (unpubl. chapter of Ph.D. diss., Stanford Univ., 1977).

25 Robert Higgs, *Competition and Coercion: Blacks in the American Economy, 1865–1914* (Cambridge, 1977); Edward Meeker and James Kau, 'Racial discrimination and occupational attainment at the turn of the century', *Explorations in Economic History*, 14 (1977), pp. 250–76.

26 E. P. LeVeen, 'British slave trade suppression policies, 1821–1865: impact and implications' (unpubl. Ph.D. diss., Univ. of Chicago, 1971), and related papers.

27 Lance E. Davis, Richard A. Easterlin, William N. Parker *et al.* (New York, 1972). A competing monument, handsome despite some cracks, is Jeffrey G. Williamson's *Late Nineteenth-Century American Development* (Cambridge, England, 1974).

28 Richard Roehl, 'French industrialization: a reconsideration', *Explorations in Economic History*, 13 (1976), pp. 233–81; P. K. O'Brien and C. Keyder, *Economic Growth in Britain and France, 1780–1914*, forthcoming.

29 G. R. Hawke, *Railways and Economic Growth in England and Wales, 1840–1870* (Oxford, 1970); Jacob Metzer, 'Railroad development and market integration: the case of Tsarist Russia', *Journal of Economic History*, 34 (1974), pp. 529–50. Hawke, it should be noted, disputes the axiom.

30 Scott Eddie, 'The terms and patterns of Hungarian foreign trade, 1882–1913', *Journal of Economic History*, 37 (1977), pp. 329–57; and a recent series of dissertations by Thomas Huertas, Rolf Dumke, Steven Webb and John Komlos.

31 R. P. Thomas and R. N. Bean, 'The fishers of men: the profits of the slave trade', *Journal of Economic History*, 34 (1974), pp. 885–914; David Galenson, 'Immigration and the colonial labor system: an analysis of the length of indenture', *Explorations in Economic History*, forthcoming.

32 Peter Temin, *Did Monetary Forces Cause the Great Depression?* (New York, 1976). Economists who imagine themselves immune from historiographical influences, by the way, should consider how completely Friedman and Schwartz broke the cake of intellectual custom on the Great Depression. Views on its history, and therefore on economics, that could be dismissed with a sneer in the early 1960s had now to be taken seriously. The extent to which forbidden thoughts may now be thought is well illustrated by an emerging interpretation of high unemployment in Britain during the 1920s as a result of – are you ready? – the dole: Daniel K. Benjamin and Levis A. Kochin, 'Searching for an explanation of unemployment in interwar Britain' (unpubl. paper, Univ. of Washington); and Stephen Easton, 'The English Poor Law and unemployment during the late 19th and early 20th centuries' (unpubl. Ph.D. diss., Univ. of Chicago, 1977).

33 A very small sample of a now very large literature might include, in addition to works mentioned elsewhere, Lance Davis and D. C. North, *Institutional Change and American Economic Growth* (Cambridge, England, 1971); J. D. Reid, Jr., 'Understanding political events in the new economic history', *Journal of Economic History*, 37 (1977), pp. 302–28, and his contribution to vol. 38; Peter Lindert and Jeffrey Williamson, 'Three centuries of American inequality', in *Research in Economic History*, 1 (1976), pp. 69–123; and R. D. Lee (ed.), *Population Patterns in the Past* (New York, 1977).

34 M. D. Morris (ed.), 'Symposium on economic change in Indian agriculture', in *Explorations in Economic History*, 12 (1975), pp. 253–331, with papers by John Hurd II, Michelle McAlpin and Tom Kessinger. The *Cambridge Economic History of India*, Vol. II (Cambridge, forthcoming – Brahma *volente*) will contain more.

35 Douglass North and R. P. Thomas, *The Rise of the Western World* (Cambridge, England, 1973) and S. Fenoaltea, 'Risk, transaction costs, and the organization of medieval agriculture', *Explorations in Economic History*, 13 (1976), pp. 129–51.

36 Gerald Gunderson, 'Economic change and the demise of the Roman Empire', *Explorations in Economic History*, 13 (1976), pp. 43–68.

37 To give some examples, occasionally exhaustive but more usually a scant handful representing many other works: Canada: Trevor O. Dick, 'Frontiers in Canadian economic history', *Journal of Economic History*, 36 (1976), pp. 34–9, and works cited there. Mexico: John Coatsworth, *An Economic History of Mexico* (New York, forthcoming), and works cited there. Brazil: Nathaniel H. Leff, 'Long-term Brazilian economic development', *Journal of Economic History*, 29 (1969), pp. 473–93; Pedro de Mello, 'The economics of labor in Brazilian coffee plantations, 1850–1888' (unpubl. Ph.D. diss., Univ. of Chicago, 1977). Australia: Noel G. Butlin, *Investment in Australian Economic Development 1861–1900* (Cambridge, 1964), and recent issues of the *Australian Economic History Review*. Japan: H. Rosovsky and K. Ohkawa, *Japanese Economic Growth – Trend Acceleration in the Twentieth Century* (Stanford, 1973); Kozo Yamamura, *A Study of Samurai Income and Entrepreneurship* (Cambridge, Mass., 1974), among many works from the same hand; A. C. Kelley and J. G. Williamson, *Lessons from Japanese Development* (Chicago, 1974). China: Dwight Perkins (ed.), *China's Modern Economy in Historical Perspective* (Stanford, 1973); Alexander Eckstein, *China's Economic Development* (Ann Arbor, 1975); Ts'ui-jung Liu and J. C. H. Fei, 'An analysis of the land tax burden in China, 1650–1865', *Journal of Economic History*, 37 (1977), pp. 359–81; the richness of Chinese historical statistics by comparison with European is astounding. India: see note 34 above. Russia: Arcadius Kahan, *The Sokha, the Spindle and the Knout: Essays in the Economic History of Eighteenth Century Russia* (forthcoming), and 'The growth of capital in Russian industrialization',

forthcoming in the *Cambridge Economic History of Europe*, Vol. VII, as cited above. West Africa: H. A. Gemery and J. S. Hogendorn (eds.), *The Uncommon Market: Essays in the Economic History of the Atlantic Slave Trade* (forthcoming). Israel: Nachum Gross and Jacob Metzer, 'Public finance in the Jewish economy in the interwar period: the expenditure side', in *Research in Economic History*, 3 West Africa: H. A. Gemery and J. S. Hogendorn (eds.), *The Uncommon Market: Essays in the Economic History of the Atlantic Slave Trade* (forthcoming). Israel: Nachum Gross and Jacob Metzer, 'Public finance in the Jewish economy in the interwar period: the expenditure side', in *Research in Economic History*, 3 (forthcoming, 1978). Italy: Jon S. Cohen, 'The 1927 revaluation of the lira: a study in political economy', *Economic History Review*, 2nd ser., 25 (1972), pp. 642–54; Stefano Fenoaltea, *Italian Industrial Production, 1861–1913* and *Public Policy and Italian Industrial Development, 1861–1913: A New Economic History* (both forthcoming); Gianni Toniolo (ed.), *Lo sviluppo economico italiano 1861–1940* (Bari, 1973); R. T. Rapp, *Industry and Economic Decline in Seventeenth-Century Venice* (Cambridge, Mass., 1976). France: George Grantham, 'Scale and organization in French farming, 1840–1880', in W. N. Parker and E. L. Jones (eds.), *European Peasants and Their Markets: Essays in Agrarian Economic History* (Princeton, 1975), itself a collection of cliometric work on European agricultural history; Paul Hohenberg, 'Change in rural France in the period of industrialization, 1830–1914', *Journal of Economic History*, 32 (1972), pp. 219–40. Central Europe: Rainer Fremdling, 'Railroads and German economic growth', *Journal of Economic History*, 37 (1977), pp. 583–604; and works cited in note 30 above. The Low Countries: Franklin F. Mendels, 'Agriculture and peasant industry in eighteenth-century Flanders', in Parker and Jones (eds), as cited above; Jan de Vries, *The Dutch Rural Economy in the Golden Age, 1500–1700* (New Haven, 1974); Joel Mokyr, *Industrialization in the Low Countries, 1795–1850* (New Haven, 1976). Scandinavia: recent issues of the *Scandinavian Economic History Review.* Ireland: Barbara L. Solow, *The Land Question and the Irish Economy 1870–1903* (Cambridge, Mass., 1971); Cormac Ó Gráda, 'Supply responsiveness in nineteenth-century Irish agriculture', *Economic History Review*, 2nd ser., 28 (1975), pp. 312–17. Great Britain: Cambridge University Press will be publishing in 1979 a collaborative *New Economic History of England, 1700–Present* that summarizes and extends cliometric work on Britain.

38 Peter Temin, as cited above.

39 Roger Ransom and Richard Sutch (Cambridge, 1977).

40 Douglass C. North, 'Economic growth: what have we learned from the past?' (unpubl. MS), p. 3.

2

Does the Past Have Useful Economics?

The answer, of course, is 'yes', and at one time the very question would have seemed impertinent. Smith, Marx, Mill, Marshall, Keynes, Heckscher, Schumpeter and Viner, to name a few, were nourished by historical study and nourished it in turn. Gazing down from Valhalla it would seem to them bizarre that their heirs would study economics with the history left out, stopping their desultory search for facts in time series at the last twenty-five years and in cross sections at the latest tape from the Bureau of the Census, passing by the experiments of history with little regard for their place in a nonexperimental science, distrusting old facts as error-ridden intrusions from another structure, abandoning historical perspectives on their political economy, and basing their theory and policy on stylized non-facts about economic development, fairy tales remembered from their youth.

Yet this is what has happened. It began in the 1940s, in some respects earlier, as young American economists bemused by revolutions in the substance and method of economics neglected the reading of history in favor of macroeconomics, mathematics and statistics. The low opportunity cost of such specialization reinforced it: American economic history by that time was, albeit with a few brilliant exceptions, neither good economics nor good history, a dim echo of the American institutionalists and through them of the German historical school. It is not surprising that immature scholars undervalued history then, still less surprising in a decade in which economists were having

It is not mere convention that impels me to thank the many colleagues who have commented on earlier drafts of this essay. I have received from them in writing the equivalent of over 100 typed pages, and many hours of conversation as well. This itself measures the vigor of historical economics, one theme here, but their contribution to the product is immeasurable. I would like to thank, therefore, the seminars in economic history at Chicago and at Northwestern; and R. Cameron, M. Edelstein, S. L. Engerman, R. W. Fogel, R. Gallman, H. Gemery, C. D. Goldin, G. Gunderson, G. Hawke, R. Higgs, G. Hueckel, J. R. T. Hughes, H. G. Johnson, E. L. Jones, A. Kahan, C. P. Kindleberger, A. Leijonhufvud, P. Lindert, P. McClelland, M. McInnis, J. Mokyr, L. D. Neal, A. Olmstead, D. Perkins, J. D. Reid, N. Rosenberg, W. W. Rostow, A. J. Schwartz, B. Solow, G. Walton, D. Whitehead, and J. G. Williamson. And I would like to apologize to George Stigler for inverting for my own purposes the title of his fine essay, 'Does economics have a useful past?' [107, 1969], *and for ignoring the useful lemma illustrated there (p. 226): 'there are not ten good reasons for anything'.*

difficulty understanding macroeconomic policy even in the short run, mathematical maximization even under narrow constraints, and statistical inference even with a simple structure. What is more surprising is that the reading and using of history was not taken up again in the early 1950s, as economists rediscovered economic growth, surprise which turns to astonishment when the neglect of history persisted into the 1970s, as they rediscovered property rights, inheritance, educational investment, social class, income distribution, and other pieces of history in economics. And what is most astonishing in this – what must make Schumpeter, say, turn back in disgust to his horn of mead and his dialogue with Marx and Smith on the historical dynamics of capitalism – is that in the late 1950s a throng of historical economists equipped with Lagrangean multipliers and Durbin-Watson statistics poured out of Purdue, Harvard, Washington, Columbia, Johns Hopkins and a widening array of new factories at home and abroad to reshape economic history into a form suited to the tastes of their colleagues in economics, yet their colleagues did not buy. The identification problem is solved: it was the demand curve, not the supply curve, that moved back. At the same price measured in an hour of reading or a month of writing, economists nowadays demand less economic history.

The result is apparent in those periodical declarations of what it is that real economists do, the general interest journals of the profession. From 1925 to 1944 the pages of the *American Economic Review*, the *Quarterly Journal of Economics* and the *Journal of Political Economy* taken together contained 6·5 percent (as weighted by size) of articles on economic history; from 1945 to 1974 they contained 3·3 percent (similarly weighted).[1] For the three journals taken separately the drift away from history was as shown in Table 2.1, and more detailed

Table 2.1 *Summary of the percentage of pages devoted to economic history, 1925–74*

	AER	*QJE*	*JPE*
1925–44	4·4	5·4	9·9
1945–74	2·2	3·3	5·4
Level at which the differences are significant (Mann-Whitney test)	·011	·021	·020

statistics tell a similar story. The *JPE* was for a long time the most historical of the journals, reflecting perhaps the reluctance with which Chicago embraced the view that economics is applied mathematics and statistics and that in the long run we are all dead. From 1929 to 1944, with a remarkable devotion to intellectuality in the face of world depression and war, the *JPE* devoted 11 percent of its pages to economic history, many of them the products of Earl Hamilton and John Nef. By 1970–4, however, the heirs of Jacob Viner and Paul Douglas devoted 2·8 percent of the pages of their journal to it. They were merely joining the trend. The journals of 1935–9, when economists were obsessed (properly) with last year's unemployment and trade statistics, contained proportionately 2·7 times more economic history than the journals of 1970–4, when economists were instead obsessed (again properly) with the origins in the very long run of growth, discrimination, legal change and the historic evils of capitalism.

These contrasts will surprise no one familiar with the literature of economics over the last fifty years, confirmed as they are in other ways.[2] To be sure, specialized journals of economic history drew off historical articles from the three major journals, as did specialized journals in other fields. The composition of the general journals is nonetheless a measure of what those who write for, edit and referee them believe is of general interest to economists. They believe history to be of small and diminishing interest. That the general journals have little economic history in view of the existence of specialized journals in economic history read exclusively by economic historians does not contradict the observation that economists are increasingly ahistorical. It restates it. Indeed, even if one were to suppose that economists read at random in all the 200-odd journals indexed in this *Journal*, the probability of them stumbling on an article on economic history in 1973–4 would have been ·028, and the number of encounters with history in the journals, like the number of deaths from horsekicks in the cavalry, would approximate a Poisson distribution.[3] Of course, economists in other fields do not in fact consult specialized journals of economic history. The drift of economic history into specialized journals and of economists out of reading these journals is doubtless attributable to the widening gap in method, closing only comparatively recently, between economics and history. In 1926 the editors of the *JPE* believed, no doubt correctly, that their subscribers would read B. J. Hovde, 'French socialism and the Triple Entente, 1893–1914', the first of three long articles cast in narrative. What is most significant, though, and least quantifiable, is the drift in economics away from using history, as distinct from merely reading it. Whether or not an economist specialized in, say, international trade reads for himself a seminal article on distributed lags in *Econometrica* or on portfolio analysis in the *Journal of Finance*, he will use their results, distilled in survey articles and in textbooks. The same cannot be said at present for economic history. Does the past have useful economics? The average American economist nowadays answers, 'No.'

The exceptions are notable, in more ways than one. It will come as a surprise to many economists that among others Armen Alchian, E. Cary Brown, Richard Caves, Donald Gordon, Reuben Kessel, Marc

Nerlove, Mancur Olson, Albert Rees, Stanley Reiter, and Arnold Zellner, none of whom do their main work in history, have in fact made contributions to it.[4] Turning away for a moment from the subject here, American economics and its relations with American history, it might be noted that in Britain such traditions of a serious amateur interest in economic history are strong: Mark Blaug, A. K. Cairncross, J. R. Hicks, R. C. O. Matthews, E. H. Phelps-Brown, R. S. Sayers, Brinley Thomas, and John Vaizey, for example, are well known in Britain as economists dealing with contemporary problems of policy and theory, yet all of them have contributed to British economic history at a high level. The postwar officers of the American Economic Association, members of the older generation trained to place history as Schumpeter did with theory and statistics at the foundation of economic science, can provide a comparable list. Among recent vice-presidents, Moses Abramovitz, Evsey Domar, Charles Kindleberger, W. Arthur Lewis and Robert Triffin show no signs of forsaking history. Nor do the words and works of postwar presidents reflect the dominant opinion of their constituents that economic history is a frill, useless to the hard, important business of formalizing another economic idea, of refining the techniques for exploiting a given set of statistics, or of deflecting current policy from a third into a second best configuration. In his presidential address to the Association in 1970, Wassily Leontief scolded those who had elected him for ignoring empirical work in favor of ever more mechanical theory and scholastic econometrics [66, 1971, p. 3]:

> Devising a new statistical procedure, however tenuous, that makes it possible to squeeze out one more unknown parameter from a given set of data, is judged a greater scientific achievement than the successful search for additional information that would permit us to measure the magnitude of the same parameter in a less ingenious, but more reliable way.

He applauded agricultural economists for a long tradition in another style, and might as well have applauded historical economists for a younger tradition in the same style [66, 1971, p. 5]:

> An exceptional example of a healthy balance between theoretical and empirical analysis and of the readiness of professional economists to cooperate with experts in the neighboring disciplines is offered by Agricultural Economics as it developed in this country over the last fifty years.

One of the agricultural economists whom Leontief undoubtedly had in mind, Theodore W. Schultz, himself a past president of the Association, regretted in 1974 that he himself had not studied economic history more diligently in his youth and argued that 'there is a strong tendency on the part of virtually all economists to undervalue the history of the economy of both high and low income countries. I doubt the wisdom of this tendency to concentrate on the immediate present' [101, 1974, p. 12]. Another postwar president, Milton Friedman, in collaboration with Anna J. Schwartz, carried a high valuation of economic history to the point of making a seminal contribution to it, as in a less extended way did Paul Douglas, John Kenneth Galbraith, Robert Aaron Gordon and J. H. Williams. And still others, such as Schumpeter, Harold Innis and Simon Kuznets, valued economic history to the point of devoting sustained effort over long careers to its enrichment.

It is apparent, however, that this older generation of American economists did not persuade many of the younger that history is essential to economics. Those they did persuade – the 'new' economic historians or 'cliometricians' – ignored the task of persuading their doubting colleagues and directed their rhetorical energies instead towards non-economists, chiefly historians. This choice of audience had the advantage of imparting emotional cohesion to the cliometricians, filling them with the enthusiasm and energy of convinced imperialists. The result was a series of conquests beginning, as I have said, in the late 1950s and widening further with each year that sharply revised American economic history and has begun recently to revise other economic histories as well. Being intellectual imperialists, however, the cliometricians forgot, as many imperialists do, that foreign adventures require domestic support, and by neglecting to solicit it, they lost it. Were other economists so disregarding of their self-interests they would court a similar fate. For thirty years after the first stirrings in the 1930s, mathematical and statistical economists pointed out to everyone who would listen that one or another piece of economics is essentially mathematical or essentially statistical until at last no one remained to be convinced. Historical economists could have pointed out with equal force that one or another piece, in some cases the same piece claimed by their more aggressive colleagues, is essentially historical. But they seldom did. Socialized inside economics as it developed after the war, they were apologetic and deferential towards their colleagues, to the point at times of imitating their colleagues' low standards of factual accuracy and wider social relevance along with their high standards of logical cogency and statistical grace. Lacking the self-confidence of the mathematical or statistical economists, the new historical economists have neglected the task of persuading others of the worth of history in economics.

I THE VALUE OF ECONOMIC HISTORY

It is not because it is difficult to do that the task has been neglected. The lines of argument are opened with little effort. For the professional economic historian the worth of economic history is that of general history, to which it contributes, and it is because he puts a high value on history, economic or not, that he chooses to study it. This justification suffices for him and for any economist who believes that history, whether or not it is directly useful in testing economic laws or framing economic policy, is collective memory fruitful of wisdom. At the least pragmatic level, indeed, the worth of economic history is that of intellectual activity generally, and nothing should be easier than convincing professional intellectuals that such activity is worthwhile. G. M. Trevelyan put the point gracefully [117, 1942, pp. viii, x]:

> Disinterested intellectual curiosity is the lifeblood of real civilization. . . . There is nothing that more divides civilised from semi-savage man than to be conscious of our forefathers as they really were, and bit by bit to reconstruct the mosaic of the long-forgotten past. To weigh the stars, or to make ships sail in the air or below the sea, is not a more astonishing and ennobling performance on the part of the human race in these latter days, than to know the course of events that had long been forgotten, and the true nature of men and women who were here before us.

One can admire historically important and economically perceptive histories of southern slaves, nineteenth-century businessmen or medieval peasants in the same way that one admires a mathematically beautiful and elegantly proven theorem in the theory of optimal control, whether or not the histories or the theorem have any practical use.

In this respect, indeed, by their attachment to the ivory tower, historical economists have much in common with mathematical economists. Further, though in their fascination with markets both activities are recognizably economic, both practitioners are likely to be met with a glassy stare and a change of subject when they speak of probate records or fixed point theorems to their colleagues in the coffee room. There remains, to be sure, one conspicuous point of asymmetry: forty years of investment in mathematizing economics and of disinvestment in historicizing economics has made it less acceptable among economists to admit ignorance of mathematics than to admit ignorance of history. The days are passing when the social sciences bridged the two cultures, literary and scientific, and economics burned the bridge long ago. Comfortable ignorance, to be sure, is not a monopoly of economists. A culture is a definition of barbarians, a definition of which people one may safely ignore; an intellectual culture is a definition of which classes of knowledge one may safely ignore. A social historian dealing habitually with inherently quantitative issues would be deeply ashamed to admit that he is ignorant of the languages, literature or political history of the societies he studies; yet admits cheerfully, with no apparent resolve to amend his ignorance, that his mathematical and statistical sophistication is that of a 10 year old child. It is meritorious in such circles to be innocent of numbers, as to be free from some mental defect. Economists have not usually carried the parallel attitude so far. It is true, nonetheless, that an applied economist dealing habitually with inherently historical issues would be ashamed to admit that he is ignorant of differential equations or identifiability, yet admits with no sense of loss that he is entirely ignorant of what occurred in the economy he studies before 1929 or 1948 or 1970.

What, then, do economists lose by their increasing inclination to define their intellectual culture to involve ignorance of the past? Why, even if they choose not to heed the lofty call of disinterested intellectual curiosity, should economists read and write economic history?

II THE PRAGMATIC VALUE OF ECONOMIC HISTORY

A *More Economic Facts*

The pragmatic answers are straightforward, the first and most obvious being that history provides the economist with more information with which to put his propositions in jeopardy. The volume of information available will come as a surprise to most economists, consumers as they are. The National Bureau of Economic Research is unusual in this, and its half-century of tillage of the past, harvested as data in thousands of regressions by economists otherwise uninterested in history, amply nourished the new historical economists of the last fifteen years. During the 1950s and 1960s many of them served an apprenticeship in economic observation, to change the metaphor, at the Bureau's social observatory in New York, contributing heavily to the two catalogues of historical objects produced in the late 1950s and the early 1960s (edited by W. N. Parker [82, 1960] and D. S. Brady [6, 1966]).[5] The publication in 1960 of another work in which the historians at the NBER had a hand, together with the Bureau of the Census and the Social Science Research Council [118, 1960], can mark the beginning of the Keplerian stage of the new economic history. The National Bureau's interests were more nomothetic than historical – an interest in quantitative history for the light it could cast on regularities and (eventually) predictabilities of the economic system rather than for the light it could cast on history itself – but it would be churlish as well as inaccurate to discount for that reason the role Moses Abramovitz, Arthur Burns, Solomon Fabricant, Raymond Goldsmith and John Kendrick among many others played in encouraging historical economics. In a discipline increasingly bored by history the Bureau was from the beginning, as Wesley Clair Mitchell put it in 1927, committed to the notion that [74, 1927, p. x]:

> business cycles consist of exceedingly complex interactions among a considerable number of economic processes, that to gain insight into the interactions one must combine historical studies with quantitative and qualitative analysis, that the phenomena are peculiar to a certain form of economic organization, and that understanding of this scheme of institutions is prerequisite to an understanding of cyclical fluctuations.

Thirty-six years later the commitment to history lived on in the ambition of Milton Friedman and Anna J. Schwartz to write an 'analytical narrative' as 'a prologue and background for a statistical analysis of the secular and cyclical behavior of money in the United States' [33, 1963, pp. xxi–xxii].

This governing idea of the Bureau – that one could in empirical work go beyond consuming historical facts to producing them, embedding the output in its appropriate historical milieu – was seized on and expanded by the young historical economists of the 1950s and 1960s. It occurred to them that the statistics most economists are content to receive from clean-looking columns of reference books could in fact be constructed for much earlier times than had been thought possible and could be brought to bear after their construction on important historical issues. Brimming from their other courses in graduate school with the new mathematical, statistical and computational techniques that flowed into the curriculum in the 1950s, they had the tools with which to reshape the historical object. To use symbolically the names of three men whose influence was more than symbolic, the students of Alexander Gerschenkron, Simon Kuznets and Douglass North were quick learners and saw that if the masters could push measures of American income or Italian industrial output or the American balance of payments back to 1869 or 1881 or 1790, they could too, and more. Robert Gallman, a student of Kuznets, laboriously reconstructed first American commodity output then GNP back to the 1830s [34, 1960; 35, 1966]; he later joined with William Parker, a student of A. P. Usher at Harvard and of Gerschenkron, Usher's successor, in a large-scale sampling of the hand-written manuscripts of the 1860 agricultural census. Richard Easterlin, another student of Kuznets, reconstructed income by state back to 1840, then turned, by way of the long swing, to the analysis of American population back to the middle of the nineteenth century [21, 1960; 22, 1961; 23, 1968]. Alfred Conrad, Paul David, Albert Fishlow, John Meyer, Goran Ohlin, Henry Rosovsky and Peter Temin, all students of Gerschenkron, made

Harvard for a time in the late 1950s and early 1960s a center of research in the new economic history by exploring with economists' eyes the voluminous quantitative records, hitherto neglected, of slavery, agricultural machinery, railways, schooling, and iron and steel in nineteenth-century America, agriculture and governmental finance in nineteenth-century Japan, and population in medieval Europe.[6] At about the same time, another example of simultaneous discovery so common when an idea's time has come, similar centers had sprung up at Rochester (where two students of Kuznets, Robert Fogel and Stanley Engerman, were exploring the records of American railways, slavery and agriculture in the nineteenth century) and at Purdue (where Jonathan Hughes and Lance Davis, students of North, together with Edward Ames, Nathan Rosenberg and a startlingly large number of other economists were reinterpreting the record of finance, business cycles and technological change from the twentieth century to the fourteenth).[7] From 1960 on, these groups gathered annually at a conference at Purdue, transferred to Wisconsin after 1969.[8] Elsewhere Gary Walton [121, 1967] and other students of North joined with North himself in a reconstruction of ocean shipping rates back to the seventeenth century [78, 1968]; Matthew Simon, also working with the fact-makers at Columbia and the NBER in the 1950s, developed balance of payments accounts for 1861–1900 [104, 1960]. Stanley Lebergott examined anew the record of American labor back to 1800 [65, 1964]. Gary Walton in collaboration with James Shepherd [102, 1972], another student of North, constructed trade accounts for the American colonies, and still another student of North, and of R. P. Thomas, Terry Anderson [2, 1972], constructed income and population statistics of New England in the seventeenth century. Roger Weiss estimated the supply of money in the American colonies [122, 1970; 123, 1974]. So it went, and goes.

To some degree these waves of fact originated inside economics. Yet once transferred to specialized historical economists such work developed a momentum of its own. To take a recent example, the successes of Friedman and Schwartz with the American monetary statistics for 1867 to 1960 inspired historical work on earlier American statistics, then on British, and now on other countries [111, Temin, 1969; 103, Sheppard, 1971]. The historical study of productivity change is another recent example of transferred momentum.[9] The early work by Abramovitz and Solow was, like that of Friedman and Schwartz, nomothetic rather than historical. In the hands of historical economists, however, it gave impetus to the construction of historical series on the quantities and prices of inputs and outputs useful far beyond their initial purpose. Whether or not the theories tested by such economic studies survive the next twist in intellectual fashion – theories of business cycles, consumption, investment behavior, growth, money, or productivity change – the urge to implement them historically continues to generate new and lasting facts.

It will seem strange to economists exposed only to older writing on history or to no writing on history at all to assert that history is a rich mine of statistical information. Badly educated economists believe there are 'no data' before the year in which the reference book nearest to hand begins its series on income or wages or exports, and twenty years ago most historians, even economic historians, would have agreed with them. Some still do, dropping with relief the task of measurement before 1900 as soon as they hit on one or another specious reason for doing so: that perfect accuracy is not attainable (estimates have errors), that no individual possesses the attributes of the average individual (distributions have variances), or that statistics dehumanize history (sets are defined for limited characteristics of the objects included). The economist should be aware that the case against statistics in history rests on such pitiable foundations, however pleasing it may be for him to suppose that the historian possesses special tools of insight superior to the spirit-killing tools of his own trade. The computer and the resulting advance in quantitative history, led by the new economic historians, have in any case given statistical agnosticism in history a quaint look.

The historical facts available for the economist's work, in truth, are voluminous beyond the wildest dreams of intellectual avarice, extending back in diminishing volume to the Middle Ages. They require only work and imagination. No Ministry of Agriculture in the thirteenth century collected statistics on English agricultural output for the benefit of twentieth-century students of agricultural economics. Yet medievalists realized long ago that the annual account of the bailiff to his lord could yield such statistics for the lands farmed by the lord himself; and they have realized more recently that all the land, farmed by the lord or by the peasants, paid tithes to the Church, itself a literate and methodical bureaucracy with a strong self-interest in examining and preserving the records of the tithe from year to year, from which output can be estimated.[10]

A large investment, of course, is necessary to put such collections of facts into usable form, and relative to the size of the investment economic historians, for all their energy, have just begun. A case in point is the astoundingly large collection of genealogical records held for baptizing the dead by the Mormon Church in Salt Lake City, records yielding detailed family histories for many generations.[11] But the student of inherited and acquired human capital could find material for his work that is less difficult than this to handle in the historical record were he to look into it. Surveys, for example, are not a recent invention. The history of Europe and its offshoots from 1086 to the present is littered with them. To take a comparatively recent example, in 1909 the United States Immigration Commission collected questionnaires from over half a million wage earners, some 300,000 of them foreign born, and from 14,000 families totaling 60,000 people, asking them about their occupation, wage income, employment, property income, earnings of the household, housing, rent paid, children, schooling, literacy, languages, money remitted abroad, money when first landed, and many other matters. The Commission surveyed employers on a comparably large scale. The results were published in forty-two volumes, which still await the curiosity of economists interested in the accumulation of human capital, the life cycle of income, the participation of women in the labor force, migration and discrimination.[12] Whenever men write down accounts of their own or others' economic activities the economist has more observations for his science. Economic historians realize that men have been doing this for a long time.

B *Better Economic Facts*

The inspiration for reconstructing the statistics of the past has not come from economics alone, with the result that economic historians can present to economists new classes of facts, richer in many dimensions than modern facts. The very deadness of the men and companies of the nineteenth century and before opens to view records closed to an economist who insists that his subjects be alive or recently deceased. Only a successful antitrust suit pries loose the records of General Electric's conspiracies in restraint of trade, yet the student of industrial organization could if he wished turn to business historians for information on the costs and benefits of collusion that would bring statistical life to his speculations on their magnitudes. The Department of Commerce, the SEC and the self-interest of the companies expose to public view some scraps of information about the costs, profits and investments of industrial firms; yet the student of investment and finance could turn to work such as Paul F. McGouldrick's *New England Textiles in the Nineteenth Century: Profits and Investment* [70, 1968] for much richer information.[13] Even for firms that have come now under close and inquisitive government regulation, such as banks, old records, once confidential and therefore candid and complete, are better than new [80, Olmstead, 1974].

Demographic history, long practiced outside of economic history but now influencing it heavily, provides still more examples of the virtues of the dead as objects of economic study. The very records of death, probate inventories and wills, are rich sources of facts (see A. H. Jones [56, 1972]). So too are counts of the once living. The 100-year rule of disclosure in, say, Britain makes it possible to do for the 1871 census of population what is impossible for the 1971 census, to scrutinize samples or, if one wishes, the entire population of all coal-mining towns (with their startlingly high fertility) or of all industrial villages (with their startlingly wide variation in family structure).[14] The critical item that is missing in any modern sample from the census is the person's name, for without his name one is unable to link the record of the census to other records. To appreciate the significance of this fact, one has only to reflect that men and governments are more methodical in their record-keeping and more bold – one might say impertinent – in their curiosity today than they were once, and when some future economic historian is able to trace people by their name (or social security number) through all the records of families, businesses, the IRS, the credit bureaus, the schools, the hospitals and the courts, our knowledge of economic behavior will, to put it mildly, increase. It has occurred to historical demographers that we need not wait until the twenty-first century (and if we wait we are liable in fact to be disappointed, for the cheapening of travel and the spread of the telephone – *sans* tap and tape – has impoverished the written record). If it is important for certain issues in labor economics, for example, to have collections of economic biographies of people, the historian stands ready to supply them in detail. The work of the Cambridge Group for the History of Population and Social Structure, building on the work of French historical demographers after the war, has developed two centuries of family histories in Britain from 'nominal record linkage', to use the jargon, applied to birth, death and marriage registers back to the sixteenth century.[15] In what is perhaps the most ambitious project of this sort to date, scholars at the University of Montreal are reconstituting the entire population of Quebec from the beginning of the colony to the French and Indian War, recording every notice of every person in the remarkably complete records of French Canada and linking them. As the age of economists and calculators dawns, statistics such as these can be linked with a widening array of records on income, property holdings, business, education and the like to provide life histories much superior to the recent samples worked over so lovingly in any current issue of the *Journal of Political Economy* or the *American Economic Review*.

The census is, of course, a survey on a massive scale, and when the manuscripts are open – i.e. when the census is old – there are few limits on economic curiosity. The Parker-Gallman work mentioned earlier, for example, matched the manuscripts of the American census of agriculture in 1860 with those of the census of population – matching that cannot be done on recent, closed censuses, that is, without the name of the respondent – and produced a full profile of those involved in farming enterprises. Because the 1860 census inquired into the wealth of those it surveyed, it is possible to examine the determinants of the distribution of wealth in 1860 at a level of detail unattainable with modern records, and Lee Soltow is currently exploiting these possibilities [106, 1975]. Roger Ransom and Richard Sutch were able to extract from the manuscript census of 1880 intimate details on a random sample of 5,283 farms in the South and to confront the issue of racial discrimination more directly than is typically possible with modern data [89, forth.]. By comparison with such rich and varied facts, the economist's usual store looks pitiably thin.

Nor are the errors in these facts larger than those in modern facts. It is naïve on two counts to believe that historical statistics have larger errors, naïve both in overestimating the quality of modern statistics and in underestimating the quality of historical statistics. When pressed an economist will usually admit that his data on, say, prices in the American economy over the last twenty years are in error to some large and unknown degree because the quality of the goods in question has improved, because the list prices correspond poorly with the transaction prices, because the definition and relevance of the sample is in doubt, or because the price index used corresponds poorly with the conceptually correct definition. He will admit, too, that these errors introduce biases of unknown sign into his multivariate regressions containing prices as an independent variable. He will run the regressions anyway, comforting himself with the mistaken reflections that his data are as good as one can get and that his estimates are in any case consistent.

Confronted on both sides by skepticism, from his colleagues in history that statistical demonstrations in history are persuasive and from his colleagues in economics that historical statistics are reliable, the historical economist cannot take this line. He has in fact developed an art of creative self-doubt that is practiced in some other fields of economics and might be with profit practiced more widely. The habit of testing the sensitivity of one's argument to possible errors in its data or possible mistakes in its analytical assumptions is widespread among scientists and historians, but is not among economists. Many, of course, understand the frailty of 'data' and act on this understanding. The tradition of the National Bureau and of the more careful empiricists outside it of publishing a full description of how data were made and where they might be wrong, in the hope (so often vain) that users will read it, fits well with historiographic traditions: in his preface to Albert Fishlow's *American Railroads and the Transformation of the Ante-Bellum Economy,* Alexander Gerschenkron drew special attention to 'the statistical appendixes in which the author offers a full insight into his laboratory and without which no real appreciation of the importance of the study and the validity of its interpretative results is possible' [27, Fishlow, 1965, p. viii]. Yet it is rare for the major journals in general economics to publish factual revisionism such as Robert J. Gordon's '$45 Billion of U.S. Private Investment Has Been Mislaid', perhaps because it is rare for economists to write it [39, 1969].[16] Zvi Griliches put his finger on the reason many economists are uninterested in the sources of data and their errors [42, 1974, p. 973]:

> Much of the problem, I think, arises because of the separation in economics between data producers and data analyzers. By and large, we do not produce our own data and, hence, do not feel responsible for it.[17]

For economic historians, required to collect their own materials and imbued with the historian's rather than the economist's attitude toward their handling, the buck stops here. Robert Fogel's *Railroads and American Economic Growth* [28, 1964] is perhaps the fullest example to date of this attitude.[18] Combining the traditions of creative self-doubt in economic history and in project evaluation, its 260 pages are directed at producing essentially one number, the benefit half of a cost-benefit study of nineteenth-century investment in American railways. Fogel began this research believing that he would confirm the assumption of the indispensability of the railways underlying earlier treatments (by Schumpeter and Rostow, for example), but found to his surprise that the facts cast doubt on it. To test this doubt, therefore, he directed his energies to estimating an upper bound on the contribution of railroads to national income and found it low; therefore, he concluded that railroads were far from indispensable for American economic growth. Historical facts are often better for economists' purposes that recent facts: they are often more detailed, voluminous and accurate, and what errors they contain are treated with respect.

But there is, of course, another sense in which they are 'better', for history performs experiments: history provides the economist not only with more rich and accurate facts but also with more variable facts. A macabre example of the point is T. W. Schultz's use of Indian statistics of agricultural output and population during the influenza epidemic of 1918–19 to argue that the marginal product of labor was positive and roughly equal to the going wage: output fell as the working population did, and labor therefore was not 'surplus', contrary to the assumption of much work on economic development, particularly Indian economic development [100, 1964, pp. 63–70]. An equally dismal experiment, the Great Depression, will remain for a long time to come the great testing ground for theories of aggregate economics, as monetarists, fiscalists and others have on occasion realized. The appreciation of the pitfalls of monetary policy was much increased by the argument of Friedman and Schwartz that, far from having little impact, it was powerfully mishandled in the 1930s; and the appreciation of the potential of fiscal policy was much increased by the argument of E. Cary Brown that, far from failing, it was not in fact tried [8, 1956] (see also L. C. Peppers [85, 1973]).

That history has performed the very experiment he wishes had been performed must occur from time to time to every economist. He must realize, too, that economics is like astronomy an observational science, taking its data and its controls, alas, as it finds them. Yet he fixes his telescope (during his infrequent trips to the observatory) on the sun, moon and nearer planets alone, for two reasons: first, he believes that these objects close to home are the only ones that provide insight into how the home planet behaves; and, second, he believes that to look beyond the near solar system, not to speak of the galaxy, is to look into another structure, where familiar laws (e.g. there are six planets, stars are little points fixed to a sphere and light moves in straight lines) might not apply. The belief that history is irrelevant to public policy will be examined below and will prove to be incorrect. The incorrectness of the belief that history might come from a different structure than the quarterly national income figures since the war and is therefore to be ignored is plain enough. To those who adopt the argument in order to limit the amount of empirical work they have to do, one can only sigh and turn back to scholars who take scholarship seriously. These innocents will always believe that 'empirical work' is a conflation of the appendix to the *Economic Report of the President* and Johnston's *Econometric Methods*. Even serious and sophisticated economic scholars are prone to adopt the assumption that the past has a different structure without testing it. The cliometricians have been forced to test the assumption at every turn, facing as they do scholars in both economics and in history who adopt it as a matter of course. Indeed, if the findings of the new economic history of the last fifteen years or so had to be put in one sentence, it would be this: in the eighteenth and nineteenth centuries men sought profit in as clear-headed and competitive a way as an economist dreaming of auctioneers and perfect markets might wish. Following Lenin and Veblen, of course, one is free to assert that the atomistic competition of the age of Smith and Mill is dead, that simple models of competitive behavior might apply to the nineteenth century but not to the twentieth. This variant assertion, however, merely reinforces the point, for it has never been tested, at any rate not in a way that would convince someone who did not believe it to begin with, despite its large role in the political economy of the last fifty years. Even if one could show that for a particular experiment (the effect of government spending on employment, say) the environment of the nineteenth century was so different from that of the 1970s that little could be learned about the present structure from the comparison, it would remain true that structures continue to change, as the often discouraging and sometimes comical results of large-scale econometric models suggest. History, like the study of other countries and cultures, is an education in structural change. A familiar example of the more usual practice is that of dropping the war years from regressions, as intrusions from another structure. Wars, however, recur, and it behooves the economic scientist, even if his interests in science extend only to its uses for today's public policy, to understand how war changes the way economies behave (see, for example, D. F. Gordon and G. M. Walton [38, 1974] and Mancur Olson [81, 1963]). Paul David put a similar point in the following way [15, 1975, p. 14]:

> An equation that fits the data well for half the available run of time-series observations and not for the rest is, for the ordinary applied economist, a failure; he will have to resist the impulse to discard the recalcitrant data in presenting his results. By contrast . . . the economic historian may hail the half-failed regression equation as nothing less than a triumph – in the sense that by uncovering the occurrence of a change in economic structure, it signals him to set to work to learn what happened in history.

Limiting one's field of vision to close objects, in any case, is as peculiar in economics as it would be in astronomy. Examples of historical experiments larger, clearer and more decisive than most that could be framed on the basis of recent experience can be generated at will. The migrations from one country or another in the last twenty years that have alarmed modern governments are dwarfed by the migrations of the nineteenth century.[19] The same can be said of the migrations of capital: if one wishes to measure the effects of foreign investment on the sending or receiving country, the British, French, Argentinian and Canadian experiences of the late nineteenth century are the best available cases in point.[20] From 1870 to 1913 Britain sent one-third of her savings abroad. If one wishes to measure the effects, burdensome or otherwise, of government debt, the British experience with the debt from the Napoleonic War or the American experience with the debt from the Civil War are the clearest experiments, taking place as they did before the Internal (or Inland) Revenue codes among other disturbing influences reached their present chaotic state (for the American case see J. G. Williamson [130, 1974]). In the 1820s the British government debt was on the order of two and a half times national income, about the same as the present ratio in the United States.[21] If one wishes to measure the impact of legal changes, the experiences in the nineteenth century and before with laws of incorporation, school attendance, child labor and the like are large and varied experiments [109, Sylla, 1969; 63, Landes and Solmon, 1972; 124, West, 1975; 99, Sanderson, 1974]. So too, if one wishes to measure the impact of floating exchange rates, are the experiences of the United States in the 1860s and 1870s, of Britain from 1914 to 1925, or of China in the 1930s. In a time of free banking, as in the United States before the Civil War, one can examine the consequences of free entry [92, Rockoff, 1974]; in a time of war and unfettered capital markets, as during the Civil War, one can examine the responsiveness of expectations to events [94, Roll, 1972]; in a time of massive new investment in public hygiene, as in American cities after the Civil War, one can examine the value of health [71, Meeker, 1972; 72, 1974]. History is society's laboratory.

C *Better Economic Theory*

The products of this laboratory affect economic ideas in ways that few economists recognize. The headline of today's newspaper, to be sure, has an effect, the more so as money for research follows the headline with a short lag. But historical findings, true or false, underlie the reaction to the headline. To pick some influential historical findings that have recently been shown to be false by cliometricians, the finding that the increase in the capital stock per man left much of the increase in income per man unexplained set off in the late 1950s an intellectual explosion in models of growth with technological change. The historical finding that the rate of savings was constant over a long period set off in the early 1950s a somewhat smaller explosion in the theory of the consumption function. The historical finding that the share of labor in income has been constant set off in the 1930s still another in the theory of the production function. The influence of economic theory on the writing of history is apparent in most pieces of new economic history, but the influence of economic history on the writing of theory is apparent only in the seminal pieces, to be forgotten in the sequel. The high ratio of historical reserves to theoretical deposits in the work of Robert Solow, Milton Friedman or Paul Douglas is not maintained in the work of their intellectual customers, with the result that the intellectual money supply is a large multiple of the factual base and subject to violent fluctuations. Rondo Cameron put the point well:

> In analogous discussions concerning the role of theory in historical research the argument is frequently made (perhaps because it is valid) that the historian will inevitably be guided by some a priori ideas. It is desirable, therefore, that these ideas be made explicit and systematized if possible. The choice, in other words, is not between theory and no theory, but explicit, consciously formulated theory and implicit, unconscious theorizing. Much the same can be said for the use of history by theorists. Even the most scornful ahistorical economist makes some use of history: his own experience, the experience of his generation, or the loose historical generalizations which abound in the folklore of even highly sophisticated societies. [9, 1965, p. 112; cf. 74, Mitchell, 1927, p. 59]

The obvious case in point is the theory of economic growth, in which a particular set of historical conventions dominate the argument. These conventions – described by Nicholas Kaldor in 1958 as 'stylized facts', a defensive usage that has been adopted widely – were developed in the

1950s, once intellectual putty but now clay, before new economic historians had begun in earnest to announce the unstylized facts. It is at least uncertain that their work will confirm the constancy of the capital/output ratio, of the rate of profit, or of the rate of growth of output per man and of the capital stock. As Robert Solow remarks at the conclusion of a brief inquiry into the factual relevance of these elements in the steady state of economic growth, 'the steady state is not a bad place for the theory of growth to start, but may be a dangerous place for it to end' [105, 1970, p. 7]. From the historical work by economists over the last two decades or so, ignored by growth theorists, it would seem so. During the second half of the nineteenth century, for example, the capital/output ratio in America rose by a factor of two, while falling by a third in Britain; during the first half of the twentieth century, the ratio in America fell 22 percent, while remaining roughly constant in Britain.[22] It may be that a fuller definition of 'capital' to include acquired human skills and a fuller definition of 'output' to include production in the household would yield different results. Economic historians, facing long periods of history in which the relation of the narrow to the full definitions have changed radically, are forced routinely to consider refinements of this sort. Whether refined or not the facts accumulated by them for the study of economic growth warrant a second look. This is perhaps most clear in the matter of technological change, the chief jewel and the chief embarrassment of the modern theory of growth. As R. R. Nelson and S. G. Winter have recently emphasized [76, 1974], historians of technology such as Paul David, Peter Temin and Nathan Rosenberg have much to tell the theorists, but the theorists' minds are fixed on other things (see, e.g., Rosenberg [95, 1972] or David [15, 1975]).

The sins of pseudo-history are not, of course, confined to mathematical theorists of economic growth. There is nothing in words as distinct from equations, however frequent the appeals in the words to the alleged experience of history, that protects looser theorizers from the error of irrelevancy. Ricardo's notion of rising land rents, Marx's of immiserization of the industrial proletariat, Lenin's of the profits from imperialism, Dennis Robertson's of foreign trade as an engine of growth, Harold Innis' of staple products as centers of growth, W. A. Lewis' of development with unlimited supplies of labor, or W. W. Rostow's of a take-off induced by great inventions and a sharp rise in the savings rate, to name a few, have not fared well in confrontation with historical fact.[23] This is not to say that theorists should forsake their blackboards or their typewriters for the nearest archive. An occasional trip to the library might help. And they should be doubtful of their own unassisted ability to summarize historical experience in a few stylized facts.

The contribution of history to theory is not confined to a supply of factual grist for the theorists' mill. The use of theory in economic history illuminates the theory and tests it, and in this respect economic history is no different from other applied economics. An application of input–output analysis to the measurement of effective protection in nineteenth-century America tests the usefulness of this tool in the same way as does an application to the measurement of effective protection in present-day Pakistan [127, Whitney, 1968; 43, Guisinger, 1970]. An agricultural economist, at least, would be comfortable with the use of simple models of supply and demand to explore the growth of the American shipbuilding, cotton textile or iron industries, and would not be surprised that use deepens them.[24] Nor would the student of international trade, aggregate economics or labor markets find anything strange in applications of models of two sector general equilibrium to the American economy before and after the Civil War or to the British economy during the Napoleonic War,[25] of money and prices to the British and American business cycle in the early nineteenth century [113, Temin, 1974], or of marginal productivity to slavery or postbellum sharecropping.[26] He might be a little surprised that such remote issues can be reached with tools perfected in the middle of the twentieth century and might, too, admire the skill with which issues long cut off from economic thinking are brought back to it. But on the whole he would perceive good economic history to be simply good applied economics.

It should be pointed out, parenthetically, that in an important sense his perception would be wrong, for good economic history must also be good history. It is this requirement that puts economic history at the highest levels on a par of difficulty with, say, econometrics at the highest levels, which requires a mastery of statistics, or mathematical economics at the highest levels, which requires a mastery of mathematics.[27] True, some new economic historians believe that economic history consists of the application of production theory or econometrics to a more or less vague notion of what happened in history, just as other economists believe that economic thinking consists of the application of Lagrangean multipliers or optimal control theory to a more or less vague notion of what is to be maximized. But the best new economic historians are historians as well as economists, just as the best economists are social scientists as well as applied mathematicians.

Even at the lower levels of historical as distinct from economic sophistication, however, reforming the economic history of the late 1950s into good applied economics, exhibiting in the reformation the power of modern economic theory, was a remarkable achievement, comparable with the reformations over the last decade in the economics of politics, property rights, labor markets and the household. For a time the new economic historians, like the new labor economists and the rest, devoted themselves to this task of intellectual arbitrage. But the theoretical rewards of economic history are greater. Any extension of economics to new subjects sets new questions with which existing theory cannot deal, and for which new theory must be created. Economic historians have been bold in this. Their theoretical boldness arises in part from the recalcitrance of the world: when the scholar's chief purpose is to understand a piece of behavior, historical or current, rather than to test a familiar economic idea (still less to develop its logic), he takes his insights from wherever he can get them, whether or not they bear the *imprimatur* of an economic bishop.[28] It arises, too, from the unusually close contact that historical economists have with another discipline, history. They have internalized the intellectual values of historians more than sociological economists have internalized those of sociologists or legal economists those of lawyers, and in consequence are peculiarly inclined to face questions for which economics has no ready answer. A case in point is the question of why political and social revolutions occur, a question that even most political scientists and sociologists, contrary to what one might expect, carefully avoid. It is impossible for a historian who wishes to write coherent history to avoid the question, even if he wished to, for revolutions, such as the American Revolution and the Civil War, are the stuff of change and change the stuff of history.[29] For this reason a good deal of the new economic history in America has centered around the causes of the Revolution and the Civil War, approaching the causes (as comparative advantage dictates) with the characteristically economic assumption of rational and informed self-interest. The new economic history made a contribution, albeit a modest one, to the understanding of the American Revolution by measuring the economic burden of the Navigation Acts and finding it small (see P. D. McClelland [69, 1969] and works cited there); it made a contribution to the understanding of the Civil War by measuring the economic burden on the South of the tariff or of the restrictions on the expansion of slavery and finding these also to be small [87, Pope, 1972; 84, Passell and Wright, 1972]. If one believes that economic interests determine political behavior, then, one can look to new economic historians for measurements of these interests. If one does not believe it, one can look to new economic historians for whatever economic measure is to the point: by showing, for example, that slavery was not economically moribund on the eve of the Civil War, the new economic historians were able to reject the theme of many historians sympathetic with the South that military intervention to abolish slavery was unnecessary.[30] In any case, the application of economics to politics raises the theoretical issue, neglected by most economists (namely, most economists to the left of Milton Friedman and to the right of Paul Sweezy), of bringing politics into economic models.[31]

The new economic history has turned increasingly in the past few years to issues such as these, central to the development of economics as a social science. The deepening of the study of American slavery, for example, notably by Fogel and Engerman in their recent book [31, 1974], has opened the issue of the role of coercion in economic society. Outside the growing band of Marxist economists, who are like their colleagues on the right unusually historically minded, the limit of thinking on the matter in economics has been an occasional remark on command compared with market economies, assuming in the background that market economies use little coercion beyond taxes, enforcement of contract and the criminal law. The assumption has never been appropriate for that quarter of the population under the age of responsibility, and in a slave society, of course, it is still less appropriate. Fogel and Engerman were able to show, however, that Southern slaveowners, capitalistic as they were, used market mechanisms as well as the whip to manipulate their slaves. In 'Slavery: the progressive institution?', a long review of the book, two other economic historians, Paul David and Peter Temin, argued that the economic theory to deal with such mixed systems of enticement and coercion does not exist [16, 1974, esp. pp. 778–83]. It may not, and this is the challenge to theory.

The challenges arise from the wide perspective forced on the economic historian by his subject. Obviously, one cannot study the long swing, if one wishes to, without long swings in income [61, Klotz and Neal, 1973]; one cannot study the long-run determinants of city size without long runs of city sizes [108, Swanson and Williamson, 1974]. But the point goes deeper than this. An economist whose attention is riveted on the present cannot be expected to ask why the institutions of the labor and capital market change, as Lance Davis and Douglass North did in *Institutional Change and American Economic Growth* [17, 1971], still less to ask why fundamental social arrangements rise and decay, as North and Robert Thomas did in *The Rise of the Western World* [79, 1973]. At a more modest level, few economists outside of agricultural economics and economic history have given serious attention to measuring (as distinct from theorizing about) managerial ability or, in more elaborate language, entrepreneurship, that phantom of the theory of the firm. The measurement was forced on economists studying agriculture by the insistence of government planners who were not economists that farmers are irrational; it was forced on economists studying the Victorian economy by the insistence of historians who were not economists that British businessmen in the late nineteenth century were irrational as well [98, Sandberg, 1974]. And even agricultural economists, on the whole exceptional among economists for their long historical perspective, cannot be expected to ask why the peculiarities of peasant land tenure have survived in many countries for centuries and why they were dissolved in land reform.

The Icelandic poet Einor Benediktsson put it this way:

To the past you must look
If originality you wish to build;
Without the teaching of the past
You see not what is new.[32]

D *Better Economic Policy*

Few intellectual activities are more mischievous when done poorly than economics or history. The power of fallacious economic reasoning or fallacious historical example to damage society is obvious: the pseudo-economics of mercantilism has been reducing trade and protecting vested interests for many centuries; the pseudo-history of the Aryan 'race' lent dignity to German fascism. The combination of bad economics and bad history in bad economic history is pernicious. To be sure, the makers of economic policy have ample opportunity for falling into error without the excuse of economic history poorly grasped. Yet, to specialize Keynes's frequently quoted remarks on the subject – frequently quoted, perhaps, because they are correct – the ideas of economic historians, both when they are right and when they are wrong, are more powerful than is commonly understood. Madmen in authority, who hear voices in the air, are distilling their frenzy from an understanding of the economic events of a few years back. Practical men, who believe themselves to be quite exempt from any historical influences, are usually the slaves of historical example.

The industrial revolution, it is said, came to Britain suddenly and simply around 1760 in a wave of gadgets, justifying policies for growth that equip illiterate peasants with computers. Foreign trade, it is said, was an engine of economic growth in Britain (and, lately, Japan), justifying a policy of impoverishing one's citizens in the pursuit of exports. Floating exchange rates, it is said, added to the chaos of the international economy in the 1930s, justifying the sacrifice of employment to the maintenance of $4·86, $2·80, $2·40 or (most recently) $2·00 to the pound sterling. Railways, it is said, were crucial to industrialization in the nineteenth century, justifying policies in nonindustrial countries in the twentieth of shoring up railways with subsidies and of eliminating trucking competition. Industrialization, it is said, brutalized the working class, justifying among most educated people a deep suspicion of capitalism. Labor unions, it is said, were responsible for a good part of the increase in wages since 1900, justifying government protection of extortionate plumbers, electricians and butchers. The competitive supply of professional services in the nineteenth century, it is said, grievously injured consumers, justifying official cartels of doctors and undertakers. Business monopoly, it is said, has spread greatly during the last century, justifying public hostility towards big business. The payment of competitive interest on demand or time deposits, it is said, created instability in the banking system, justifying laws to forbid it. Air pollution, it is said, is worse now than it was once, justifying draconic policies to combat it. Fossil fuel, it is said, is being used at a faster rate relative to proven reserves now than fifty years ago, justifying national goals of subsidizing new fuels and abandoning international trade in oil. Whether these are good or bad policies, to the extent that their public propaganda and their private inspiration rest on false historical premises – and most of them to a large extent do – their rationale is full of doubt.

One could add cases in point without limit, but two of the more important will suffice. The muddle of exchange rates in the 1920s and 1930s led to the development of the elasticities approach to the balance of payments, which to this day dominates theory and policy. The approach has been under attack now for several years on logical ground, but the development of an alternative will depend on a reinterpretation of past experience with exchange rates.[33] The muddle of employment in the 1930s and the interpretation of the muddle by Keynes and others led to the postwar policy of full employment and to a concentration on fiscal methods to achieve it. Their interpretation bears rethinking. As Hugh Rockoff remarked in a recent survey of the American experience with free entry to banking, 'One purpose of history is to broaden our conception of the possible' [93, 1975, p. 176]. The apprehension of true history as well as the correction of false contributes to public policy because an economist whose memory is limited to the recent past has a narrow conception of the possible. We may in our praise and criticism of present governments be willing or unwilling slaves of historical example, but slaves we are.

E *Better Economists*

In the light of all this, it is not surprising that Smith and Marshall, Schumpeter and Keynes were deeply historical in their thinking. An economist, least of all a cliometrician, cannot argue that there are no substitutes for history in the production of important economics, no more than he can argue that there was no substitute for the railway in American economic growth. Some important economics has been written by historical illiterates, although it must be admitted that cases are difficult to find. The work of Edgeworth as distilled in modern textbooks, for example, seems a likely candidate until one reads the work itself and stumbles over tags from Herodotus. In much of the work of J. R. Hicks it is not obvious that history plays a part, yet he lectured on medieval history in one of his early academic appointments, has been by his own account a lifelong reader of the *Economic History Review*, and published in 1969 *A Theory of Economic History* [48, 1969, p. v] (see also [47, 1953]). History is a stimulus to the economic imagination, defining and stretching the limits of economic craft. An economist learns from his other studies how to see, to label and to repair the pieces of the economic building. From history he learns whence the building came, how its neighbors were built and why a building in one place was and will be built differently from one in another. The wider questions that face economics are historical. If history is useful to an economist's work, it is still more useful to his education.

It would be unreasonable to propose in the style of the German historical school that history dominate the education of economists, that abstractions of maximization be abandoned in favor of the concreteness (or, more commonly in practice, the verbal abstractions) of history. The reaction to this unreasonable proposal, indeed, explains some of the drift towards present-mindedness in modern economics. Yet, as the English economic historian T. S. Ashton said [3, (1946) 1971, p. 177]:

> The whole discussion as to whether deduction or induction is the proper method to use in the social sciences is, of course, juvenile: it is as though we were to debate whether it were better to hop on the right foot or on the left. Sensible men with two feet know that they are likely to make better progress if they walk on both.

An economist hopping along without a historical leg, unless he is a decathalon athlete, has a narrow perspective on the present, shallow economic ideas, little appreciation for the strengths and weaknesses of economic data, and small ability to apply economics to large issues. If we interrogate our students, we will find that they believe economic research to consist chiefly of a passing acquaintance with the latest pronouncement of the Council of Economic Advisers, the latest assumption relaxed in an economic model and the latest revision in the local canned regression program. One does not have to look beyond their teachers to find where they acquired this peculiar set of notions.

For fifteen years or so cliometricians have been explaining to their colleagues in history the wonderful usefulness of economics. It is time they began explaining to their colleagues in economics the wonderful usefulness of history. Wonderfully useful it is, a storehouse of economic facts tested by skepticism, a collection of experiments straining the power of economics in every direction, a fount of economic ideas, a guide to policy and a school for social scientists. It is no accident that some of the best minds in economics value it highly. What a pity, then, that the rest have drifted away. Does the past have useful economics? Of course it does.

NOTES

1 This difference, treating each of the fifty years as an observation, is significant at the ·00003 level. Because the distribution for the earlier period was bimodal, and

plainly therefore non-normal, I used the Mann-Whitney U test. The underlying evidence is available on request. Briefly, for 1925–63 the number of pages in articles on history in the three journals was calculated from all their appearances in the various history classifications in the *Index of Economic Journals* [1, 1961–5]. Its definition of 'history' is 'articles concerned primarily with a period 20 years or more earlier than the beginning date of the volume' [1, 1961, p. xi]. The definition imparts a downward bias to the number of pages recorded as history in earlier years, because the volumes of the *Index* for those years cover a wider span: to qualify as history an article in 1939 had to concern events 34 years before; one in 1949, 29 years before; one in 1963, 23 years; and one in 1974, only 20. A correction would accentuate the postwar fall. For 1964–74 the number of pages in articles on history was calculated from the journals themselves, classifying doubtful cases as history. The total number of pages available for all subjects was calculated from the journals, including supplements sent to subscribers and excluding advertisements, administrative matter and book reviews in book review sections (not classified in the *Index*). The AER after 1969 is not defined to include the *Journal of Economic Literature*; if one were to adopt the alternative definition, the recent evaporation of history from the journals would be somewhat more pronounced. The percentages divide the pages of history by total pages, weighting journals in the total by their number of total pages. Unweighted averages of the three behave in much the same way.

2 Martin Bronfenbrenner would not agree [7, 1966]. He measured the column inches of Class 5 (Economic History) relative to the total in the *Index* volumes, arriving at:

1886–1924	1·21%	1950–4	1·44%
1925–39	1·49	1955–9	1·64
1940–9	1·49	1960–3	1·47

This he described as an 'upturn . . . with some slight decline since 1960' [7, 1966, p. 544]. In this calculation, however, he neglects the articles classified as History but appearing in other parts of the index (such as 9.51, Security and Money Markets, History), which are, ignoring the double-counting, 80 percent of the total; and he does not notice the sharp downward bias in the earlier volumes imparted by the definition of 'history' in the index (an article appearing in 1924 would have to be concerned chiefly with events before 1866, 58 years before, to qualify as history). A. W. Coats' assertion that economic history has occupied 'an increasing share of the total periodical literature' [12, 1971, p. 32] is based on Bronfenbrenner's figures.

3 The figure is the share of column inches of history titles in the index of the *Journal.* In 1973–4 these included all articles in history, not merely those fitting into Class 5 of the *Index.* Highly specialized journals of economic history, such as *Agricultural History,* are not indexed in the *Journal*; they were in the *Index.*

4 60, Kessel and Alchian, 1959; 8, Brown, 1956; 10, Caves, 1971; 11, Chambers and Gordon, 1966; 77, Nerlove, 1965; 81, Olson, 1963; 90, Rees, 1961; 54, Hughes and Reiter, 1958; 137, Zellner and Murphy, 1959. It was Reiter who invented the word 'cliometrics', a joke that caught on.

5 The earlier volume contains most of the papers delivered to the joint meeting of the Conference on Income and Wealth and the American Economic History Association at Williamstown in 1957, a meeting that celebrated the marriage between the NBER and the new economic history. Recently, it is sad to report, the marriage has been drifting towards separation.

6 The monument to this work is Part One of Rosovsky, ed. [96, 1966]. Conrad and Meyer's work is collected in [14, 1964].

7 The products of the Purdue school (*floruit* 1958–66) are gathered in *Purdue Faculty Papers in Economic History* [88, 1967].

8 The role of foundation financing for this and other projects in cliometrics was

critical. The Ford Foundation supported the Purdue meetings for a time, and the Rockefeller Foundation supported a generation of Gerschenkron's students at Harvard. A brief gap in the middle 1960s was filled after 1968 by the National Science Foundation, which has continued since then to encourage cliometrics. When some future historian of economic thought applies refined measures to this history, he will find, I think, that the intellectual marginal product of these grants was extraordinarily high.

9 It is not widely appreciated outside British economic history that the 'residual' (in its price dual form) was invented in the 1920s for a historical study of British and American industry by G. T. Jones in his posthumous book *Increasing Returns: A Study of the Relation Between the Size and Efficiency of Industries, with Special Reference to the History of Selected British and American Industries, 1850–1910* [57, 1933, p. 33]. As we shall see again below, reading history has even its theoretical rewards.

10 Skeptics will find a look at J. Z. Titow convincing on the wealth of data derivable from bailiffs' accounts [116, 1972]. There does not appear to be a use of the tithe in the English literature, but it has become a commonplace in the French, as in J. Goy and E. Le Roy Ladurie [41, 1972].

11 See the article by Clayne Pope and Larry Wimmer on these records, forthcoming in *Historical Methods Newsletter*.

12 See R. Higgs [50, 1971] for a brief description and use of the *Report*. Higgs used the published volumes, but the manuscript questionnaires, if they have survived, would be still more revealing. The *Report*, incidentally, is a good example of the need for historical sophistication in interpreting historical statistics. It was a nativist and racist document, in the candid style of the age of the Big Stick and the White Man's Burden.

13 Gavin Wright described this impressive study as 'the most "vertically integrated" study of econometric history to date. McGouldrick has performed every "stage of production" himself, from the basic source work with a sample of Waltham-Lowell type textile firms (1836–86) to sorting out the various conceptual problems involved in measuring the capital stock, output, capacity, etc., and finally, to regression analysis of dividend and investment behavior' [132, 1971, p. 440].

14 See E. A. Wrigley [135, 1972], especially the essay by Michael Anderson on the use of the British census manuscripts for the study of family structure.

15 A selection from the work of the Cambridge Group is worth including in any reading list for the new labor economics. For a nontechnical summary, see E. A. Wrigley [134, 1969], and for a recent example in detail of such work, T. P. R. Laslett [64, 1972].

16 That George Jaszi of the US Department of Commerce was able to argue in a comment that Gordon had discovered nothing new makes the other point: details of data, even important details, are not interesting to economists [55, 1970]. In his reply to Jaszi, Gordon asserts that 'the economics profession and particularly production function investigators had remained ignorant of government owned, privately operated capital' [40, 1970, p. 945] before his article. This appears to be correct.

17 Having drawn on Griliches' thinking here, it would be impolite to add that the studies on which he comments make no attempt to remove errors by remeasurement and embark instead, to repeat Leontief's acerbic remark quoted earlier, on 'devising a new statistical procedure, however tenuous, that makes it possible to squeeze out one more unknown parameter from a given set of data' [66, 1971, p. 3].

18 Fogel's calculations were for 1890. Fishlow's *American Railroads* is a similar study for the early nineteenth century [27, 1965]. Together they constitute a brilliant reinterpretation of the role of transportation in American growth, for which they were awarded in 1971 the Schumpeter Prize. The account of Fogel's experience derives from conversations with him.

19 There is a voluminous literature by historical economists on these: B. Thomas [114, 1954], R. A. Easterlin [22, 1961], and many more, among them P. Hill [52, 1970], L. Neal and P. Uselding [75, 1972] and A. C. Kelley [58, 1965].

20 See Michael Edelstein [24, 1974] and works cited there. The seminal work on the case of a receiving country is Jacob Viner [120, 1924]. The other books from the Taussig school of international finance published at Harvard in the 1920s and 1930s were also richly historical: J. H. Williams [128, 1920], H. D. White [126, 1933] and W. F. Beach [4, 1935]. Taussig himself as a young man wrote history [101, 1888].

21 One must include gross social security wealth, gross of the present value of social security taxes (as estimated by Martin Feldstein [26, 1974, p. 915, col. 3]). In 1971 GNP was on the order of $1,000 billion, the gross government debt $400 billion, and Feldstein's estimate of gross social security wealth $2,000 billion, for a ratio of about 2·4. In 1821 the GNP of the United Kingdom was on the order of £340 millions (based on the P. Deane and W. A. Cole [19, 1962] estimate for Great Britain increased by an estimate of Irish income at two-thirds the British level per capita) and the funded and unfunded government debt £840 million [73, Mitchell, 1962, pp. 8, 366, 402], for a ratio of about 2·5. The ratio of payments of interest to GNP in the UK in 1821 was 9 percent, about the same as interest, income security and veterans benefits and services to GNP in the USA in 1971, namely, 8 percent [73, Mitchell, 1962, p. 396; 119, *Economic Report of the President*, 1975, p. 325]. These comparisons could be refined to include local governments and non-interest-bearing debt.

22 For the United Kingdom this is the ratio in 1855, 1900 and 1958 of fixed reproducible capital net of depreciation to net domestic product (see C. H. Feinstein, Tables 43 and 20, with an allowance for capital consumption based on Table 1 [25, 1972]); for the United States the ratios in 1844–53, 1894–1903 and 1958 of depreciable capital to net national product (Gallman's Table 2.9 in Davis *et al.* [18, 1972]). The two books from which these figures come, incidentally, illustrate the role of social observatories in the encouragement of new economic history: Feinstein's is one of a series published under the auspices of the National Institute of Economic and Social Research (the British equivalent of the NBER) and the Cambridge Department of Applied Economics (an interpretive volume by Feinstein and R. C. O. Matthews is to follow); eight of the twelve authors of the Davis *et al.* book have worked at the NBER, and the book itself amounts to an interpretive summary of the long inquiry by them and others (notably Simon Kuznets) at the Bureau into trends in American economic growth.

23 See, in order, P. Lindert [68, 1974]; R. M. Hartwell [46, 1970]; R. P. Thomas [115, 1968]; I. B. Kravis [62, 1970]; E. J. Chambers and D. F. Gordon [11, 1966]; A. C. Kelley, J. G. Williamson and R. J. Cheetham [59, 1972]; and W. W. Rostow, ed. [97, 1963]. The work by Fishlow and Fogel on the American railway in the nineteenth century was in part motivated by Rostow's large claims for it as the critical innovation in American growth.

24 See among many others C. K. Harley [45, 1973], R. B. Zevin [138, 1971] and R. W. Fogel and S. L. Engerman [29, 1969], reprinted in Fogel and Engerman [30, 1971]. This book [30, 1971], incidentally, is a good selection of work on America by new economic historians, as is P. Temin [112, 1973].

25 See C. Pope [87, 1972], P. Passell and G. Wright [84, 1972], P. Passell and M. Schmundt [83, 1971], G. Hueckel [53, 1973] and, the most ambitious work to date along these lines, J. G. Williamson [130, 1974]. Cliometricians have been among the few economists to use non-linear general equilibrium models empirically.

26 C. D. Goldin [36, 1973; 37, 1976] and Fogel and Engerman [31, 1974] are recent examples of a large literature on slavery deriving from the early work of Conrad and Meyer [13, 1958]. J. D. Reid, Jr. [91, 1973] is an example of an equally large literature on sharecropping by cliometricians, among them Robert Higgs [51,

1974], Stephen DeCanio [20, 1974] and Roger Ransom and Richard Sutch [89, forth.].

27 Any economic historian has had the experience of colleagues announcing to him that they, too, are economic historians. It usually develops that they have run a regression back to 1929. The effect is similar to that of an economist who uses arithmetic announcing to his colleagues in mathematical economics that he, too, is a mathematical economist.

28 A good example is J. G. Williamson, especially ch. V [129, 1964]. After using without success the usual theories to explain the American balance of payments in the nineteenth century, he developed finally what is now known as the monetary theory, anticipating by several years its first theoretical statement. P. B. Whale, beginning with a similar historical problem, had done the same in 1937 [125, 1937].

29 Coherence was sacrificed for the gains from specialization in the collective volume by Davis, Easterlin, Parker and others [18, 1972], in so many other ways such a fine summary of the work of the cliometricians. Its focus on the economic revolution (its subtitle was 'An economist's history of the United States') required it to bypass the contributions of new economic history to political history. The Revolution, Jackson and the Second Bank, the tariff, slavery, the Civil War, and the free coinage of silver occupy, according to the index, 20 pages in total, smaller than the single entry 'Canals'.

30 This was explicit in Conrad and Meyer [13, 1958], although it was not put on a firm base until Y. Yasuba [136, 1961]. Cf. G. Gunderson [44, 1974].

31 Violent revolution and civil war are not the only political events to attract the attention of new economic historians: see J. Pincus [86, 1972] on the causes of early nineteenth-century tariffs; E. P. LeVeen [67, 1971] on the British suppression of the slave trade; R. B. Freeman [32, 1972] – an example of fine historical work by a non-historian – on the rise of educational discrimination in the South; R. Higgs [49, 1971, ch. IV] and J. Bowman and R. H. Keehn [5, 1974] on agrarian protest in the late nineteenth century; and G. Wright [133, 1974] on the political economy of New Deal spending.

32 I owe this quotation to Jon Sigurdsson of the Icelandic Economic Development Institute.

33 Presently much of the effort of the International Trade Workshop at the University of Chicago is devoted to applying the 'monetary' approach to the experience of England, France and Japan before World War II.

REFERENCES*

1 American Economic Association, *Index of Economic Journals*, vols I–VI (Homewood, Ill.: Irwin, 1961–5).

2 Anderson, T. 'The economic growth of seventeenth-century New England: a measurement of regional income', unpublished doctoral dissertation (University of Washington, 1972).

3 Ashton, T. S., 'The relation of economic history to economic theory', *Economica*, N. S., 13 (May 1946), pp. 81–96; reprinted in *The Study of Economic History*, ed. N. B. Harte (London: Frank Cass, 1971), pp. 161–80.

4 Beach, W. F., *British International Gold Movements and Banking Policy, 1881–1913,* (Cambridge: Harvard University Press, 1935).

5 Bowman, J. and Keehn, R. H., 'Agricultural terms of trade in four midwestern

*A complete bibliography on American economic history useful to economics, even if confined to 'cliometrics' in its recent incarnation, would run to many hundreds of items. This selection misses much important work. Items 18, 30, 49, 88, 112, 130 and 132 contain alternative selections.

states, 1870–1900', *J. Econ. Hist.*, 34 (Sept. 1974), pp. 592–609.

6 Brady, D. S. (ed.), *Output, Employment, and Productivity in the United States after 1800*, Conference on Research in Income and Wealth, Studies in Income and Wealth, Vol. 30 (New York: National Bureau of Economic Research; distributed by Columbia University Press, 1966).

7 Bronfenbrenner, M. 'Trends, cycles, and fads in economic writing', *Amer. Econ. Rev.*, Supplement, 56, 2 (May 1966), pp. 538–52.

8 Brown, E. C., 'Fiscal policy in the 'thirties: a reappraisal', *Amer. Econ. Rev.*, 46, 5 (Dec. 1956), pp. 857–79.

9 Cameron, R., 'Has economic history a role in an economist's education?', *Amer. Econ. Rev.*, Supplement, 55, 2 (May 1965), pp. 112–15.

10 Caves, R., 'Export-led growth and the new economic history', in *Trade, Balance of Payments and Growth*, ed. J. N. Bhagwati *et al.* (Amsterdam: North Holland, 1971).

11 Chambers, E. J. and Gordon, D. F., 'Primary products and economic growth: an empirical measurement', *J. Polit. Econ.*, 74, 4 (Aug. 1966), pp. 315–32.

12 Coats, A. W., 'The role of scholarly journals in the history of economics: an essay', *J. Econ. Lit.*, 9, 1 (March 1971), pp. 29–44.

13 Conrad, A. H. and Meyer, J. R., 'The economics of slavery in the ante-bellum South', *J. Polit. Econ.*, 66 (April 1958), pp. 95–130; reprinted in [14, 1964].

14 Conrad, A. H. and Meyer, J. R., *The Economics of Slavery and Other Studies in Econometric History* (Chicago: Aldine, 1964).

15 David, P. A., *Technical Choice, Innovation and Economic Growth: Essays on American and British Experience in the Nineteenth Century* (New York and London: Cambridge University Press, 1975).

16 David, P. A., and Temin, P. 'Slavery: the progressive institution?', *J. Econ. Hist.*, 34 (Sept. 1974), pp. 739–83.

17 Davis, L. E. and North, D. C., *Institutional Change and American Economic Growth* (Cambridge: Cambridge University Press, 1971).

18 Davis, L. E., Easterlin, R. A., Parker, W. N. *et al.*, *American Economic Growth: An Economist's History of the United States* (New York: Harper & Row, 1972).

19 Deane, P. and Cole, W. A., *British Economic Growth, 1688–1959* (Cambridge: Cambridge University Press, 1962).

20 DeCanio, S., *Agricultural Production, Supply and Institutions in the Post-Civil War South* (Cambridge: MIT Press, 1974).

21 Easterlin, R. A., 'Interregional differences in per capita income, population, and total income, 1840–1950', in [82, Parker, 1960].

22 Easterlin, R. A., 'Influences in European overseas emigration before World War I', *Econ. Dev. Cult. Change*, 9 (April 1961), pp. 331–51.

23 Easterlin, R. A., *Population, Labor Force, and Long Swings in Economic Growth: The American Experience* (New York: NBER; distributed by Columbia University Press, 1968).

24 Edelstein, M., 'The determinants of U.K. investment abroad, 1870–1913: the U.S. Case', *J. Econ. Hist.*, 34, 4 (Dec. 1974), pp. 980–1007.

25 Feinstein, C. H., *National Income, Expenditure and Output of the United Kingdom, 1855–1956* (Cambridge: Cambridge University Press, 1972).

26 Feldstein, M., 'Social security, induced retirement, and aggregate capital accumulation', *J. Polit. Econ.*, 82, 5 (Sept/Oct. 1974), pp. 905–26.

27 Fishlow, A., *American Railroads and the Transformation of the Ante-bellum Economy* (Cambridge: Harvard University Press, 1965).

28 Fogel, R. W., *Railroads and American Economic Growth: Essays in Econometric History* (Baltimore: Johns Hopkins Press, 1964).

29 Fogel, R. W. and Engerman, S. L., 'A model for the explanation of industrial expansion during the nineteenth century: with an application to the American iron industry', *J. Polit. Econ.*, 77, 3 (May/June 1969), pp. 306–28.

30 Fogel, R. W. and Engerman, S. L. (eds), *The Reinterpretation of American Economic History* (New York: Harper & Row, 1971).

31 Fogel, R. W. and Engerman, S. L. *Time on the Cross: The Economics of American Negro Slavery,* 2 vols (Boston: Little, Brown, 1974).

32 Freeman, R. B., 'Black-white income differences: why did they last so long?', unpublished manuscript (Harvard University, 1972).

33 Friedman, M., and Schwartz, A. J., *A Monetary History of the United States 1867–1960* (Princeton: Princeton University Press for the NBER, 1963).

34 Gallman, R. E., 'Commodity output, 1839–1899', in [82, Parker, 1960].

35 Gallman, R. E., 'Gross national product in the United States, 1834–1909', in [6, Brady, 1966].

36 Goldin, C. D., 'The economics of emancipation', *J. Econ. Hist.*, 33, 1 (March 1973), pp. 66–85.

37 Gallman, R. E., unpublished manuscript on urban slavery, forthcoming (Chicago: University of Chicago Press, 1976).

38 Gordon, D. F. and Walton, G. M., 'A new theory of regenerative growth and the experience of post World War II West Germany', unpublished manuscript (University of Indiana, Oct. 1974).

39 Gordon, R. J., '$45 billion of U.S. private investment has been mislaid', *Amer. Econ. Rev.*, 59, 3 (June 1969), pp. 221–38.

40 Gordon, R. J., 'Reply to comment by G. Jaszi', *Amer. Econ. Rev.*, 60, 5 (Dec. 1970), pp. 940–5 (see [55, Jaszi, 1970]).

41 Goy, J. and Le Roy Ladurie, E., *Les Fluctuations du produit de la Dîme* (Paris: Mouton, 1972).

42 Griliches, Z., 'Errors in variables and other unobservables', *Econometrica*, 42, 6 (Nov. 1974), pp. 971–98.

43 Guisinger, S. E., 'The theory and measurement of effective protection – the case of Pakistan', unpublished doctoral dissertation (Harvard University, 1970).

44 Gunderson, G., 'The origin of the American Civil War', *J. Econ. Hist.*, 34, 4 (Dec. 1974), pp. 915–50.

45 Harley, C. K., 'On the persistence of old techniques: the case of North American wooden shipbuilding', *J. Econ. Hist.*, 33, 2 (June 1973), pp. 372–98.

46 Hartwell, R. M., 'The standard of living controversy: a summary', in *The Industrial Revolution*, ed. R. M. Hartwell (Oxford: Blackwell, 1970).

47 Hicks, J. R., 'An inaugural lecture', *Oxford Econ. Pap.*, N.S., 5 (June 1953), pp. 117–35.

48 Hicks, J. R., *A Theory of Economic History* (Oxford: Clarendon Press, 1969).

49 Higgs, R., *The Transformation of the American Economy, 1865–1914: An Essay in Interpretation* (New York: Wiley, 1971).

50 Higgs, R., 'Race, skills, and earnings: American immigrants in 1909', *J. Econ. Hist.*, 31, 2 (June 1971), pp. 420–8.

51 Higgs, R., 'Patterns of farm rental in the Georgia cotton belt, 1880–1900', *J. Econ. Hist.*, 34, 2 (June 1974), pp. 468–82.

52 Hill, P., 'The economic impact of immigration into the United States', unpublished doctoral dissertation (University of Chicago, 1970).

53 Hueckel, G., 'War and the British economy, 1793–1815, a general equilibrium analysis', *Explor. Econ. Hist.*, 10, 4 (Summer 1973), pp. 365–96.

54 Hughes, J. R. T. and Reiter, S., 'The first 1,945 British steamships', *J. Amer. Statist. Assoc.*, 53 (June 1958), pp. 360–81.

55 Jaszi, G., '$45 billion of U.S. private investment has been mislaid: comment', *Amer. Econ. Rev.*, 60, 5 (Dec. 1970), pp. 934–9 (see R. J. Gordon's 'Reply' [40, 1970]).

56 Jones, A. H., 'Wealth estimates for the New England colonies about 1770', *J. Econ. Hist.*, 32, 1 (March 1972), pp. 98–127.

57 Jones, G. T., *Increasing Returns* (Cambridge: Cambridge University Press, 1933).

58 Kelley, A. C., 'International migration and economic growth: Australia, 1865–1935', *J. Econ. Hist.*, 25, 3 (Sept. 1965), pp. 333–54.

59 Kelley, A. C., Williamson, J. G. and Cheetham, R. J., *Dualistic Economic Development: Theory and History* (Chicago: University of Chicago Press, 1972).

60 Kessel, R. A. and Alchian, A. A., 'Real wages in the North during the Civil War: Mitchell's data reinterpreted', *J. Law Econ.*, 2 (Oct. 1959), pp. 95–113.

61 Klotz, B. P. and Neal, L. D., 'Spectral and cross-spectral analysis of the long swing hypothesis', *Rev. Econ. Statist.*, 55, 3 (August 1973), pp. 291–8.

62 Kravis, I. B., 'Trade as a handmaiden of growth: similarities between the nineteenth and twentieth centuries', *Econ. J.*, 80, 320 (Dec. 1970), pp. 850–72.

63 Landes, W. M. and Solmon, L. C., 'Compulsory schooling legislation: an economic analysis of law and social change in the nineteenth century', *J. Econ. Hist.*, 32, 1 (March 1972), pp. 54–91.

64 Laslett, T. P. R., *Household and Family in Past Time* (Cambridge: Cambridge University Press, 1972).

65 Lebergott, S., *Manpower in Economic Growth: The American Record since 1800* (New York: McGraw-Hill, 1964).

66 Leontief, W., 'Theoretical assumptions and nonobserved facts', *Amer. Econ. Rev.*, 61, 1 (March 1971), pp. 1–7.

67 LeVeen, E. P., 'British slave trade suppression policies 1821–1865: impact and implications', unpublished doctoral dissertation (University of Chicago, 1971).

68 Lindert, P. H., 'Land scarcity and American growth', *J. Econ. Hist.*, 34, 4 (Dec. 1974), pp. 851–84.

69 McClelland, P. D., 'The cost to America of British imperial policy', *Amer. Econ. Rev.*, Supplement, 59, 2 (May 1969), pp. 370–81.

70 McGouldrick, P. F., *New England Textiles in the Nineteenth Century: Profits and Investment* (Cambridge, Mass.: Harvard University Press, 1968).

71 Meeker, E., 'The improving health of the United States, 1850–1915', *Explor. Econ. Hist.*, 9, 4 (Summer 1972), pp. 353–74.

72 Meeker, E., 'The social rate of return on investment in public health, 1880–1910', *J. Econ. Hist.*, 34, 2 (June 1974), pp. 392–421.

73 Mitchell, B. R. with Deane, P., *Abstract of British Historical Statistics* (Cambridge: Cambridge University Press, 1962).

74 Mitchell, W. C., *Business Cycles: The Problem and its Setting* (New York: NBER, 1927).

75 Neal, L. and Uselding, P., 'Immigration, a neglected source of American economic growth: 1790–1912', *Oxford Econ. Pap.*, N.S., 24, 1 (March 1972), pp. 68–88.

76 Nelson, R. R. and Winter, S. G., 'Neoclassical vs. evolutionary theories of economic growth: critique and prospectus', *Econ. J.*, 84, 336 (Dec. 1974), pp. 886–905.

77 Nerlove, M., 'Two models of the British economy: a fragment of a critical survey', *Int'l. Econ. Rev.*, 6, 2 (May 1965), pp. 127–81.

78 North, D. C. 'Sources of productivity change in ocean shipping, 1600–1850', *J. Polit. Econ.*, 76, 5 (Sept./Oct. 1968), pp. 953–70.

79 North, D. C., and Thomas, R. P., *The Rise of the Western World* (Cambridge: Cambridge University Press, 1973).

80 Olmstead, A. L., 'New York City mutual savings bank portfolio management and trustee objectives', *J. Econ. Hist.*, 34, 4 (Dec. 1974), pp. 815–34.

81 Olson, M., *The Economics of Wartime Shortage, a History of British Food Supplies in the Napoleonic Wars and in World Wars I and II* (Durham: Duke University Press, 1963).

82 Parker, W. N. (ed.), *Trends in the American Economy in the Nineteenth Century*, Conference on Research in Income and Wealth, Studies in Income and Wealth, Vol. 24 (Princeton: Princeton University Press, 1960).

83 Passell, P. and Schmundt, M., 'Pre-Civil War land policy and the growth of

manufacturing', *Explor. Econ. Hist.*, 9, 1 (Fall 1971), pp. 35–48.

84 Passell, P. and Wright, G., 'The effects of pre-Civil War expansion on the price of slaves', *J. Polit. Econ.*, 80, 6 (Nov./Dec. 1972), pp. 1188–1202.

85 Peppers, L. C., 'Full-employment surplus analysis and structural change: the 1930s', *Explor. Econ. Hist.*, 10, 2 (Winter 1973), pp. 197–210.

86 Pincus, J., 'A positive theory of tariff formation applied to the 19th-century United States', unpublished doctoral dissertation (Stanford University, 1972).

87 Pope, C., 'The impact of the ante-bellum tariff on income distribution', *Explor. Econ. Hist.*, 9, 4 (Summer 1972), pp. 375–421.

88 *Purdue Faculty Papers in Economic History 1956–1966* (Homewood, Ill.: Irwin, 1967).

89 Ransom, R. and Sutch, R., unpublished book manuscript on post-bellum southern agriculture, forthcoming.

90 Rees, A. E., *Real Wages in Manufacturing, 1890–1914* (Princeton: Princeton University Press, 1961).

91 Reid, J. D., Jr., 'Sharecropping as an understandable market response: the post-bellum South', *J. Econ Hist.*, 33, 1 (March 1973), pp. 106–30.

92 Rockoff, H. T., 'The free banking era: a reexamination', *J. Money, Credit, Banking*, 6, 2 (May 1974), pp. 141–67.

93 Rockoff, H. T., 'Varieties of banking and regional economic development in the United States, 1840–1860', *J. Econ. Hist.*, 35, 1 (March 1975), pp. 160–81.

94 Roll, R., 'Interest rates and price expectations during the Civil War', *J. Econ. Hist.*, 32, 2 (June 1972), pp. 476–98.

95 Rosenberg, N., *Technology and American Economic Growth* (New York: Harper & Row, 1972).

96 Rosovsky, H. (ed.), *Industrialization in Two Systems: Essays in Honor of Alexander Gerschenkron, by a group of his students* (New York: Wiley, 1966).

97 Rostow, W. W. (ed.), *The Economics of Take-off into Sustained Growth* (New York: St Martin's, 1963).

98 Sandberg, L. G., *Lancashire in Decline: A Study in Entrepreneurship, Technology and International Trade* (Columbus: Ohio State University Press, 1974).

99 Sanderson, A. R., 'Child-labor legislation and the labor force participation of children', *J. Econ. Hist.*, 34, 1 (March 1974), pp. 297–9.

100 Schultz, T. W., *Transforming Traditional Agriculture* (New Haven: Yale University Press, 1964).

101 Schultz, T. W., 'Lingering doubts about economics', unpublished paper (University of Chicago, 1974); *Amer. Econ. Rev.*, forthcoming.

102 Shepherd, J. F. and Walton, G. M., *Shipping, Maritime Trade, and the Economic Development of Colonial North America* (Cambridge: Cambridge University Press, 1972).

103 Sheppard, D. K., *The Growth and Role of U.K. Financial Institutions, 1880–1962* (London: Methuen, 1971).

104 Simon, M., 'The United States balance of payments, 1861–1900', in [82, Parker, 1960].

105 Solow, R. M., *Growth Theory: An Exposition* (Oxford: Clarendon Press, 1970).

106 Soltow, L., *Men and Wealth in the United States, 1850–1870* (New Haven: Yale University Press, 1975).

107 Stigler, G. J., 'Does economics have a useful past?', *Hist. Pol. Econ.*, 1, 2 (Fall 1969), pp. 217–30.

108 Swanson, J. A. and Williamson, J. G., 'Firm location and optimal city size in American history', in *The New Urban History: Quantitative Explorations by American Historians*, ed. L. F. Schnore (Princeton: Princeton University Press, 1974).

109 Sylla, R., 'Federal policy, banking market structure and capital mobilization in the United States, 1863–1913', *J. Econ. Hist.*, 29, 4 (Dec. 1969), pp. 657–86.

110 Taussig, F. W., *The Tariff History of the United States* (New York: Putnam, 1888).
111 Temin, P., *The Jacksonian Economy* (New York: Norton, 1969).
112 Temin, P. (ed.), *New Economic History: Selected Readings* (Harmondsworth, England: Penguin, 1973).
113 Temin, P., 'The Anglo-American business cycle, 1820–60', *Econ. Hist. Rev.*, 2nd ser., 27, 2 (May 1974), pp. 207–21.
114 Thomas, B., *Migration and Economic Growth* (Cambridge: Cambridge University Press, 1954).
115 Thomas, R. P., 'The sugar colonies of the old empire: profit or loss for Great Britain?', *Econ. Hist. Rev.*, 2nd ser., 21, 1 (April 1968), pp. 30–45.
116 Titow, J. Z., *Winchester Yields* (Cambridge: Cambridge University Press, 1972).
117 Trevelyan, G. M., *English Social History* (London and New York: Longmans, Green, 1942).
118 US Bureau of the Census, *Historical Statistics of the United States, Colonial Times to 1957* (Washington, DC: USGPO, 1960).
119 US President, *Economic Report of the President* (Washington, D.C.: USGPO, 1975).
120 Viner, J., *Canada's Balance of International Indebtedness, 1900–1913* (Cambridge, Mass.: Harvard University Press, 1924).
121 Walton, G. M., 'Sources of productivity change in American colonial shipping, 1675–1775', *Econ. Hist. Rev.*, 2nd ser., 20, 1 (April 1967), pp. 67–78.
122 Weiss, R. W., 'The issue of paper money in the American colonies, 1720–1774', *J. Econ. Hist.*, 30, 4 (Dec. 1970), pp. 770–84.
123 Weiss, R. W., 'The colonial monetary standard of Massachusetts', *Econ. Hist. Rev.*, 2nd ser., 27, 4 (Nov. 1974), pp. 577–92.
124 West, E. G., 'Educational slowdown and public intervention in 19th-century England: a study in the economics of bureaucracy', *Explor. Econ. Hist.*, 12, 1 (Jan. 1975), pp. 61–87.
125 Whale, P. B., 'The working of the pre-war gold standard', *Economica*, N.S., 4 (Feb. 1937), pp. 18–32.
126 White, H. D., *The French International Accounts, 1880–1913* (Cambridge, Mass.: Harvard University Press, 1933).
127 Whitney, W. G., 'The structure of the American economy in the late 19th century', unpublished doctoral dissertation (Harvard University, 1968).
128 Williams, J. H., *Argentine International Trade Under Inconvertible Paper Money: 1880–1900* (Cambridge, Mass.: Harvard University Press, 1920).
129 Williamson, J. G., *American Growth and the Balance of Payments, 1820–1913* (Chapel Hill: University of North Carolina Press, 1964).
130 Williamson, J. G., *Late Nineteenth-Century American Development: A General Equilibrium History* (London and New York: Cambridge University Press, 1974).
131 Williamson, J. G., 'Watersheds and turning points: conjectures on the long-term impact of Civil War financing', *J. Econ. Hist.*, 34, 3 (Sept. 1974), pp. 636–61.
132 Wright, G., 'Econometric studies of history', in *Frontiers of Quantitative Economics*, ed. M. D. Intriligator (Amsterdam: North Holland, 1971).
133 Wright, G., 'The political economy of New Deal spending: an econometric analysis', *Rev. Econ. Statist.*, 56, 1 (Feb. 1974), pp. 30–8.
134 Wrigley, E. A., *Population and History* (London: Weidenfeld & Nicolson, New York: McGraw-Hill, 1969).
135 Wrigley, E. A. (ed.), *Nineteenth-Century Society: Essays in the Use of Quantitative Methods for the Study of Social Data* (Cambridge: Cambridge University Press, 1972).
136 Yasuba, Y. 'The profitability and viability of plantation slavery in the United States', *Econ. Stud. Quart.*, 12 (Sept. 1961), pp. 60–7; reprinted in [30, Fogel and Engerman, 1971].

137 Zellner, A. and Murphy, G., 'Sequential growth, the labor-safety-valve doctrine and the development of American unionism', *J. Econ. Hist.*, 19, 3 (Sept. 1959), pp. 402–21.

138 Zevin, R. B., 'The growth of cotton textile production after 1815', in [30, Fogel and Engerman, 1971].

Part Two

Enterprise in Late Victorian Britain

3

From Damnation to Redemption: Judgments on the Late Victorian Entrepreneur

DONALD N. McCLOSKEY and LARS G. SANDBERG

In the 1890s it became clear that Britain had lost the industrial leadership of the world to Germany and the United States. Each year the statistics of trade and output brought fresh evidence that the trend established in the 1870s of slower industrial growth in Britain than in the new industrial nations was continuing. New products and new markets were being developed by German chemists and salesmen and by American engineers and plant managers while British businessmen fought a rearguard action on economic battlefields where they had once stood unchallenged. Such military metaphors as this last flowed naturally from the pens of journalists and scholars describing this humbling experience, and there was much talk of commercial 'invasion' and industrial 'defeat'. Anthropomorphic metaphors, as well, of 'youthful' foreign nations usurping the place of 'old' Britain, were called on to bolster the frail illusion of understanding the turn of events. And when metaphor proved unsatisfying, it was natural that attention should turn to the men at the top. When an army is outmaneuvered, who is to blame for its defeat but its incompetent generals? When an economy grows old, who is to blame for its decrepitude but its aging businessmen? Increasingly after the 1890s in the editorial columns of trade journals and in the pages of government reports, for one industry after another, blame for the British lag behind Germany and America was put on British management.

On the level of journalism and schoolbook history there is no difficulty in meting out praise or blame: if great entrepreneurs, independent of circumstances, were responsible for Britain's relative rise before 1870, then surely bad entrepreneurs must have been responsible for her relative decline after 1870. The reasoning involved is the same as that underlying the perennial political cry in troubled times, 'throw the

Without implicating him in the views expressed here, we should like to thank Peter Lindert of the University of Wisconsin for his incisive comments on a draft of this essay.

rascals out'. When the British cotton textile industry fell on bad times after World War I, it was suddenly discovered that entrepreneurs before the war had lacked foresight. Similarly the once lionized New England cotton textile managers were found to be incompetent when their industry began to shrink in the face of southern competition.[1] The American coal industry, whose technical efficiency was renowned the world over before World War I, was found by the Coal Commission of the troubled 1920s to have fatal flaws in management. In short, any competitive rise or fall in an industry's output is in this view attributable to good or bad management. The British decline, then, was seen to be a clear case of bad management.

A more sophisticated view was that bad management, although important, was nonetheless only a part of the reason for Britain's relative decline. A number of contemporary intellectuals, from all sections of the political spectrum, among them Hobson, Veblen and Marshall, took this position. In 1903, Marshall, for example, wrote:

> Sixty years ago England had . . . leadership in most branches of industry . . . It was inevitable that she should cede much . . . to the great land which attracts alert minds of all nations to sharpen their inventive and resourceful faculties by impact on one another. It was inevitable that she should yield a little of it to that land of great industrial traditions which yoked science in the service of man with unrivalled energy. It was not inevitable that she should lose so much of it as she has done.[2]

Marshall's great student, Clapham, chided the less rational of the critics of British performance for judging entrepreneurial skill by the mere size of American versus British output: 'Half a continent is likely in course of time to raise more coal and make more steel than a small island, although this fact still surprised people between 1890 and 1910.'[3] Yet for all his reasoned caution and carefully balanced examples, Clapham too believed that he had uncovered case after case of less than satisfactory management in steel, in coal, in textiles and in the new industries. A student of his, Duncan Burn, developed this theme in detail for the steel industry, in his influential book, *The Economic History of Steelmaking 1867–1939, A Study in Competition*, which formed the capstone of the Marshallian tradition in the study of entrepreneurial failure.[4]

The heirs of Hobson, occupied with labor and social history, had less to say on the subject, although they could not be blamed for noting when the occasion arose that the capitalists themselves believed their house to be in disarray. It was the heirs of Veblen and Schumpeter, taking a sociological view of the matter, who in the 1950s carried on the development of the hypothesis of entrepreneurial failure. An important factor in this work was a group of economic historians, especially Americans, who developed the argument in the late 1940s and 1950s that the linchpin of economic history is the entrepreneur.[5] With the revival at about the same time of general scholarly interest in the performance of the late Victorian economy, the British entrepreneur became a case in point.[6] The most forceful and eloquent application of the entrepreneurial approach to Britain was David Landes' contribution to *The Cambridge Economic History of Europe*, published in 1965.[7] Building on an earlier piece presented in 1954 to a conference sponsored by the Harvard University Center in Entrepreneurial History ('Entrepreneurship in Advanced Industrial Countries: The Anglo-German Rivalry'), Landes crystallized the long-standing argument that the contrast between German and American industrial triumphs and British defeats could best be explained by emphasis on 'the importance of this human factor – the success of entrepreneurial and technological creativity on one side, the failure on the other'.[8] Similar conclusions emerging in the 1960s from other publications, such as Derek Aldcroft's influential article, 'The entrepreneur and the British economy, 1870–1914', published in 1964,[9] added up to a broad indictment of British entrepreneurs in the late nineteenth century, namely, that:

(1) They failed to adopt the best available techniques of production in many industries, ranging from ring-spinning and automatic weaving in cotton to the mechanical cutter and the electrification of mines in coal.
(2) They underestimated the growing importance of science, investing little in laboratories and technical personnel for research or for the effective exploitation of foreign research.
(3) They overinvested in the old staple export industries such as cotton and iron, and were slow to move to the industries of the future such as chemicals, automobiles and electrical engineering.
(4) They were bad salesmen, especially abroad.[10]
(5) They were insufficiently aggressive in organizing cartels to extract monopoly profits from the world at large.

The development of this damning catalogue marked the high point in the historiographic career of the hypothesis of entrepreneurial failure, for although accorded the honor of serious consideration in many writings on the Victorian economy by this time the hypothesis was already under attack from several quarters.[11]

The first line of attack was to admit that late Victorian entrepreneurs did in fact neglect to install the best available industrial equipment, but to explain this neglect in terms other than entrepreneurial failure, shifting the explanation from sociological to economic variables. One such variable, which Veblen himself thought important, while not on this account forgoing the pleasure of damning British entrepreneurship, was the age of British industrial equipment. Britain, it was argued, was burdened with the equipment of an earlier generation of industrial technology while foreign late-comers to industrialization had the advantage of a fresh start. An oft-cited example of the burden of the past is the alleged inefficiency of Britain's tiny coal cars on the railways. The difficulty with moving to larger coal cars was that of 'interrelatedness', as Frankel called it in an influential article on the economic burden of the past:[12] sidings, loading equipment, tracks, and so on were designed to accommodate the small cars, and consequently changing the cars would require massive investment in these interrelated pieces of equipment as well. Charles Kindleberger, in his stimulating if inconclusive *tour de force, Economic Growth in France and Britain, 1851–1950*,[13] favored an institutional rather than a technological version of the hypothesis. The difficulty, Kindleberger argued, was not so much that large investments were needed to overcome the disadvantages of Britain's early start in industrialization, but that the benefits and costs of the investments were not centered in one economic unit. The railways, for example, owned the sidings, but the collieries owned the coal cars. Consequently, as in the technological version of the hypothesis, the long-standing neglect of the larger cars was rational from the point of view of the individual entrepreneurs involved.

Although one might well doubt that these obstacles to fresh investment could be large enough to offset the advantage Britain got from having the capital to begin with before her rivals and still more that the obstacles would necessarily be greater in Britain than elsewhere,[14] both forms of the interrelatedness argument have been mildly fashionable. For all their fashionability, however, little work has been done to establish their quantitative significance, leaving supporters of the entrepreneurial hypothesis free to attribute some substantial part of the reluctance to install new industrial equipment to entrepreneurial failure. The only attempt to show that interrelatedness was quantitatively significant, indeed, is a paper by Paul David applying the argument in both the technological and institutional form not to industry but to agriculture.[15] David's success in explaining the British lag in the adoption of the mechanical reaper on these grounds, however, says little about the applicability of the argument outside of agriculture, for interrelatedness is peculiarly a problem of capital in land. Farmers as a group have to work with land as they find it, in the case of nineteenth-century Britain with land in the ridge-and-furrow configuration appropriate to earlier agricultural techniques but highly inappropriate to an age of drainpipes and mechanical reapers. Industrialists, however, need not work with the equipment of their predecessors: unlike the farmer with his land, they can abandon their old plant and equipment.

A similar paucity of quantitative evidence has dulled the impact of the attempt to focus attention on another variable, the growth of demand. Slower aggregate growth in Britain than in the industrializing countries may have meant that it was rational to keep an older capital stock: a slowly growing capital stock, like a slowly growing human population, has a higher average age and therefore includes less up-to-date components. This explanation, based again on the allegedly antique character of British equipment, was a popular alternative to entrepreneurial failure among contemporaries,[16] especially for the steel industry, where it seemed most likely to apply, and has been adopted by subsequent doubters of the entrepreneurial hypothesis such as I. Svennilson and H. J. Habakkuk.[17] Like the interrelatedness argument, the age-of-capital argument received its formal theoretical baptism in the 1950s long after it had been proposed in the historical literature, emerging as technological change 'embodied' in new capital equipment. And again, only one attempt has been made to use the logic developed in the theoretical literature to derive an estimate of its quantitative significance, by Peter Temin in 'The relative decline of the British steel industry, 1880–1913', published in 1966.[18] Temin arrived at the startling conclusion that slower British growth could account for a 15 percent lag in productivity in steelmaking behind that of Germany and America, a large enough effect, were it true, to destroy the hypothesis of entrepreneurial failure: a 15 percent difference is surely enough to account for any difference attributable to bad management. Fortunately for the hypothesis of failure, it is not true. Temin's argument rests on two demonstrably false propositions: first, that productivity growth in the American steel industry was 3 percent per year (in fact it was only 1·3 percent per year); second, that productivity change fell in proportion to the fall in the growth of output in Britain (in fact it did not).[19] These and other revisions reduce the estimate of the embodiment effect from 15 percent to less than 1 percent.

The various attempts to explain the neglect of the newest equipment on economic grounds, then, did not succeed in dislodging the hypothesis of failure. The difficulty was that the new variables were usually introduced in the same non-quantitative way that adherents of the hypothesis of failure introduced entrepreneurship itself. In his development of the hypothesis Landes discussed a variety of economic arguments, discarding them one by one on qualitative grounds to arrive at his final result. Kindleberger's and Habakkuk's methods in developing alternative hypotheses were similar, carrying the discussion through casual empiricism and more or less cogent reasoning on the alternative arguments suggested in the literature towards the one position that seemed to them tenable. Another example of this procedure is a book by A. L. Levine, *Industrial Retardation in Britain, 1880–1914*, published in 1967.[20] Apparently unaware of Landes' work,

Levine nonetheless reached much the same conclusion by much the same route. After arguing, in the manner of Landes, that there existed a lag of British industry behind German and American industry in matters of technology and organization, Levine marshalled a good sample of contemporary and retrospective testimony on the various possible explanations, discarded them in sequence and came finally to the judgment that the 'technical and organizational lag in British industry was, more than anything else, a question of entrepreneurial responses'.[21] This sort of *qualitative* argument by isolation has the critical difficulty that the size of the isolated residual variable, whether sociological or economic, is left a matter of faith rather than fact. Few who were not already convinced of the importance of entrepreneurship would be converted to the faith by Levine's argument, or even by Landes' more sophisticated and eloquent argument, because it does not rest on some indubitable line of fact or logic. At each step the reader is invited to accept without quantitative evidence a judgment on the quantitative significance of an alternative factor in order to arrive at the final result that the effect of the residual factor, whether entrepreneurship, interrelatedness or embodiment, was 'large'.

The uncertainties in using a qualitative argument to arrive at a quantitative result are common enough in historical writing, although a sanguine observer might hope that economic history, with its potential for drawing on clear economic theories and concrete economic facts, would be able to avoid them more often than it does. The theories were clear in the economic alternatives to the hypothesis of entrepreneurial failure, but the facts for making them general explanations were lacking. The entrepreneurial hypothesis itself was built on a somewhat narrow base of fact, consisting of the one presumably well-founded case of failure in iron and steel provided by Burn's book and a few considerably less well-founded cases in chemicals, electrical engineering and a handful of other industries.[22]

The second line of attack on the hypothesis of failure consisted of a broadening of this base of fact through the detailed narrative study of the performance of individual industries. Although not directed at this particular issue alone, the narrative studies greatly modified the picture of poor entrepreneurship. S. B. Saul led the attack with a series of papers centering on the engineering industries, published over the last decade or so,[23] and this approach reached a climax in the publication of a set of industry studies in 1968 entitled *The Development of British Industry and Foreign Competition 1875–1914*[24] under the editorship of one of the framers of the hypothesis of entrepreneurial failure, D. H. Aldcroft. There was much in these essays, in Saul's work and in similar work elsewhere[25] to support the hypothesis, but only in a mild and modified form. Saul argued that the consulting engineer system was an important cause of economic inefficiency in the making of railway engines and automobiles, but rejected the typically uniform condemnation of British entrepreneurship in these industries, as well as in machine tools and electrical engineering. A similar revision of the journalistic picture of widespread failure emerged from work on cotton textiles, shipping and other industries. Indeed, Aldcroft's own indictment of British entrepreneurs was substantially less sweeping in his introduction to the 1968 volume than it had been in his earlier work, although he still insisted that entrepreneurial failure characterized a good part of industry:

> [T]he fact that some industrialists were slow to adopt new techniques does not necessarily mean that they were inefficient or lacked enterprise . . .
>
> On the other hand, neither must one adopt an unduly complacent attitude when discussing the performance of British business in this period. As we have already seen there was considerable room for improvement in many branches of British industry . . . But the problem was not always simply one of a failure to innovate on the part of industrialists.[26]

Earlier industry studies, such as Burn's on iron and steel, had yielded the conclusion that entrepreneurs had failed; apparently close study of other industries along similar non-quantitative lines could yield the opposite conclusion on British performance in the aggregate. It was perhaps Charles Wilson's close study of the marketing successes of Unilever in soap, for example, that motivated him to propose an interpretation of British performance precisely the reverse of the hypothesis of failure: he argued that over a substantial part of British industry, especially among the 'miscellaneous industries and incorporeal functions', as Giffen called them, vigorous entrepreneurship prevailed.[27]

As close as Wilson's position on entrepreneurial failure is to his own, Saul remarks at one point in his useful survey of the period, *The Myth of the Great Depression, 1873–1896*, that he is not convinced by Wilson's essay because Wilson 'argues by example'.[28] This is a common criticism and is valid not only for Wilson's work, but for Saul's own, and that of virtually all the disputants, at least to the extent that they wish to draw general inferences for or against British entrepreneurs from their own particular sample of entrepreneurial performance. A case, after all, is merely a case, and little effort has been expended in constructing a truly random sample of British behavior, properly weighted for the importance of each industry. The rules of the game of example and counterexample, indeed, discourage a random choice of cases: in comparing British with German enterprise, supporters of the hypothesis of failure have felt free to ignore the apparently clear cases of good performance of British agriculture and retail trade, while opponents of it have until recently remained silent on the apparently clear cases of poor performance in the slow adoption of ring-spinning in cotton and the basic process in steel. Short of a truly random sample of sectors to be studied intensively or a national assessment of performance based on productivity in creating national income, larger samples, whether statistical in nature or not, are of little help. The industries in W. Hoffmann's index of industrial output, to take as an example a vein of data that has been worked hard and long by students of the period, do not constitute a random sample of the statistical universe of British entrepreneurial performance, weighted as they are towards old industries making commodities and away from new industries providing services. International comparisons of productivity using similar indices of output in the United States and Germany would yield biased readings: it could well have been that as a mature industrial nation in 1870 Britain already had achieved an advanced technology in the basic industries of the industrial revolution and was well advised to concentrate the search for productivity improvement in services and light industries, which are underrepresented in the standard indices of industrial output.

One swallow, then, does not make a summer, nor do scattered cases of entrepreneurial success or failure make or break the hypothesis of general entrepreneurial failure. More important still, while the first, economic attack on the hypothesis had the enlightenment of economic theory without the discipline of economic fact, the second, narrative attack too often consisted of fact without theory. The facts in the sources were brought to life with makeshift economics or, worse yet, the economic logic of the sources themselves. The judgment of acquittal of the British cotton textile managers rendered by R. E. Tyson on the charge that they irrationally ignored ring-spinning, for example, rested primarily on the testimony of Melvin Copeland in 1912.[29] Copeland was reputable and well-informed, and as it happens his impressionistic assessment of the economics of ring-spinning can be verified by more cogent methods,[30] but to accept his assessment without further inquiry is to accept his implicit economic theory, that is to say, his particular brand of the more or less vague and contradictory intellectual machinery of makeshift economics. Without redoing the economics and reevaluating the facts, there is little reason to accept his favorable judgment over the unfavorable judgment of many equally qualified observers of the industry.

Furthermore, the manner of proof in the work of Saul, Wilson and the rest was similar to that in the work of Landes and Aldcroft in that it attempted a qualitative rather than a quantitative isolation of entrepreneurial performance. The same measures of performance were used, namely, an industry's output or an industry's speed in adopting allegedly critical innovations indicative of entrepreneurial skill. Neither of these measures is adequate on theoretical grounds, the measures of output because they confound influences of demand with those of supply and the measures of indicative innovations because they neglect the variability in the advantage to be gained from different innovations in different countries. The flaw in using a mere output measure to gauge entrepreneurial performance is clear enough, despite its perennial popularity. The use of indicative innovations – such as ring-spindles and automatic looms in textiles, machine cutters in coal and the basic process in steel – is less obviously flawed. The usual way of identifying these innovations is to rely on hindsight together with the faulty lemma that any innovation eventually adopted should have been adopted, if it was available, earlier. Clapham remarked of the basic process in steel, for example, that 'it is hard to believe that a process employed so extensively in 1925 and 1913 might not have been employed to advantage rather more than it was in 1901 and earlier'.[31] This may well be true, but the mere fact that the process was adopted in 1925 sheds little light on the appropriateness of adopting it in 1901.

What is required, but is seldom forthcoming in works using such measures to damn or praise British entrepreneurs, is a close examination of the economics of each innovation, to determine whether something other than entrepreneurial vigor might account for the rate of adoption in Britain and abroad. Interpreting indicative innovations as reflections of vigor often yields absurd implications. The by-product coke oven was adopted first in Germany, next in Great Britain, and last in the United States, and the lag of Britain behind Germany has been used to support the argument for entrepreneurial failure in Britain. But few would suggest that American entrepreneurial vigor in steel was inferior to British, despite the slower adoption of the by-product oven in America. Apparently, then, the rate of adoption reflects the ranking of some other variable among the three countries – perhaps the price of labor relative to coal – rather than the ranking of entrepreneurial quality. The point applies to other indicative innovations as well. Before they can be used as indicators of entrepreneurial ability the record of adoption of each must be examined for the influence of less intriguing but more measurable variables. To use output or indicative innovations as measures of performance without the necessary theoretical and empirical groundwork leaves in doubt the very fact to be explained, the existence of British failures in entrepreneurship.

The most recent development in the debate on the entrepreneurial hypothesis has been a direct attack on this premise that there were indeed economically relevant failures, an attack grounded in economic theory and using quantitative information relatively intensively. The present writers have contributed to this work,[32] and other work of a similar nature by Roderick Floud, Charles Harley, Peter Lindert and

Keith Trace is published in a volume of papers and discussion arising out of a conference on quantitative British history held in 1970.[33]

The assertions of failure imply a comparison with superior performance elsewhere, and the standard of comparison used most often in earlier work is the performance of entrepreneurs in Germany and the United States. The new quantitative work has adopted as well the procedure used in the older literature of comparing performance in Britain and abroad one industry at a time. As inadequate as this procedure is for proving or disproving the hypothesis of entrepreneurial failure in the aggregate, ignoring as it does the possibility that British performance was better or worse in other industries, it is adequate for the purpose of accepting or rejecting the particular allegations of failure made in the previous literature.

To measure the distance between British and foreign performance a measuring rod is needed. Two related questions are involved, both of which require a quantitative measure of performance. First, assuming that there were failures, were they important for the performance of the British economy as a whole? To prove that British businessmen neglected certain new techniques in production and marketing does not prove that this neglect was of great consequence for the British economy. Second, were there in fact failures? That is, whether or not it would have made a great deal of difference to the economy as a whole, would British businessmen have done better to adopt American and German habits of enterprise? The measuring rod used in the new quantitative work to answer these questions is the profit foregone by choosing British over foreign methods. The adoption of foreign methods, in other words, is viewed as a potential investment, and entrepreneurial failure as a failure to make such investments as were profitable. The existence of profitable but unexploited investments is used to gauge whether British entrepreneurs could have done better, and the size of the foregone earnings to gauge the significance for economic growth of their failures to do so, a reasonable enough approach, for if these failures did not yield lower profits they are failures only in a peculiar sense of the word.

In applying the criterion of the profitability of imitating foreign methods, the new work has distinguished carefully between prospective and retrospective opportunities for profit. The point is sometimes made that Britain's traditional attitudes towards new techniques in production and marketing, and towards cartels, research and new industries, were profitable enough in the prewar economic world, but proved disastrous afterwards. It is surely driving the theme of the irony of history too far, however, to expect British entrepreneurs to have anticipated in 1913 the trick history was about to play on them. Indeed, a truly prescient entrepreneur in, say, cotton textiles would have avoided investment in virtually any type of cotton equipment in the years just before 1913, certainly in the very capital intensive automatic looms: if the unforeseeable events of the 1920s and 1930s are to be made retrospectively foreseeable almost any case of slow adoption of new machinery becomes a rational anticipation of the collapse of Britain's traditional exports. That is, one cannot have it both ways, criticizing British entrepreneurs on the one hand for not investing in capital intensive new methods in the making and marketing of the old staple exports and on the other for putting too much capital into the very same industries. In any case, the issue is what investments in imitation British entrepreneurs could have made that would have been profitable, from their point of view at the time the decisions were made.

Any of the alleged categories of failure could be examined from this point of view, although in fact only one, the putative failures to adopt the best available technique of production, has been so examined in the new work. The opportunities foregone in neglecting the best technique have been expressed in a variety of ways and this gives a misleading impression of heterogeneity of purpose in the new work. The various measures used are essentially identical. Higher profits can be achieved if more output can be produced with the same inputs, that is, if productivity can be raised. The measuring rod for entrepreneurial failure, then, can be expressed indifferently as the money amount of profit forgone, as the proportion by which foreign exceeded British productivity, as the distance between foreign and British production functions, or as the difference in cost between foreign and British techniques. All of these give the same result and each can be translated exactly into any one of the others. The only fundamental methodological variety in the studies is that some deal with particular innovations, such as the ring-spindle or the steamship, and others with entire industries. When the accusations of entrepreneurial failure are confined to a number of readily identifiable innovations, the logic of comparing actual and potential productivity can be applied to these alone. Peter Lindert and Keith Trace, for example, measured the profit foregone, expressed as an absolute money amount, in the slow adoption of the Solvay soda process in British chemicals. Charles Harley reconstructed the production and cost functions for sail and steamships, through which he was able to examine the speed with which entrepreneurs replaced one with the other as their relative profitability changed.[34] When the accusations of failure are made for an industry's entire mode of doing business the comparisons must be broader. Roderick Floud, for example, measured productivity change over time in a British machine tool firm, with a view in part to comparing that performance with performance elsewhere.[35] But the underlying logic in all the studies is uniform.

So too, on the whole, are their findings. Taken together, the quantitative work is most damaging to the hypothesis of entrepreneurial failure, rejecting repeatedly the presumption of missed opportunities underlying the hypothesis. From one point of view the findings are not very surprising, for any significant gain in output to be had from adopting foreign methods would yield a much larger proportional gain in profits to alert entrepreneurs, profits which would be proportionately larger the smaller was the initial share of entrepreneurial profits in costs. Technical communication in the late nineteenth century was surely good, and if businessmen could not be convinced of the superiority of a new technique through reading their trade newspapers, the ringing cash register of even one competitor who did become convinced would do the job. The only case of entrepreneurial failure quantified in detail by the new studies, the slow replacement of the Leblanc soda process in preference to the Solvay process, documented, along with several successes, in the paper by Lindert and Trace, makes the point, for British soda-making was in the hands of a tightly organized cartel protected by substantial barriers to entry after 1890. But in a competitive milieu, even a brief period of irrationality would be eroded by the expansion of better managed firms, and there is little doubt that the British economy was on the whole competitive. In cotton textiles, for example, there is no evidence that firms installing automatic looms at the time the industry was beginning to be criticized for ignoring them, in the first decade of the twentieth century, expanded faster or made larger profits than their more conservative competitors.[36] This fact by itself, even without the confirming calculation of profitability, suggests that the slow conversion to automatic looms was a rational response to economic conditions, not a failure.[37]

From another point of view it is indeed somewhat surprising that only one minor failure was detected in these many studies, for there must surely be no country at any time that has not experienced to some degree the consequences of mistakes and irrationalities on the part of its businessmen. The relevant historical question is whether one can explain the different pattern of economic growth in Britain contrasted with Germany and the United States by the difference in the amount of entrepreneurial failure. In order to be able to accomplish this, the failures must have been larger in Britain than elsewhere and must have been important. The new quantitative studies are, of course, subject to error. But within any reasonable bounds of the error, there is little doubt that in the industries examined the failures, if they existed, were neither large nor important. The social loss from poor management is the lost output. If the lost output was as much as 5 percent in the basic industries usually considered poorly managed – steel, coal, cotton, chemicals and railways – British national income would have been lower than it could have been by only a little over 1 percent.[38] It might well be inferred from these studies, in short, that the hypothesis of relatively slow adoption of new techniques has little to contribute to the understanding of British growth in the later nineteenth century.

The new quantitative work represents a substantial advance in the understanding of the late Victorian economy, but it is not beyond criticism. The advance in precision is sometimes gained at the expense of a narrow focus on the question of how rapidly British entrepreneurs adopted new processes of production, neglecting the other items in the catalogue of failure. The proponents of the hypothesis of failure have not satisfactorily demonstrated that there was indeed underinvestment in research, in the new industries, in marketing or in the formation of cartels. But whether they have established their case or not these issues would deserve treatment in a full study of the hypothesis, and could indeed be treated in much the same way as investments in new processes. Although the economic theory of the adoption of new processes is unusually well-developed, there are nonetheless adequate tools available for putting many of the other assertions into testable form.

The assertion that there was underinvestment in the new industries, for example, is not difficult to test. One relevant statistic would be the marginal rate of return on the capital that was in fact invested in them: if it was unusually high, the argument would deserve some consideration, and the appropriate weight to be put on it in explaining British growth could be inferred from the income to be gained from eliminating the disparity in marginal returns. The alleged British inability to form cartels and extract monopoly gains from the world at large, as it is said the Germans did, can be tested as well. Late in the period at least the British exhibited more skill in this regard than they have usually been credited with – witness Lever in soap and Courtauld in rayon.[39] It may be doubted, too, whether the gains in foreign markets would offset the misallocation from monopoly in domestic markets. In any case, the extent of the gain in foreign markets from combination could be measured and set against the loss. The profit foregone from bad marketing, if it existed, could be estimated too, perhaps by viewing expenditure on marketing as an investment in shifting the demand curve. It is not clear that these experiments in applied economics would yield results unfavorable to British entrepreneurs. The comparisons in the literature with American and German performance in marketing, in cartel formation and in investing in the new industries, usually assume that it is obvious that foreign behavior in these matters was to be emulated. It is not often realized that the estimates of the profitability of these activities might well show that the Americans and Germans pursued them too much, rather than the British too little.

The alleged reluctance to invest in research is an especially good case in point. H. W. Richardson, in common with many other students of the industry, argues that there was too little investment in research in

British chemicals,[40] and the same has been said of other industries. Whether more research was individually or even nationally profitable, however, is by no means clear. There is a good argument to be made for being a 'fast second' in research, that is, as T. C. Barker put it in his study on the glass industry in the volume edited by Aldcroft, 'to stand by watchfully while others poured their fortunes into development . . . and to be sure to obtain a license for a successful process as soon as it became a paying proposition'.[41] The fruits of research, in other words, are to some extent commonly consumed goods for which investment by an individual firm would be irrational: America and Germany may have been investing too much.

British investment in research may in any case have been constrained compared to the American or German by the relative shortage in Britain of scientifically educated personnel, and, for most of the period, by Britain's peculiar patent system. A calculation of the rationality of more research would have to allow for these constraints. Unless one attempts to explain the constraints themselves as responses to entrepreneurial demand, as Landes, for one, does, they should be looked on as external conditions imposed on entrepreneurs, and their results should not be accounted failures.

A broader issue is involved here. The new quantitative work has chosen to focus on the rationality or lack of it of entrepreneurs in a given market environment. This focus is perhaps defensible, for the literature does allege that there were such irrationalities. Individual rationality, however, does not necessarily produce aggregate rationality, and the literature on entrepreneurial failure can be interpreted as arguing in part that there were not only individual but also aggregate irrationalities. Entrepreneurs in British chemicals may have been well advised to invest little in research on dyes, given the scarcity of British technicians trained in chemistry. From the national point of view, however, more investment in training chemists may have been desirable. This issue, the issue, as Paul David put it, of market failures above and beyond any individual entrepreneurial failures,[42] is not treated in the quantitative work. This is not to say, however, that it is out of reach of standard economic and statistical tools. The social return to technical education, for example, could be estimated and comparisons made with German and American rates of return. There is no presumption that the expected return in the late nineteenth century, disallowing the misuse of hindsight involved in arguing that these investments paid off most in the new technological environment of the twentieth century, was high, but this and similar questions need more work.

The tools used in the quantitative work, in common with those used elsewhere to study the hypothesis of entrepreneurial failure, do appear to break down in one respect. Entrepreneurship has always been studied as a residual, because it is not a variable that can be measured directly. Argument by identifying a residual category is a respectable procedure, but it has the inevitable hazard that other variables besides the one of interest may be affecting what remains from the influence of directly measured variables. It may be possible to show that the adoption of the ring-spindle in cotton or the basic process in steel was unprofitable, but it still may be that entrepreneurship was bad, offset by still other unmeasured variables. This objection to the residual methodology does not have great force. With any reasonably complete theory of how economic change takes place the major variables will appear in the accounting. One may speculate on offsets to poor entrepreneurship, but the speculations become less interesting with each successive demonstration that the behavior of British industries can be fully explained with conventional variables such as factor prices and available technology. Occam's razor is a good precept in these matters, and it cuts deep into the hypothesis of entrepreneurial failure.

In a related context, that of studies of productivity change, the residual has been called, rightly, 'a measure of our ignorance'. The range of our ignorance of the influence of entrepreneurship on British economic performance has been narrowed greatly by its intensive study. The study has progressed from journalistic generalization, through qualitative statement and counterstatement, and finally to quantitative assessment. The process is by no means complete, for nothing less than a full and detailed explanation of late Victorian economic performance would be required for its completion, and that accomplishment is far beyond the horizon. It is fair to say, however, that the late Victorian entrepreneur, who started his historiographic career in damnation, is well on his way to redemption.

NOTES

1 See Irwin Feller, 'The draper loom in New England textiles, 1894–1914: a study of diffusion of an innovation', *Journal of Economic History*, 16 (September 1966), pp. 320–47, and L. G. Sandberg, 'Comment' (on Feller's article), *Journal of Economic History*, 18 (December 1968), pp. 624–7.

2 'Fiscal policy of international trade', in Alfred Marshall, *Official Papers* (London: Macmillan, 1926), p. 405. Cf. his *Principles of Economics*, 8th edn. (London: Macmillan, 1920), pp. 298ff. and *Industry and Trade*, 4th edn. (London: Macmillan 1923), pp. 86ff. Also T. Veblen, *Imperial Germany and the Industrial Revolution* (New York: Macmillan, 1915), p. 128 and J. Hobson, *Incentives in the New Industrial Order* (New York: Thomas Seltzer, 1923), pp. 78–83.

3 J. H. Clapham, *An Economic History of Modern Britain*, Vol. III (Cambridge: Cambridge University Press, 1938), p. 122.

4 (Cambridge: Cambridge University Press, 1940). Cf. T. H. Burnham and G. O. Hoskins, *Iron and Steel in Britain, 1870–1930.* (London: Allen & Unwin, 1934), who concluded, after a lengthy assessment of the extenuating circumstances, that 'if a business deteriorates it is of no use blaming anyone except those at the top' (p. 271).

5 The center for this work was the Harvard Business School, which published the

movement's journal, *Explorations in Entrepreneurial History*. Arthur H. Cole was one of the key figures and his paper 'An approach to the study of entrepreneurship', *Journal of Economic History*, 6 (Supplement, 1946), pp. 1–15, reprinted in Frederic C. Lane and Jelle C. Riemersa (eds), *Enterprise and Secular Change: Readings in Economic History* (Homewood, Ill.: Irwin, 1953) – itself an important text for the new approach – is a good statement of the central argument.

6 This revival in interest was largely a result of an apparently solid statistical case for British economic failure presented by E. H. Phelps-Brown and S. J. Handfield-Jones and D. J. Coppock. See Phelps-Brown and Handfield-Jones, 'The climacteric of the 1890s: a study in the expanding economy', *Oxford Economic Papers* (October 1952), pp. 266–307, and Coppock, 'The climacteric of the 1890s: a critical note', *Manchester School*, 24 (January 1956), pp. 1–31. Coppock successfully moved the climacteric from the 1890s to the 1870s. For a recent summary of the issue, see S. B. Saul, *The Myth of the Great Depression, 1873–1896* (London: Macmillan, 1969).

7 'Some reasons why', pp. 553–84 in David S. Landes, 'Technological change and development in Western Europe, 1750–1914', chapter 5 in H. J. Habakkuk and M. Postan (eds), *The Cambridge Economic History of Europe*, Vol. VI (Cambridge: Cambridge University Press, 1965), reprinted with minor revisions and an extension to the present in Landes, *The Unbound Prometheus* (Cambridge: Cambridge University Press, 1969).

8 Landes, 'Some reasons why', p. 582.

9 *Economic History Review*, 2nd ser., 17 (August 1964), pp. 113–34.

10 A seminal work in the transformation of this allegation from journalistic to scholarly opinion was R. J. S. Hoffman's *Great Britain and the German Trade Rivalry, 1875–1914* (Philadelphia: University of Pennsylvania Press, 1933), which used British consular reports to paint a singularly unfavorable picture of British salesmanship in Latin American, continental, and other markets invaded by the Germans.

11 Opinions in the textbooks of the last decade or so are a useful barometer of professional opinion on this matter. R. S. Sayers, *A History of Economic Change in England, 1880–1939* (London: Oxford University Press, 1967), and W. H. B. Court, *British Economic History 1870–1914, Commentary and Documents* (Cambridge: Cambridge University Press, 1965), were largely silent on the issue. The rest devoted a good deal of attention to it. W. Ashworth, *An Economic History of England 1870–1939* (London: Methuen, 1960), thought the suggestion 'that leaders of business and technology were less ingenious and adaptable than either their fathers or their foreign contemporaries . . . a very doubtful one' (p. 241). E. J. Hobsbawm, *Industry and Empire* (London: Pantheon, 1968), agree finding the several versions of the sociological explanation 'all quite unconvincing' (p. 153). S. B. Saul, *The Myth of the Great Depression*, cited above, was willing to grant entrepreneurship a residual role, but a small one (see pp. 46ff). P. Mathias, *The First Industrial Nation* (London: Methuen, 1969), was more sympathetic to the hypothesis: 'Undoubtedly, however, such failure to innovate was wide-spread and undoubtedly the more aggressive adoption of new techniques would have led to greater industrial investment and possibly to better records in exports' (p. 415). Cf. S. Pollard and D. W. Crossley, *The Wealth of Britain 1085–1966* (New York: Schocken, 1969), p. 227.

12 M. Frankel, 'Obsolescence and technological change in a maturing economy', *American Economic Review*, 45 (June 1955), pp. 296–319. See also D. F. Gordon, 'Obsolescence and technological change: comment', *American Economic Review*, 46 (September 1956), pp. 646–52, and Frankel's 'Reply' following Gordon.

13 (Cambridge, Mass.: Harvard University Press, 1964), especially chs 6 and 7. See also C. P. Kindleberger, 'Obsolescence and technical change', *Oxford Institute of Economics and Statistics*, Bulletin no. 23 (August 1961), pp. 281–97.

14 The existence of small coal cars on the railways, by the way, seems a doubtful

example on which to base the argument: the cars are still small to this day, twenty years after nationalization and eighty years after their alleged economic inferiority first emerged.

15 'The landscape and the machine: technical interrelatedness, land tenure, and the mechanization of the corn harvest in Victorian Britain', in D. McCloskey (ed.), *Essays on a Mature Economy: Britain After 1840, Papers and Proceedings of the MSSB Conference on the New Economic History of Britain, 1840–1930* (London: Methuen, 1971). See the discussion following the paper for a balanced assessment of how well David made his case.

16 Such as S. J. Chapman, speaking of steel in *Foreign Competition* (1904), p. 4, quoted with approval in H. J. Habakkuk, *American and British Technology in the 19th Century* (Cambridge: Cambridge University Press, 1962), p. 208: 'The up-to-date character of many American works is as much an effect as a cause of the expansion of the industry in America.'

17 Svennilson, *Growth and Stagnation in the European Economy* (Geneva: 1954), p. 123, and Habakkuk, *American and British Technology*. See Landes' review of Habakkuk's book, D. S. Landes, 'Factor costs and demand: determinants of economic growth', *Business History*, 7 (January 1965), pp. 15–33.

18 In Henry Rosovsky (ed.), *Industrialization in Two Systems: Essays in Honor of Alexander Gerschenkron* (New York: Wiley, 1966).

19 See D. N. McCloskey, 'Economic maturity and entrepreneurial decline: British iron and steel 1870–1913' (unpublished Ph.D. dissertation, Harvard University, April 1970), ch. 6. A revised version of this dissertation is to be published as a book by the Harvard University Press.

20 (London: Weidenfeld & Nicolson, 1967).

21 Levine, *Industrial Retardation.* Levine emphasizes the embodiment argument as a contributing factor, as did Habakkuk.

22 Burn's and Burnham and Hoskin's books (cited earlier) on the steel industry were the only full-length studies of entrepreneurial failure in an industry until recently, and it was natural that the framers of the entrepreneurial hypothesis drew on them heavily. One index of the steel industry's dominance in the literature on entrepreneurial failure is that some third of the footnotes in an early version of Landes' sub-chapter, 'Some reasons why', in his contribution to the *Cambridge Economic History of Europe*, Vol. VI (same title, comprising chapter 3 in 'Entrepreneurship in advanced industrial countries: the Anglo-German rivalry', cited above) deal with it. But the gross output of iron and steel was only 4·4 percent of national income in 1907.

23 S. B. Saul, 'The American impact on British industry, 1895–1914', *Business History*, 3 (December 1960), pp. 19–38; 'The motor industry in Britain to 1914', *Business History*, 5 (December 1962), pp. 22–44; 'The export economy 1870–1914', *Yorkshire Bulletin of Economic and Social Research*, 5 (18 May 1965); 'The market and the development of the mechanical engineering industries in Britain, 1860–1914', *Economic History Review*, 2nd ser., 20 (1967); 'The machine tool industry in Britain to 1914', *Business History*, 9 (January 1968), pp. 22–43; 'The engineering industry', in Aldcroft (ed.), cited below.

24 (London: Allen & Unwin, 1968).

25 Such as R. A. Church, 'The effect of the American export invasion on the British boot and shoe industry', *Journal of Economic History*, 28 (June 1968), pp. 223–55, and A. E. Harrison, 'The competitiveness of the British cycle industry, 1890–1914', *Economic History Review*, 2nd ser., 22 (August 1969), pp. 287–303.

26 Aldcroft (ed.), *Development of British Industry*, p. 34f.

27 C. Wilson, 'Economy and society in late Victorian England', *Economic History Review* (August 1965), pp. 183–98. See also his *The History of Unilever* (New York: Prager, 1968) [first published by Cassell, 1954], Vol. I, especially Part I.

28 Cited above. The quoted phrase is in the useful annotated bibliograpy, p. 62.

29 R. E. Tyson, 'Cotton textiles', in Aldcroft (ed.), p. 122. Compare M. Copeland, *The Cotton Manufacturing Industry of the United States* (Cambridge, Mass.: Harvard University Press, 1912), especially pp. 66–73 and 90–2.

30 Cf. L. G. Sandberg, 'American rings and English mules: the role of economic rationality', *Quarterly Journal of Economics*, 83 (February 1969), pp. 25–43.

31 J. H. Clapham, *Economic History of Modern Britain*, p. 148.

32 D. N. McCloskey, 'Productivity change in British pig iron, 1870–1939', *Quarterly Journal of Economics*, 82 (May 1968), pp. 281–96; L. G. Sandberg, 'American rings and English mules', cited above; D. N. McCloskey, 'Did Victorian Britain fail?', *Economic History Review*, 2nd ser., 23 (December 1970), pp. 446–59; L. G. Sandberg, 'Lancashire in decline', unpublished book-length manuscript; and D. N. McCloskey, 'Economic maturity and entrepreneurial decline: British iron and steel 1870–1913', cited above.

33 McCloskey (ed.), *Essays on a Mature Economy*, cited above, including Roderick Floud, 'Changes in the productivity of labour in the British machine tool industry', Charles K. Harley, 'The shift from sailing ships to steamships, 1850–1890', and Peter H. Lindert and Keith Trace, 'Yardsticks for Victorian entrepreneurs'. Other studies in this volume bearing directly on the hypothesis of failure are the paper by Paul David mentioned above and a paper by one of the present writers, D. N. McCloskey, 'International differences in productivity: coal and steel in America and Britain before World War I'.

34 Other examples of single-innovation studies are McCloskey's 'Economic maturity and entrepreneurial decline', chapter 4 (on the basic process of steelmaking), Sandberg's 'American rings and English mules', and David's 'The landscape and the machine' (on the mechanical reaper), all cited above.

35 See also D. N. McCloskey, 'Productivity change in British pig iron' and 'Did Victorian Britain fail?' cited above.

36 Cf. Sandberg, 'Lancashire in decline', chapter 4.

37 This argument is relevant to a subsidiary hypothesis in the literature, that Britain as a whole in the late nineteenth century suffered from the disinterest of the third generation of industrial dynasties in making profits. In a competitive milieu the social loss from this behavior, which is the loss from the mismanagement of the real capital in the hands of indolent grandsons, is minimized by the entry of new firms, the declining market shares of the old, and the hiring of competent managers by wealthy heirs who know their own limitations.

38 The value of output of these industries in 1907 was roughly £500 million. Five percent of £500 million is £25 million, or 1·2 percent of 1907 national income. The source for the value of output is the 1907 census of production. For a full development of the argument see McCloskey, 'Economic maturity and entrepreneurial decline', chapter 1, cited above.

39 See Wilson, *The History of Unilever*, cited above, and D. C. Coleman, *Courtaulds* (London: Oxford University Press, 1969), Vol. II. See also Lindert and Trace on United Alkali and McCloskey, 'Economic maturity and entrepreneurial decline', chapter 3, on the successful cartel in Bessemer steel rails.

40 Aldcroft (ed.), *Development of British Industry*, p. 302. Compare the similar judgment of Lindert and Trace regarding dyestuffs in McCloskey (ed.), *Essays on a Mature Economy.*

41 ibid., p. 324.

42 See the 'General discussion on the performance of the late Victorian economy' in McCloskey (ed.).

4

International Differences in Productivity? Coal and Steel in America and Britain before World War I

The assumption that the New World has yielded unusually high returns to the factors of production has been a part of our thinking from the time of Adam Smith and before. It is a congenial assumption, suggesting as one might wish that the right to life, liberty and the pursuit of happiness had material as well as moral advantages. The evidence for it, however, has been collected somewhat casually. In the nineteenth century Anglo-American comparisons were made with scattered data on real wages, that is, data on labor's marginal product. After the first British census of production in 1907 they were made with data on labor's average product. In either case the comparisons reflected the productivity of one factor of production alone, although, to be sure, the excess of American over British labor productivity was so large that it appeared that no reasonable allowance for larger inputs of other factors could account for it. The findings for the 1920s of A. W. Flux, the director of the British census, that real value added per worker in British manufacturing was half the American average was confirmed in later studies by L. Rostas for the late 1930s, by M. Frankel for the late 1940s and, most thoroughly, by a series of studies by the Organization for European Economic Co-operation and the Cambridge Department of Applied Economics on real national income in Europe and America for the early 1950s.[1] The OEEC–Cambridge studies, which were based on careful international comparisons of price levels rather than on the par exchange rate and included all sectors of the economy rather than manufacturing alone, found that British gross national product per worker was about half the American level and value added per worker in manufacturing alone was still lower.[2]

In his study of *Why Growth Rates Differ* Edward Denison attempted to explain this gap in the levels of income per worker for 1960.[3] The gap between the United States and the United Kingdom was then 41

I should like to thank Michael Edelstein of Columbia University, Stanley L. Engerman of the University of Rochester, Peter Temin of MIT, and the members of the Columbia University Seminar on Economic History, for their helpful comments on earlier drafts of this essay.

percent of the American level. He found that only 11 percentage points of it could be explained by total factor input corrected for quality and a mere 0·7 percentage points by misallocation and economies of scale; the rest, or about three-quarters of the total gap in 1960, had to be attributed as a residual to 'lags in the application of knowledge, general efficiency and errors and omissions'.[4] This result is both disappointing and remarkable. It is disappointing because it implies that even an imaginative use of conventional economic theory leaves the greater part of productivity differences unexplained.[5] It is remarkabe because it implies that the productivity of the British economy was very far behind: as Denison put it, the level of total productivity, after allowing for economies of scale, the quality of the labor force, misallocation and conventionally measured inputs of capital, was about 20 percent lower in the United Kingdom in 1960 than it had been in the United States in 1925. The gap was apparently a large, persistent fact.

Explanations of the fact have consumed many hours of after-dinner conversation, and their origin in the mental haze of brandy and cigars is sometimes apparent in their printed expression. After a nod towards the evidence, the writer loosens his tie and his standards of logic, and launches on one of several speculations. In reading the literature of Anglo-American comparison, one is struck by the attraction that certain of these speculations appear to have, irrespective of their empirical merit: repeatedly the story is told of cheap land causing mechanization, a large free trade area encouraging economies of scale, rapid growth of industrial plant permitting the use of the most modern equipment in the New World, and the inevitable 'clogs to clogs in three generations' crushing the spirit of enterprise in the Old.

The persistence of the gap through many generations creates difficulties for some of these. For example, it is plausible perhaps that the vigor of an immigrant population yielded higher productivities, but the mass immigrations were confined to the second half of the nineteenth century, too late to explain any American superiority before 1850 and too early to explain it after 1920. Allyn Young, among others, doubted that there was evidence of greater vigor in the United States and supposed instead that economies of national scale were the dominant factor.[6] On the other hand, as E. Rothbarth pointed out, the scale of the American economy was not always larger than the British.[7] He suggested that the higher ratio of land to labor was the true cause of American superiority. Yet land was not always an important factor of production: indeed, by the time estimates of factor shares are available, in the late nineteenth century, the share of land in national income was well below 10 percent in the United States and below 15 percent in the United Kingdom.[8] Though for particular industries, as will be shown later, the amount and quality of land in the United States may explain high labor productivities, for the economy as a whole it is doubtful that it can. If the arguments had been framed in quantitative terms, such difficulties as these would have been immediately apparent and would have inspired more critical examination of the explanations of American superiority, but they have generally been left in the prequantitative form in which the after-dinner speakers first expressed them. And many of them, of course, do not seem to fit easily into quantitative categories. This is especially true of the assertion, which has done good service as a residual explanation when others have proved wanting, that American businessmen were able to seize and retain a technological lead over Europe.

It is not generally recognized how puzzling would be the existence of a persistent and large American technological lead. If the difference between American and British production functions were as little as 10 percent, say, and the share of entrepreneurial returns in total costs as much as 30 percent, the adoption of American methods would increase returns to entrepreneurship by at least a third: a British firm could reduce its costs by 10 percent and take the reduction in additional profit.[9] With the easy transport and communication that developed during the nineteenth century between the United States and the United Kingdom, with the frequent migrations of managers and the absence of a language barrier between the two, and with the competitive markets of both, it is hardly credible that such a large reward for imitation would go unclaimed. Recently D. W. Jorgenson and Z. Griliches have expressed skepticism about the significance of technological change, or costless increases in output for a given input, over time, asserting that 'the accumulation of knowledge is governed by the same economic laws as any other process of capital accumulation. Costs must be incurred if benefits are to be achieved.'[10] If this view has some plausibility for technical change between two years it has still more for technical differences between two countries. Investment in imitation is surely a less risky undertaking than investment in research, especially when the imitation can take the form of the mere purchase of improved machinery or the hiring of better managers from the leader. It would be strange if large technical differences persisted.

But this line of reasoning seems to be contradicted by the large, persistent gap in residual productivity.[11] The national comparisons of Denison register a gap of 35 percent between the average levels of total productivity in the two countries and the earlier studies of labor productivity suggest that the same order of magnitude of difference has existed for a century and a half. One necessary downward revision should be mentioned. National comparisons give an exaggerated impression of the typical degree of American superiority. To get a true impression the comparisons must be made at the level of industrial detail corresponding to individual firms, because the national comparisons ignore intermediate inputs. If the United States had typically a 20 percent advantage in efficiency, the advantage would be amplified by the cheapness of intermediate inputs, yielding a national productivity difference larger than 20 percent.[12] If the United States, for example, produced iron ore and coal, as well as finished iron and steel, with 20 percent less inputs than the United Kingdom did, the total direct and indirect resource costs of American iron and steel would be more than 20 percent less than British resource costs. Put the other way, the national difference of 35 percent in productivity corresponds to a smaller difference at the level of industrial detail where comparisons of costs and decisions to innovate take place. This is the level of the firm. The higher the typical share in total costs of purchases from other firms, the lower will be the productivity difference. In the United States the share was around 44 percent of costs, implying a typical difference in productivity of about 20 percent.[13]

A gap of 20 percent is still large. In view of it, one strategy of research would be to examine in detail the channels of technological flow in an attempt to find where they were blocked. Another, which will be pursued here, is to subject the difference in productivity to creative disbelief. The working hypothesis for this task is that British and American industries operated on substantially the same production functions. The appropriate production functions are those for the products of individual industries including materials in costs as well as value added. For practical reasons the industries must have easily measured inputs and outputs and must be few in number. To offset their fewness they must be large. In order to put the working hypothesis in the most jeopardy, finally, they should be industries whose technological performance in late nineteenth-century Britain by the conventional measures was bad. Two industries that satisfy these requirements are coal and steel.

COAL

Historical opinion on the performance of the British coal industry before 1913 is not uniformly unfavorable. The industry grew much more slowly than the American or German industries, but there are adequate explanations from the side of demand for this, as there is for the worldwide shrinkage in the market for coal after the early 1920s, an event that casts a shadow back on the prewar history of the industry. Clapham, for example, concluded that in the quarter century before 1913:

> The whole industry, though full of conflict, was active and expanding both commercially and geographically. Its best units were admirably equipped.[14]

Still, he noted that most British mines ignored equipment that had become common abroad. The mechanical coal-cutter is the best known, but the list includes as well steel pit props, electric haulage of coal and concrete and cement liners for shafts and tunnels. A. J. Taylor, the leading student of the industry, has emphasized these deficiencies, and his views are more representative of historical opinion on the matter than Clapham's. He mentions diminishing returns to land and other extenuating circumstances, yet concludes that

> It is still valid to speak of a hard core of recognizable inefficiency existing in the pre-1914 coal industry . . . in terms of diminished labour effort, unwillingness to accept innovation and the failure to provide a structure for the industry suited to the opportunities and needs of the twentieth century. . . . In all this the experience of coal was no doubt symptomatic of trends which were widely operative in British industry, more particularly in its older and deeper rooted sectors.[15]

This assertion does not bear up under close examination.

The chief evidence that an unwillingness to accept innovation altered the industry's history is that after the 1880s output per man-year in British coal mining declined, which, were this by itself an acceptable measure of productivity, would certainly suggest that there was an important failure of spirit in industry. The evidence of productivity is certainly more relevant to the issue than selected cases of the slow adoption of new equipment: indeed, the only way to determine whether the equipment was an important and profitable novelty is to perform a productivity calculation before and after its adoption. The average product of British labor, however, is a poor indicator of the course of British productivity. Average product fell, to be sure, but it fell or stagnated everywhere in Europe before World War I and does not suggest therefore any peculiarly British failure.[16] On the contrary it suggests that the natural conditions of coal mining dominated the determination of the average product of labor, driving it down as the coal beds were depleted. The rise in the average product in the United States during the period does not contradict this interpretation, since American coal reserves were so enormous that their depletion, except in the anthracite region, was negligible.[17] And comparisons of the level of the average product in various countries confirm it, suggesting that American product per man was high because the margin of cultivation of coal reserves had not been pushed far and that Belgian product, for example, was low because the margin had been pushed very far indeed. In comparing American and British productivity, however, most observers have resisted attributing all the difference in labor's average product to differences in the input of land. A resolution of the issue requires an estimate of how large the impact of the quantity and quality of cooperating factors was on the average product of labor.

The estimation of the average product of British and American labor is not as straightforward as the mass of statistics on the industry, the result of thorough and sustained official scrutiny in both countries, might lead one to hope. The data requirements of productivity measurement are great and in making comparisons between countries the sources of error are great as well. The output of coal, for example, seems to be a simple concept, but is not. Differences in the quality of coal mined may bias the measurement of output in one country in terms of another, because coal with good qualities and therefore high value per ton warrants more intensive mining at higher cost – that is, lower productivity. A similar problem afflicts the measurement of labor input. Ideally each quality of coal and labor should be weighted by its economic value in one country to form an index for one country in terms of the other, but the data are not good enough to do this.[18] Even the comparison of the crude aggregates, presented in Table 4.1, which is based on the British Census of Production 1907 and the American Census of Mines and Quarries of 1909, is difficult. Through the statistical haze, nonetheless, comes the impression that output per man in Britain was half or perhaps a little more than half that in America before World War I.

The input of capital cannot explain any of this difference, since capital per man was about the same in the two countries. Horsepower per man,

Table 4.1 *Yearly output per man employed, UK 1907 and USA 1909*

	Output (millions of long tons)	*Wage earners employed (millions)*	*Tons of output per wage earner year*
UK	267	0·812	325
USA	408	0·667	613

Sources:

USA: US Bureau of the Census, Thirteenth Census, Vol. XI, *Mines and Quarries 1909* (Washington, DC: Govt Printing Office, 1913), pp. 186ff. The employment figure given on p. 186 excludes coke workers, as it should to be comparable with the British figure. It relates to 15 December. December, however, was the month of peak employment in the industry (100 compared to 93·4 for the entire year; ibid., p. 30). The figure given here is corrected for this overstatement.

UK: Board of Trade, *Final Report on the First Census of Production of the United Kingdom (1907)* (London: HMSO, 1912), pp. 42ff. The employment figure has been reduced by an allowance for iron miners working in mines under the Coal Mines Regulation Act (which are included in the definition of the coal industry in the British census). It relates to four Wednesdays during the year and reflects the normal absenteeism of 10 percent: the census figure is roughly 10 percent below the Home Office figures, which relate apparently to people employed whether actually working or for example, according to the census data was virtually identical in the two: 2·82 per man in Britain and 2·85 in America. Horsepower statistics are very crude measures of capital, since they reflect only the stock of a certain kind of equipment rather than all equipment, structures and inventories together, yet there is reason to accept their surprising testimony that high American wages did not lead to higher capital per man. The reason is that capital was a substitute for land as well as labor: bad and expensive coal land, such as Britain had relative to America, could be worked profitably only by investing in deep shafts and long tunnels to ferret out the coal. This heavier capital investment meant, for example, that British mines were much larger than American mines. It is plausible, then, that the substitution of capital for labor in the United States was matched by a substitution of capital for land in the United Kingdom. In any case, only if the measure is very much in error would capital have any great effect on output per man because capital's share in total costs was small. In the United Kingdom its share was around 12 percent and in the United States only 4 percent.[19]

Land's share was small, too, but its small weight in the calculation of productivity was offset by the enormous differences in its quantity and quality in the two countries. The ideal measure of land input, like the ideal measures of coal output and labor input, would add up different units weighted by their value in producing coal.[20] This value – the coal land's price – is determined by characteristics such as its closeness to consumers, the ease of mining it and the quantity of coal it contains. If the separate effects on price could be measured with acceptable accuracy, the production function, as it were, for land in terms of these characteristics of quality could be written down and the land input in the two countries compared precisely. The price of coal land classified by quality, however, is not available. Fortunately, the case to be made here, that differences in resource endowments explain most of the difference in output per man, can rest on a very rough approximation to the ideal programme.

The sheer quantity of coal land per worker was clearly larger in America than in Britain. The exact meaning of the 'sheer quantity' of land is somewhat elusive. Is it coal land in existence or coal land in use, tons of reserves under the ground or acres of land on the surface? The unit of measurement chosen should satisfy the specification of the production function that doubling it and all other inputs results in a doubling of output. Moreover, the unit represents a property right that

---

Table 4.1 *Sources* contd:
not. The hours worked per year by each of these wage earners was probably somewhat higher in the UK than in the USA; the eight-hour day was introduced in unionized mines in the USA in 1898 and by 1909 the day was 8·6 hours (US Geological Survey, *Mineral Resources of the United States 1922* (Washington, DC: Govt Printing Office, 1925), p. 503). In the UK the eight-hour day was introduced in 1908, after the census.

is bought and sold and should therefore correspond to the unit employed in these transactions. The situation is obscured by the differences in mineral property rights in America and Britain: in America the surface land and everything under it was sold as one, while in Britain the surface and mineral rights were sold separately, often to the extent of selling different seams under one surface to different mining companies.[21] A reasonable compromise is to take the right to mine a certain quantity of tons of coal reserves as the unit of land. In any case, it should be the number of the units, however defined, that mining companies actually own or lease. Land that contains coal but is not considered worth holding by the coal companies should not be included in the coal industry's inputs. The American census gives acres of coal land owned or leased by the industry, but the British census does not and there is no corresponding statistic available in other sources. There are no statistics on the land 'in use', however, that might be defined. The only alternative is to use the tons of reserves in actively mined regions as an estimate of the land employed in the industry.[22] This is a crude procedure and it is prudent therefore to bias it in the direction of lowering the American measure of land employed. Accomplishing this by using in the measure only the reserves of the six most intensively mined states (Pennsylvania, West Virginia, Ohio, Indiana, Maryland and Arkansas), American land input in 1910 in terms of reserves was about 400,000 million metric tons.[23] Total reserves were eight times this: many of them lay fallow in the Rocky Mountains, to be sure, but the reserves of such large coal-producing states as Illinois and Kentucky are also excluded from this figure. In comparable units, the entire reserves of the United Kingdom, whether intensively mined or not, were about 100,000 million metric tons.[24] British land input, then, was a quarter of the American and land input per worker was in the ratio of 0·205 to 1·000. The difference is about 80 percent of the American level of land per worker. The difference in output per worker was 47 percent of the American level. Since the share of land was about 0·08 in costs, the difference in the quantity of land per worker explains about 6·4 percentage points of the total difference of 47 points.

Not only was the quantity of coal land large in America compared with Britain, but, more important, its quality was high. American seams were generally thicker, closer to the surface, freer from faults, flatter and drier than British seams.[25] American coal land in 1910 had been blessed with a fortunate geological history and a brief industrial history. In using the meagre data to count these blessings, it is important to keep in mind that the quality of land to be worked was to some extent a matter of choice. If unusually thin seams were to be worked profitably in competitive circumstances they must have been unusually close to the surface, have been unusually free from faulting, or have had some other compensating virtue. Thick seams, on the other hand, would have been worked at great depths and with very faulted contours.[26] The result is that a simple plot of output per man against one of these qualities (such as thickness, shallowness, faultlessness) will give an impression of the impact of the quality biased towards no impact at all: as the thickness of seams rise, for example, their average depth will increase, reducing on that account output per man and resulting in an understatement of the true impact of changing thickness alone. It is important, therefore, to hold the other variables constant.[27]

There is widespread evidence that in the range usually observed the thickness of seams had a large effect on output per man. One of the few opportunities to control for depth as well as thickness for a good-sized sample is the data collected for forty-eight American shaft mines by Carroll Wright as Commissioner of Labor in his *Sixth Annual Report 1890, Cost of Production: Iron, Steel, Coal, etc.*[28] A regression of output per man on thickness, depth, and the size of the screen separating coal into 'screenings' and more valuable large sizes, yielded an R^2 of 0·39, which is hardly impressive, and a coefficient on depth insignificantly different from zero. It is not too surprising that in the shallow American mines depth was unimportant (the average in Wright's sample was only 178 ft compared with a British average of around 1,000 feet).[29] The effect of seam thickness, however, is clear and strong: the coefficient is five times its standard error and the elasticity of output per man with respect to seam thickness is over 0·5. The weight of evidence, indeed, is that the effect of thickness was even greater, with an elasticity of around 1. In an unusual sample of outputs per tonnage worker an seam thicknesses collected for 1921 in Illinois, for example, the implied elasticity in the range of 5·5 ft is about 1·2.[30] The consequences are important. The average seam worked in Britain in 1924, when the matter was first investigated systematically, was 50 in.; the average in America in 1920–2 was about 65 in.[31] With an elasticity of about 1, this difference would explain about 25 percentage points of the total difference of 47 percent in the average product of labor.

The 15·6 percent difference remaining after the effects of land and thickness are extracted is more than explained by the great depth of British mines. The effect of depth can be approached through its close correlation with thickness. In contrast with the United States, in which the distances between coal markets created wide divergences in price, the United Kingdom was one market for coal. The market as well as technology worked to limit the dispersion of behavior in the industry. All combinations of thickness and depth could be observed in the United States because a poor combination was protected by the distance to a competitor. British mines, however, were all forced to lie close to the same curve of equal average product relating thickness and depth.[32] The slope of this curve expresses, then, the change in thickness required to compensate for a given change in depth. The elasticity of thickness with respect to depth appears to have been in 1924 about 1·2.[33] Since the average depth of mines in the early 1920s was about 1,000 ft in Britain and only 280 ft in the United States, the equivalent change in thickness is very high. Any reasonable elasticity of output per man with respect to thickness, then, will permit the depth of the coal to explain the remaining difference in average product. Indeed, the quantity and quality of land available to the American industry explains much more than is necessary to absolve the British industry of the change of failure, especially in view of the biases introduced against this hypothesis in the course of the argument. A weaker argument, weighted still more against the hypothesis of British competence, would suffice.

The exercise is crude, to be sure, but its very crudeness suggests that it requires no delicate and uncertain inquiry to explain the difference between labor productivity in the American and British industries in terms of the large differences between the resources with which the two worked. The case for a failure of masters and men in British coal mining before 1913, in short, is vulnerable to a most damaging criticism: there was clearly no failure of productivity.

STEEL

It is commonly believed, with even more conviction than for the coal industry, that the steel industry in late nineteenth-century Britain performed poorly. The managers in coal could be excused on the grounds that the quality of the natural resource with which they worked was deteriorating, but the steelmakers could not: indeed, the chief history of the industry, D. Burn's *The Economic History of Steelmaking 1867–1939*,[34] faults them for ignoring, in the phosphoric ores of Lincolnshire, the natural resources they did have. Burn emphasizes repeatedly the 'personal deficiencies', 'attachment to routine' and 'inadequate education' of British managers, and T. H. Burnham and G. O. Hoskins in their history of the industry sum up a similar indictment as follows: 'There is, in fact, good evidence to believe that the British iron and steel industry would not have declined so fast or so far during the period reviewed had the men at the head possessed greater vision and a bolder and more energetic capacity for organization, direction and administration'.[35] This view of the industry is widely accepted. The steel industry, in fact, almost invariably plays a large role in discussions of American technological superiority. If most observers believe that British coal mining was inferior, virtually all believe that British steelmaking was.

The evidence for a large technological difference in steel, as in coal, is dubious and it is fairly easy to show that the difference did not exist. In coal it was convenient to begin with the average product of labor in measuring productivity, since labor costs were 60 to 70 percent of the total. In steel the direct costs of labor were much smaller. Most of the costs were materials, especially pig iron, but because the materials were used in relatively fixed proportion to output during the period the measure cannot use their average product. In any case the data on quantities of labor and pig iron used in steel production are poor. The way around this obstacle is to use the inputs' prices relative to the price of output rather than their quantities – that is, their marginal rather than their average products.[36]

The best sources for comparing prices of inputs and outputs in steel, as for comparing their quantities in coal, are the prewar censuses of production in the United States (1909) and the United Kingdom (1907). Market prices reported regularly in the trade journals are useful checks, but the census data has the critical advantage of wide coverage. Wide coverage has drawbacks, too, often concealing rather than curing the heterogeneity in such categories as 'American pig iron' or 'British wage earners'. Market prices, in contrast, refer to a specific commodity at a specific location sold under specific terms, although it is often difficult to determine exactly what these specifications were. The average values in the censuses, then, must be handled with care. For example, the British census gives values and quantities for 'thick plates', which include ship plates and boiler plates, while the American census gives data for 'plates and sheets', which include sheets as well. Since sheets required much more rolling than plates, they were more expensive per ton and their effect of raising average values must be removed if the American industry is not to appear spuriously inefficient.[37] A similar problem of heterogeneity occurs in the measure of pig iron input. Low phosphorous (or 'acid', 'Haematite' or 'Bessemer') pig iron was more expensive because it was cheaper to use and more costly to make than other varieties. Because the British industry used more of it than the American industry the categories given in the censuses must again be broken down into more detail to avoid spurious productivity differences.[38]

The results of the various corrections are exhibited in Table 4.2, which gives the names and average values of comparable American and British products. The values that it was necessary to estimate are bracketed. The marginal product of pig iron implied by this table – that is, the ratio of the price of pig iron to the price of a steel product – is invariably higher in Britain. This is not surprising, since labor was, of course, much cheaper relative to pig iron in Britain than in America, causing labor to be used intensively and raising the marginal product of pig iron. What is surprising, in view of the usual assumption of overwhelming American superiority, is that this higher marginal product of pig iron in Britain is not outweighed by a correspondingly lower marginal product of labor. That is, as shown in Table 4.3, the

Table 4.2 *Rolled iron and steel: census values of labor and pig iron inputs and major products*

USA 1909		*UK 1907*	
American name	*American value*	*British name*	*British value*
(dollars/ton or man-year)		(shillings/ton or man-year)	
Bessemer pig iron	[$15·70]	Haematite pig iron	72·5s
Other pig iron	[$14·68]	Other pig iron	55·4s
Average, all pig used	$15·10	Average, all pig used	[65·3s]
Yearly earnings, wages	$679	Yearly earnings, wages	[1,690s]
Plates ≤ gauge 16	[$36·10]	Plates ≤ 1/8″ thick	138·7s
Rails	$28·38	Rails (including train) rails	120·0s
Bars and rods	$31·97	Steel bars, angles	133·8s
Structural shapes	$30·90	Girders, beams	128·0s
Black plates and sheets	$49·00	Black plates and sheets	188·0s

Source: The source for the USA is the 1909 Census, pp. 238–40, and for the UK the 1907 Census, pp. 101–3 (see sources for Table 4.1). The coverage is roughly half of the value of rolled products and steel (i.e. excluding cast iron) in both the UK and the USA. The bracketed figures were estimated as described in previous footnotes. The UK average value of pig used was estimated from the average values given in the census (for forge and foundry, haematite, and basic) weighted by estimates of the haematite and non-haematite pig iron used to make steel and wrought iron (i.e. excluding cast iron and exported pig iron). These estimates, in turn, were based on the acid/basic proportions of steel output and an assumption that all puddling was done with non-haematite pig.

uniformly high price ratio of pig iron to steel in Britain was just barely offset by a uniformly low price ratio of labor to pig iron, leaving very small differences in the total productivity of the American and British industries.

On this reckoning, which agrees with the pattern of comparative advantage that might be expected, the American industry was slightly superior in the making of rails, bars and structural shapes, and the British industry in the making of plates and sheets. The assumption that the share of labor was the same for each product when it was not imparts a small bias to the results, as can be seen from the steady relative improvement of British performance as the degree of fabrication (and labor intensity) increases from rails to sheets. If this bias were corrected, the productivity differences would be more uniform from product to product, with perhaps a 2 or 3 percent average superiority for the American industry.

The negligible difference in output for a given input suggests that entrepreneurial failure had little to do with the relative positions of the British and American supply curves, especially in view of certain biases

Table 4.3 *Productivity differences for major steel products*

	Marginal products of pig iron USA 1	UK 2	*% difference in marginal products of pig iron (USA higher = +)* 3	*% difference in total productivity (USA higher = +)* 4
Heavy plates	·418	·471	−11·92	−1·57
Rails	·533	·545	− 2·22	+8·13
Bars, rods, etc.	·473	·488	− 3·13	+7·22
Structural shapes	·488	·510	− 4·41	+5·94
Black plates and sheets	·308	·348	−12·20	−1·85

Source: Table above. Columns 1 and 2 are the average price of pig iron divided by the price of the product. Column 3 is [(1)−(2)]/[1/2(1)+1/2(2)]. Column 4 is column 3 minus the share of labor (assumed to be 0·192, which is the American value and is high for the UK) times the percentage difference in the price ratio of labor to pig iron (*W/P*). That is, column 4 is (denoting percentage differences in the variables with asterisks)

$$A^* = (P_I/P)^* + S_L(W/P_I)^*$$

The result assumes that labor and pig iron are the only two factors of production. In the United States they accounted for about 0·68 percent of the costs of production, excluding steel inputs into steel in the total cost.

against the British industry in the measure. Two years of productivity growth between the years of the British and American censuses would account for some of the difference. Moreover, 1907 and 1909 in the two countries were at different stages of the business cycle. The productivity measurements assume that the industries were in long-run equilibrium, that is, that their cost curves were horizontal. When a cyclical increase in demand has raised output to a new peak, straining capacity, this assumption is violated and productivity appears lower than it is. It is likely, in fact, that the British industry suffered more from this downward bias in the measure.[39] In any case, though the measure in steelmaking as in coal mining is crude, the result is plain: the total productivities of the American and British industries before the war, when the allegations of American skill and British ineptitude were already many decades old, were virtually indistinguishable.

The apparent lack of any failure of productivity in coal and steel suggests that the traditional contrast between managerial vigor in America and sloth in Britain may be in need of critical reexamination. The measures of productivity proposed here are far from perfect and apply to only two industries. Yet the alleged superiority of American over British technique does not register in either, even though the superiority in coal and steel has usually been thought to have been especially great. Apparently, technology in these two industries was international. This is not a very surprising conclusion, given the ample means of communicating knowledge and the strong incentives to use it. In this view, the differences between the Old World and the New were differences in the quantity and quality of inputs, not in vigor and technology.

DISCUSSION

Chairman: S. B. Saul
Prepared comments: D. Landes
Landes: The coal and steel sections of the paper are not strictly comparable. The argument in the section on coal uses labor productivity, while that on steel uses total productivity. One question that comes to mind, then, is whether using labor productivity in steel might not give rather different results. In the section on coal McCloskey begins his argument by observing that 'average product fell, to be sure, [in England] but it fell or stagnated everywhere in Europe before World War I and does not suggest therefore any peculiarly British failure'. This observation is based on Taylor's table of average labor productivity per man, and while McCloskey is, literally speaking, correct, his interpretation is a strange one in an otherwise carefully quantitative paper. The variations in behavior brought out by the table are more striking than the particular uniformity he used. For example, in Germany labor productivity does level off after the 1880s, but over the whole period from the 1870s to the war there is a rise in productivity of one-third. Over the same period, American productivity in bituminous coal doubles, while British productivity suffered a slight net decline.

In the subsequent calculations of the importance of the two geological factors in coal mining, thickness and depth of seam, a great deal depends on the particular elasticities chosen. In the argument on this point, McCloskey uses two small samples, which imply elasticities of output per man with respect to seam thickness ranging from 0·5 to 1·2. The calculation then proceeds on the assumption that the elasticity is 'around 1'. If the elasticity of 0·5 had been chosen instead, the significance of seam thicknesses in explaining output per man would be cut in half.

Having arrived at some estimates of the elasticities, the question becomes what the differences in the thickness and depth of seams actually were. Here McCloskey uses data from the 1920s, when they first became available. In applying these data to the Anglo-American comparison in 1907–9, however, the difficulty arises that British seams were becoming thinner and deeper as time went on, whereas American seams, it is argued in the paper, were not. The sharpness of the contrast in geological conditions, then, may not have been as great in 1907–9 as it was in the 1920s, and the power of the geological explanation is reduced, by an unknown amount.

The methodology underlying the calculations for coal raises some other questions. Taylor gives prominence to the increase in absenteeism in British mines. What one would like to see is some attempt to bring variables such as these, some of which are perhaps less quantifiable than absenteeism, into the analysis. The importance of other factors than the geological is suggested, too, by the great regional variations exhibited in one of Taylor's tables in the rate of growth of output per man in Britain in the late nineteenth century. By 1924, the paper notes, British output per man was uniform among districts, with mining concentrated on seams with similar geological characteristics. But the evidence from Taylor suggests that the correlation between geological conditions and output per man derived from the 1924 data might not hold at earlier times. That is, some factors other than geology were at work.

In the steel industry the argument is based on total productivity, measured, assuming that the industry was competitive, by the ratio of the prices of pig iron input and of steel output. The essential results are exhibited in Table 4.3. One problem with this procedure is that the ratio might fluctuate from year to year, leaving one in doubt as to which year to choose for the comparison. And, in fact, in McCloskey's Ph.D. thesis, from which the argument on the steel industry is taken, there appears a chart of the marginal product of pig iron in the production of steel, which does show substantial fluctuations from year to year. Another problem is that the measure focuses on steel alone: one might wonder, for example, whether similar results would emerge from a study of the industry as a whole, including pig iron.

There are a few larger issues suggested by the paper. Is it really relevant to compare British with American, rather than German, performance? The traditional story of the enormous superiority of American technology must certainly be revised in light of this and similar papers, but it remains to be seen whether the alleged German superiority was also illusory. Finally, McCloskey is troubled by the large residual gap in productivity between countries that Denison finds, and argues that such differences cannot be believed. If one starts from the other point of view, however, and believes in differences among people in different countries and the slowness of the transmission of technology that these differences imply, then the large residual gap in productivity is not troubling at all. This position, of course, is a matter of faith. But so, too, is McCloskey's position that the differences are unbelievable and must be explained.

McCloskey: On the issue of the view of the world or working hypothesis with which one starts, his has the advantage that it has observable implications. If you suppose to begin with that technology is international, you have a concrete standard against which to judge the truth of the supposition, by seeing whether you can or cannot explain international differences in total productivity. This may have something to do with the way the burden of proof is left with those who doubt rather than with those who support the hypothesis of entrepreneurial failure: the working hypothesis of the latter group gives them few ways of proving the truth or falsehood of their position.

The coal and steel sections of the paper do not really use different methodologies. The one uses average product and the other marginal product, but there is between these two what mathematicians call a relationship of 'duality'. The simplest way to see that this is true is to consider the simple case of one input, call it 'L', which is purchased at the wage 'w', and one output, call it 'Q' which is sold at a price 'p'. In competitive equilibrium there are no supernormal profits, so $PQ-wL=0$. That is, $pQ=wL$, or $Q/L=w/p$. This last says that the average product of labor (Q/L) is the same as the marginal product (w/p). A change or difference in the average product would therefore equal a change or difference in the marginal product. In the general case, in other words, a measure of productivity based on quantities (a generalized average product) would give the same result as one based on prices (a generalized marginal product). The first part of the paper uses a quantity measure and the second part a price measure, but there is no difference in principle or in the results that they would give between the two.

It might be useful to mention the economic assumptions that lie behind productivity measures in this paper and in the others concerned with productivity at the conference. First, the industry is assumed to be perfectly competitive, so that no monopoly profits are being earned and, in the one-factor case, $pQ=wL$. Second, to make certain of this last result, long-run equilibrium is assumed. No Marshallian quasi-rents are being earned: entrepreneurs have had time to adjust their employment of each factor to the desirable level given the prices of the factors and the price of the output. Third, to facilitate the calculation given the difficulty of finding yearly data on the shares of the factors of production in costs, the shares are assumed to be constant. An equivalent assumption is that the production function of the industry is of the Cobb-Douglas form.

Feinstein: Returning to one of Landes' points, it was not helpful to make comparisons in the British coal industry with the United States. Conditions were so different there that one learns very little from the comparison. Germany would be a more sensible choice. Furthermore, the argument of the paper is that by 1907 the British industry could do no better. But in fact in later years it *did* do better. The question is, then, were there improvements that were achieved after the war that could have been achieved before it?

McCloskey: Feinstein's question was identical to the one he had asked in the paper. The question that is answered by a productivity calculation is precisely: was some other technique of production (in this case the American) superior to the one used in Britain? And the calculation involves the same logic, too, if the question is one of profitability, as in the paper by Lindert and Trace. The comparison with the United States is relevant (although, of course, it would be desirable to bring Germany, Belgium and France into the comparisons as well) because the United States had so much higher labor productivity in coal that contemporaries and historians have taken it for granted that technology there was superior, while conceding that geological conditions were better in the United States. The point of the paper is that the geological conditions can explain the entire large difference in labor productivity. Although some doubt is cast on the calculations for 1907–9 that used postwar data on geological conditions, the change in conditions in fifteen years are not enough to alter the results significantly.

Trace: There would have been pressure to open up new fields, as in Kent and the Midlands, which may indeed have altered the results.

McCloskey: These fields were known very early, and were in fact exploited when it became profitable to do so. As was argued in the paper, the British industry was geographically concentrated by comparison with the American industry and there was therefore strong pressure to open up new fields gradually as the balance of geological conditions warranted. This point answers one of Landes' questions as well. The paper did not say that geological conditions were uniform, but only that in all mines the increment to labor productivity from exploiting thickness was carefully balanced against that from exploiting shallowness. In the United States, by contrast, mining was widely scattered and many mines that worked seams that were both thin and deep could survive: there was more deviation possible from a single line of equal average product as a function of depth and thickness.

Thomas: It is not clear how the physical conditions could be separated from entrepreneurial performance in the explanation of average product per man.

McCloskey: The purpose of the paper is to estimate the magnitudes of the geological effects. The argument, then, is that once these have been properly measured there is no residual productivity difference to be explained by entrepreneurship.

Landes: He objected to precisely this residual procedure. If one started with the entrepreneurial explanation, one could exclude geological conditions just as well.

Lindert: Landes' point could be made in another way: even if 100 percent of the difference was explained, it would still not follow that the one factor, entrepreneurship, was unimportant, so long as there were still other factors to be taken into account.

McCloskey: The point he began with was relevant here: if one does start with the entrepreneurial hypothesis, there are no guides as to how to put the argument in quantitative form.

NOTES

1 A. W. Flux, 'Industrial productivity in Great Britain and the United States', *Quarterly Journal of Economics*, 48 (November 1933), pp. 1–38; L. Rostas, *Comparative Productivity in British and American Industry* (Cambridge: Cambridge University Press, 1948); M. Frankel, *British and American Manufacturing Productivity* (Urbana: University of Illinois Press, 1957); M. Gilbert and I. B. Kravis, *An International Comparison of National Products and the Purchasing Powers of Currencies* (Paris: OEEC, 1954); M. Gilbert *et al., Comparative National Products and Price Levels* (Paris: OEEC, 1958); D. Paige and G. Bombach, *A Comparison of National Output and Productivity of the United Kingdom and the United States* (Paris: OEEC, 1959).

2 Gilbert and Kravis, op. cit., p. 22, recalculated from per capita to per worker; Paige and Bombach, op. cit., p. 21. Taking as 100 the geometric average of American manufacturing value added per employee in British and American prices, the British level given in Paige and Bombach for 1950 was only 36·5.

3 Washington, DC: Brookings Institution, 1967.

4 Denison, op. cit., p. 332. His findings for the other Western European countries studied were much the same.

5 Denison's theoretical framework is essentially the Cobb-Douglass production function under conditions of equilibrium and perfect competition. A slightly more general framework is that of K. J. Arrow, H. B. Chenery, B. S. Minhas and R. M. Solow in 'Capital-labor substitution and economic efficiency', *Review of Economics and Statistics*, 43 (August 1961), pp. 225–50. They, too, find large unexplained differences in productivity between countries, in their case between the United States and Japan.

6 'Increasing returns and economic progress', *Economic Journal*, 38 (December 1928), pp. 527–42.

7 'Causes of the superior efficiency of U.S.A. industry as compared with British Industry', *Economic Journal*, 56 (September 1946), pp. 383–90. Recent work on early national income by R. Gallman for the United States and C. H. Feinstein for the United Kingdom suggests that at the par of exchange the income of the two was approximately equal in the 1850s. The argument has the further difficulty that Britain sold to a world market: the market for British cotton textiles, for example, was surely larger than the American market throughout the nineteenth century.

8 Series 66, p. 141, in US Bureau of the Census, *Historical Statistics of the United States* (Washington, DC: Govt Printing Office, 1960) estimates rent as around 8 percent of American national income from 1870. P. Deane and W. A. Cole in *British Economic Growth, 1688–1959* (Cambridge: Cambridge University Press, 1964), p. 247, estimate rent, including apparently some rents of buildings, at around 13 percent from 1860 to World War I.

9 The basis for the estimate of a 30 percent share is the sum of entrepreneurial income and dividends in American national income in the late nineteenth century given in *Historical Statistics* at the place cited above. The reason the share in national income is an upper bound on the relevant share is that, as discussed below, the share relevant to a particular industry's production function would include intermediate goods as well as value added.

10 'The explanation of productivity change', *Review of Economic Studies*, 34 (July 1967), pp. 249–84, at p. 274. E. Denison has subjected this article to searching criticism, pointing out, among other things, that they did not offer evidence for the assertion quoted here ('Some major issues in productivity analysis: an examination

of estimates by Jorgenson and Griliches', *Survey of Current Business*, 49, no. 5, pt II, May 1969, pp. 1–27).

11 Denison himself admits that he is puzzled by it and remarks that his 'inability to decompose residual productivity or analyze it satisfactorily is surely the greatest gap in the present study' (Denison, op. cit., p. 340).

12 Cf. E. D. Domar, 'On the measurement of technological change', *Economic Journal*, 71 (December 1961), pp. 709–29.

13 It can be shown, as in Domar, op. cit., that the typical productivity measure is the national measure multiplied by the share of inputs not purchased from other firms. In the 1947 input–output table for the American economy (given in H. B. Chenery and P. G. Clark, *Interindustry Economics*, New York: Wiley, 1959, p. 222) purchased inputs were 44 percent of total domestic sales. In the first British Census of Production it was found that 58 percent of the costs were purchased from other firms (*Final Report on the First Census of Production of the United Kingdom (1907)*, London: HMSO, 1912, p. 19). For a similar group of industries in the American input–output table (excluding, that is, agriculture, fishing, transport, trade and services), 47 percent were purchased from other firms.

14 J. H. Clapham, *An Economic History of Modern Britain* (Cambridge: Cambridge University Press, 1938), Vol. III, p. 168.

15 'The coal industry', chapter 2 in D. Aldcroft (ed.), *The Development of British Industry and Foreign Competition 1875–1914* (London: Allen & Unwin, 1968), p. 69.

16 Cf. Taylor, op. cit., p. 46.

17 In anthracite mining output per man-day declined after 1899, while in bituminous it continued to rise (US Geological Survey, *Mineral Resources of the United States 1917* (Washington, DC: Govt Printing Office, 1920), pt II, p. 932).

18 Because the price of any particular ton of coal or man-hour of labor reflects many different quality components, the components would need to be separated by some such method as regressing coal prices on BTUs per ton and other qualities. The analysis should not include costless quality differences in the inputs such as the presence of more vigorous men in America than in Britain; it should include education, experience and other qualities of the inputs requiring investment.

19 The share of capital and land, calculated as a residual from labor and materials, was 19 percent in the UK in 1919 (*Report of the Coal Industry Commission* (Sankey Commission), SP 1919 XI, p. xii) and 12 percent in the United States in 1909 (*Census of Mines and Quarries*, pp. 183–229). Assuming that land and capital earned roughly similar returns, these can be split into land and capital by using their shares in total asset values. C. H. Feinstein's data on the coal industry in his *Domestic Capital Formation in the United Kingdom 1920–1939* (Cambridge: Cambridge University Press, 1965, pp. 80ff.) imply that the depreciated value of fixed capital in historical prices plus the value of stocks in trade was £146 million in 1920, while the value of coal deposits and surface land was £96 million. According to D. B. Creamer, S. P. Dobrovolsky and I. Borenstein's *Capital in Manufacturing and Mining* (Princeton: Princeton University Press, 1960, pp. 274ff.) in the United States in 1909 the value of capital ($486 million) was much smaller in relation to all land used in the industry ($1,064 million) than in the United Kingdom. The upshot is that while the estimates of the shares of land in Britain and America are about the same (7·5 and 8·2 percent), the British share of capital (11·5 percent) is much higher than the American (3·8 percent).

20 Strictly speaking, a conversion of the stock of land into a flow of services from land is required. Jorgenson and Griliches (op. cit.) criticized J. W. Kendrick for aggregating stock of capital rather than service flows and the same point applies to land. The fullness of utilization of coal land may have been different in the two countries, yielding different flows from the same stock.

21 Incidentally, the pattern of coal land tenure is a good example of the effect of economic conditions on legal arrangements. In the United Kingdom, apparently,

land was expensive enough to overcome the high transaction costs of selling mineral rights and surface rights separately and to warrant more specialization between ownership of the rights and exploitation of the rights (over two-thirds of American coal acreage was owned outright by the mining companies; in Britain, however, ownership of coal by the mines was exceptional).

22 It might seem reasonable to weight the reserves by the share of the region – the state in America and the county in Britain – in total output. It is not: although this weighting scheme corresponds with what one does unconsciously in assessing the size of actively used coal reserves, it yields a statistic that varies with the degree of detail chosen, as an arithmetic example can make clear. Suppose there were three districts with outputs of 1, 1 and 1 and with reserves of 2, 3 and 4. If the statistic were calculated taking all three districts separately, it would be 9/3. Taking the first and second together, it would be 14/3.

23 12th International Geological Congress, *The Coal Resources of the World* (Toronto: Morang, 1913), Vol. II, article by M. R. Campbell, 'The coal reserves of the United States', pp. 525–39. The definition of the intensity of mining is the ratio of 1909 output to the states' total reserves. The definition and the truncation at six states is highly arbitrary. The implicit assumption is that in these states the exploitation of coal land was as intense per ton of reserves as in Britain. For Pennsylvania and Maryland this is no doubt true. For the others it is less plausible.

24 To make the comparison with the United States (whose reserves were given for seams greater than 2 ft in thickness at a depth of less than 3,000 ft), the British reserves of 171,000 million metric tons (International Geological Congress, op. cit., p. 628, with Scotland's probable reserves estimated on the basis of the ratio of 'probable' to 'actual' in England and Wales) had to be reduced by estimates of the British reserves between 3,000 and 4,000 ft deep and 1 to 2 ft in thickness (the estimates were 25 percent of the total to correct for the different standards of depth and 20·7 percent (given in Colliery Guardian, *Digest of Evidence Given Before the Royal Commission on Coal Supplies (1901–05)* (London, 1905–7), Vol. I, p. xxxii) to correct for the different standards of thickness. This procedure entails the assumption that depth and thickness were not correlated. They would be at shallower depths and greater thicknesses because of selective mining of the shallower and thicker seams, but at these far limits of depth and thickness the assumption is reasonable.

25 See, for example, F. G. Tryon and M. H. Schoenfield, 'Comparison of physical conditions in British and American coal mines', *Coal and Coal Trades Journal* 57, pp. 934, 956–7, 1087–9, 1202–6 (4 parts), autumn weeks of 1926. Tryon was the chief statistical adviser to the United States Coal Commission and was in charge of the US Geological Survey coal statistics. Tyron and Schoenfield use the data on British mines collected for the Royal Commission on the Coal Industry (the Samuel Commission) of 1926. A table, also from the Samuel Commission, on the conditions of coal mining in the major coal-mining countries is reproduced in the League of Nations, International Economic Conference, *Memorandum on Coal*, Vol. I (Geneva, 1927), p. 39, as well as in Tryon and Schoenfield, op. cit., p. 1203.

26 This point is made repeatedly in the testimony of the witnesses to the Royal Commission on Coal Supplies (1901–5). See Colliery Guardian, op. cit., Vol. I, chapter I, 'The working of thin seams'; chapter II, section 3, 'Evidence as to thickness of seams worked at great depths'.

27 Errors in the independent variables will also bias the coefficient on thickness in a regression explaining output per man downward. Unfortunately, simultaneous equation bias, of which this is a classic case (because there exists another relation among the variables, namely, the conditions of profit maximization), works in the other direction.

28 Revised edn (Washington, DC: Govt Printing Office, 1891), pp. 199ff.

29 Cf. Tryon and Schoenfield, op. cit., p. 1205, speaking of the 1920s: 'In the

bituminous mines of the United States, no marked correlation between average thickness and average depth of working has yet developed simply because the readily accessible coals have not been exhausted.'

30 *Report of the U.S. Coal Commission* (Washington, DC: Govt Printing Office, 1925), part II, p. 1079.

31 Estimated from Tryon and Schoenfield, op. cit., p. 1088. American bituminous seams in 1920 averaged 63 inches and anthracite seams in 1922 80 inches. 1922 was a depressed year in anthracite mining and the figure of 80 inches may therefore be too high: in bad years thin seams were not mined. 1920 and 1924 were prosperous years for coal in the United States and Britain.

32 Output per man was very uniform in the UK compared with the US; cf. Tyron and Schoenfield, op. cit., p. 1204.

33 Tryon and Schoenfield, op. cit., p. 1205, give the average depth of coal in seams under 2 ft in thickness as 517 ft, between 2 and 4 ft as 876 ft, between 4 and 6 ft as 1163 ft, and over 6 ft as 1351 ft.

34 Cambridge: Cambridge University Press, 1940.

35 Burn, op. cit., pp. 303, 213, 11; and Burnham and Hoskins, *Iron and Steel in Britain 1870–1930* (London: Allen & Unwin, 1943), p. 271.

36 The equivalence of measures of productivity using prices and quantities has received attention recently. See, for example, D. W. Jorgenson, 'The embodiment hypothesis', *Journal of the Political Economy* 74, 1–17, February 1966, p. 3n. An early use of the price measure, familiar to economic historians, is G. T. Jones, *Increasing Return* (Cambridge: Cambridge University Press, 1933), esp. p. 33 (Jones' index can be shown to be identical to the price measure given in Jorgenson). It should be emphasized that the price measure is not merely an approximation to the quantity measure: with consistent data it is identical to it and is therefore not more volatile or uncertain.

37 The average value of plates and sheets is given in the American census as $40·00 per long ton (US Bureau of the Census, Vol. X, *Manufactures 1909* (Washington, DC: Govt Printing Office, 1913), p. 240). The census gives tonnages, but not values, of plates and sheets by gauge (ibid., p. 238). Assuming that a gauge of 17 or lighter is comparable to the British category of 'sheets', and assuming further that sheets sold at the black plate and sheet price (a high estimate of the true price) of $50·00 per ton (given at p. 240), the heavy plate price can be estimated at $36·10 per ton.

38 The object was to break the American census value of pig iron used in steelworks and rolling mills ($15·10 per ton; ibid., p. 252) into Bessemer and non-Bessemer prices, comparable to the values reported in the British census. The census gives tonnages for five types of pig iron; the American Iron and Steel Institute's *Statistical Report for 1913* gives 1909 market prices for pig iron similar to each of the five types; from this information and the average census value it is possible to infer the appropriate census values for the Bessemer type and for the rest.

39 1907 was a peak year for British steel output and was not surpassed until 1912. In 1909, the American industry produced about 3 percent more steel than in the previous peak, but the previous peak was three years before and was surpassed in 1910: the industry had ample time to adjust and was not pressed much beyond its previous peak output until 1910.

5

Did Victorian Britain Fail?

Few beliefs are so well established in the credo of British economic history as the belief that the late Victorians failed. Statistical economists and literary historians, Englishmen and foreigners, late Victorians and moderns have accepted some version of it. The three senses in which Britain is said to have failed are that output grew too slowly because of sluggish demand, that too much was invested abroad because of imperfect capital markets, and that productivity stagnated because of inept entrepreneurship. The three are closely related. Slower growing demand, partly an inevitable consequence of new competition in world markets and partly an avoidable consequence of the shortcomings of British merchants and manufacturers, is said to have slowed British growth and, consequently, to have dulled the incentive to invest at home. The obstacles to investment were multiplied by imperfect capital markets, which channeled funds abroad to an even greater extent than warranted by the sluggish markets at home. In this milieu entrepreneurs had few opportunities to invest in new technologies. Again, however, the obstacles were multiplied by the inadequate response of the economy, for entrepreneurs were slow to take up even the limited opportunities open to them. Productivity, therefore, is said to have stagnated, worsening Britain's position in foreign markets, driving still more investment abroad and closing the circle of failure. Few historians subscribe to the whole of this dismal tale, but many believe parts of it. The argument of this essay is that these beliefs are ill founded.

I

Since the early 1930s when W. Hoffmann found that British industrial growth slowed noticeably after 1870, historians have suspected a failure in output growth. In a companion study to Hoffmann's, W. Schlote found that export growth also slowed after 1870. The correlation between industrial and export growth was suggestive and its discovery timely, for the new economics of the 1930s seemed to provide it with a

I should like to thank Professors P. David, S. L. Engerman, R. W. Fogel, P. Lindert, P. F. McGouldrick, J. R. Meyer, C. Pope and R. Sylla for their comments on a version of this essay presented in January 1969 to the Purdue Conference on the Application of Economic Theory and Quantitative Techniques to Problems of Economic History.

theoretical rationale. Aggregate demand, after all, determines output, and exports were a large part of Britain's aggregate demand. To many economists and historians it has seemed that this insight, though used by its discoverers to explain relatively brief periods of mass unemployment in the 1920s and 1930s, could also be used to explain the slow growth of the British economy in the forty years after 1870.[1]

One systematic use of the demand explanation of the late Victorian decline is a paper by J. R. Meyer, 'An input–output approach to evaluating British industrial production in the late 19th century'.[2] Because it makes the argument in a simple form and arrives at a concrete conclusion against which the significance of criticisms can be measured, it makes a particularly good text for an examination of the hypothesis. As Meyer puts the argument,

> Under almost any set of realistic assumptions, increments of industrial exports should increase the value of total production by more than their own value . . . This means that the indirect as well as direct effects of the late-nineteenth-century export decline must somehow be evaluated . . . About the best means now known for obtaining such measurements is the Leontief input–output table. The author has constructed such a table for the British economy of 1907 . . . The level of industrial activity that would have been generated if exports had maintained the 1854–1872 rates of growth, everything else assumed unchanged, was found by replacing the actual exports with the theoretical exports [and using the input–output table] to arrive at the implied direct and indirect requirements of industrial output . . . the results tend to support the hypothesis that if the rate of growth in industrial exports had been maintained, the United Kingdom could have sustained its former high-level advance in industrial production . . . The input–output results . . . [substantiate] the plausibility of retarded exports as an explanation of nineteenth-century stagnation in the United Kingdom.[3]

There are a number of criticisms of the argument that make it seem overelaborate or incomplete but do not change its central conclusion. One such criticism is that the exercise in input–output analysis is unnecessary. If it is appropriate to speak of one rate of growth for all the many types of British exports, this rate will produce an identical rate of growth of gross output simply because the matrix of interindustry requirements is assumed in input–output analysis to be a matrix of constants. And it is entirely appropriate to speak of one rate of growth of final demand in the present context. The hypothesis under consideration is that the falling average rate of growth of exports after 1870 retarded industrial production. The argument is not about the product composition of export growth but about its average rate, the one rate of growth that characterizes its behavior. Little is gained by carrying out the input–output calculations, for the result that they will give has been assumed. Meyer's data imply, for example, that if exports had grown at 4·8 percent per year from 1872 to 1907, as they did from 1854 to 1872, then industrial output would have grown at 4·7 percent per year.[4] The near equality of the two rates is not surprising.

Although gross output and final demand must grow at the same rate if the assumptions of input–output analysis are met, they do not appear to have done so, and this is another difficulty with the argument. Hoffmann's index of industrial output, which is essentially a gross output index, grew at about 1·69 percent per year from 1872 to 1907 while real exports grew at 2·36 percent and real national income at 2·40 percent.[5] The difference of 0·7 percent per year between the growth of final demand and gross output is inconsistent with the assumption in input–output analysis of fixed intermediate requirements. It took less and less intermediate output to produce the final output of the economy. Neglecting this development (which may with some justice be called 'productivity change') will lead to an incorrect estimate of the hypothetical rate of growth of industrial output.

Neither of these criticisms, however, alters the broad conclusion. The hypothetical rate of growth of gross output as a whole (and industrial gross output as a part of it) can be recalculated using the more economical argument that its growth must equal the hypothetical growth of final demand minus the growth of the ratio of final demand to gross output. The rate of growth of exports from 1854 to 1872 is taken to be the hypothetical rate of growth of final demand from 1872 to 1907 in the relevant sense. It matters little whether exports alone or all of final demand (consumption, investment, exports and government spending) are treated as the exogenous variable, for they grow at similar rates. The change in the ratio of final demand (Imlah's index) to gross output (Hoffmann's index) is calculated from the observed change in the period 1872–1907. Subtracting it from the hypothetical growth of final demand yields a gross output growth rate of 4·37 – 0·67 = 3·71 percent per year from 1872 to 1907 had exports grown as they did from 1854 to 1872. This is indeed far above the growth rate of 1·69 percent per year in industrial output actually achieved from 1872 to 1907 and is higher even than the rate of 2·98 percent per year achieved from 1854 to 1872. The emphasis on exports appears to be justified.[6]

The argument that Britain's output grew more slowly because of slower-growing exports, however, assumes that aggregate demand alone determined output, when in fact there were constraints of supply.[7] Indeed, there is evidence that they were the only binding constraints. If faltering export demand after 1872 held back the growth of the British economy there would have been increasing unemployment as actual output, cut by the insufficiency of aggregate demand, fell more and more behind potential output. But unemployment after 1872 was low and did not increase with time: the trade union figures suggest that unemployment late in the period 1872–1907 was lower than it was early in the period. The Victorian economy was at full employment and the growth of real output was determined by the growth of the factors of production, such as fixed capital and skilled labor, not by aggregate demand. This, then, is the decisive criticism of the demand theory: in the situation of the Victorian economy it is more plausible to assume that supply created its own demand than that demand would have created its own supply.

The argument is that the hypothetical growth rate of 3·71 percent per year was impossible. Clearly, if all factors of production were inelastic in supply and if productivity change were exogenous, the achieved rate of growth would have been the limit of possibility. The question, then, is whether productivity change and the supplies of factors of production were responsive enough to the demands of the economy to permit a 3·71 percent rate of growth.

The supply of labor was in all likelihood insufficiently responsive to the pressures of export demand in the late nineteenth century to permit so high a growth rate. Unemployment was low and the rural pool of underemployed labor was by this time small.[8] Had all emigration from the United Kingdom ceased and had all these emigrants been of working age, the labor force might have grown at 1·6 percent per year rather than at 1 percent as it did from 1871 to 1911, but this is still low relative to the hypothetical growth of gross output.[9] If capital and labor were not substitutable, then, the slow growth of the labor force in the United Kingdom would have limited output growth. To put it the other way, had output grown at 3·71 percent per year from 1872 to 1907 instead of 1·69 percent the labor force at the end of the period would have had to have been twice as large as the actual labor force and two-fifths larger than the entire population aged 15 and over.[10]

If capital and labor *were* substitutable, an increase in capital per man could substitute in some degree for these improbable increases in the labor force. The magnitude of the necessary capital accumulation, assuming that the elasticity of substitution between capital and labor was unity, can be estimated from an equation of the sources of growth:

$$\overline{Q}_{go} = s_k \overline{K} + s_l \overline{L} + \overline{T}'$$

in which $\overline{Q}_{go}$ is the proportional growth rate of gross output in the economy, $\overline{K}$ and $\overline{L}$ the growth rates of capital and labor, s_k and s_l their shares in national income, and $\overline{T}'$ the rate of productivity change defined to correspond with gross output.[11] The growth equation can be solved for the rate of growth of capital,

$$\bar{K} = \frac{1}{s_k}[\bar{Q}_{go} - s_l \bar{L} - \bar{T}']$$

and placing the appropriate values in the right-hand side of the new equation yields the necessary rate:[12]

$$\bar{K} = \frac{1}{0 \cdot 442}[0 \cdot 0371 - 0 \cdot 52\,(0 \cdot 0102) - 0 \cdot 0050] = 0 \cdot 0609$$

This 6·09 percent per year rate of capital growth is in the vicinity of four times the actual rate in the late nineteeth century.[13] The hypothetically higher capital growth would have had to have come from a great increase in the ratio of savings to income. Indeed, the disproportionate growth in capital would make the task more difficult because the capital–output ratio would rise, raising the savings ratio necessary for a given rate. Englishmen would have had to have saved about 42 percent of their income – that is to say, an incredibly high proportion of it – for gross output to grow at its hypothetical rate of 3·71 percent per year.[14]

The argument, of course, can be made the other way around: from a reasonable upper bound on the savings ratio one can deduce upper bounds on the growth of capital and output. An assumption about the outcome of such an exercise underlies much of the discussion of British opportunities at the end of the nineteenth century. As a matter of arithmetic higher savings are always possible, but the relevant historical question is whether the late Victorians were profligate in consumption compared with foreigners at the time or with Englishmen before. The evidence suggests that they were not. American savings ratios were higher than British ratios, but the difference was small. For example, from 1886 to 1900, by all accounts a period of low British savings, the British ratio of net investment to net national income averaged 10·4 percent, while the American ratio averaged 13·7 percent, a difference of 3·3 percent of income.[15] Nor were savings a much higher share of national income before 1870: the savings ratio averaged 12·8 percent from 1858 to 1873. Given the probable range of error in the estimates, the differences are insignificant. More important, if the order of magnitude of the deficiency in the savings ratio were 3 or 4 percent of income, making up the deficiency would have had a small impact on the rate of growth of income. British emulation of the American standard of thrift, for example, would have raised the rate of growth of domestic capital by about a half of its former rate and the rate of growth of income by less than a tenth.[16] In other words, the route to significantly higher income growth by way of a rise in the savings ratio was not open to late Victorian England.

II

It is likely, then, that there were binding resource limitations on the growth of the British economy in the late nineteenth century. By reallocating resources, of course, any one sector of the economy could have grown faster: industry could have grown at the expense of services and exports at the expense of production for home consumption had labor and capital been allocated differently. The most popular target for hypothetical reallocation has been Britain's enormous holdings of capital abroad in the late nineteenth century. The common view is that if investors had been restrained from sending abroad a third of the savings available for capital formation, Britain would have been better off. It is clear that in this case Britain's domestic capital stock would have grown half as fast again. It is not clear, however, that exchanging domestic for foreign capital would have raised British national income. The question is how bringing capital home could be expected to increase income and how large the increase would have been.

If world capital markets were functioning efficiently, of course, a prohibition of investment abroad would have reduced British national income. Most of the supporters of the hypothesis of immiseration by capital exports have accepted the assumption that the enlightened self-interest of investors in perfect capital markets maximizes national income.[17] Their case has rested, therefore, on two themes: first, that investors were not enlightened; and, second, that capital markets were not perfect.

The main sort of unenlightened behavior is said to have been investment in foreign projects with a high risk of default. Even J. M. Keynes, however, who led the attack in the 1920s on investment abroad, did not base his argument on a supposition that Englishmen invested in risky projects abroad, any more than in risky projects at home, without demanding interest compensation for the risk. His primary point was, rather, that in default the physical capital abroad was lost to Englishmen: 'If the Grand Trunk Railway of Canada fails its shareholders . . . we have nothing. If the Underground System of London fails its shareholders, Londoners still have their Underground System.'[18] The significance of the point depends on the magnitude of the defaults and in the period 1870–1913, as A. K. Cairncross has observed,[19] they were small. Even in the 1870s, which was 'probably the least remunerative decade in the sixty years before the war', defaults on investments abroad were 'a comparatively small amount'.[20] Defaults were not an important drain on British capital before the war.

The more common theme than the loss from default in the literature of immiseration by capital exports is the perversity of Britain's imperfect capital market. The City, the story goes, was expert at channeling British savings into foreign trade credit and railway bonds, but inexpert at serving the industrial hinterlands of Britain itself.[21] Keynes, for example, emphasized the Colonial Stock Act of 1900 and similar Acts before it which permitted British trust funds to be invested in colonial railway and governmental bonds, giving, he claimed, an artificial incentive to investment abroad. The effect was 'to starve home developments by diverting savings abroad and, consequently, to burden home borrowers with a higher rate of interest than they would need to pay otherwise'.[22]

The logic of this and similar arguments based on an artificial preference by some lenders for lending abroad is not compelling. If borrowers in the colonies were, in fact, offering lower interest rates than borrowers with similar credit standing at home, there would be an incentive for British lenders who, unlike the trustees, had no special motive for investing in colonial securities to move out of them into domestic securities, raising the low-colonial interest rates. The evidence on the differential between home and foreign interest rates for securities of similar quality suggests that the common source of funds for home and foreign investment was, in fact, effective in equalizing the rates. Indeed, interest rates for securities abroad were normally slightly higher than securities at home with the same risk.[23]

The qualification 'with the same risk' requires emphasis. In 1911–13 the average return on all capital at home was more than 10 percent, while the return on capital abroad was less than 5 percent.[24] The capital abroad, however, was held in safe bonds, while the capital at home had to be held on balance in equity. Englishmen owned their own capital stock and the risk of ownership required compensation in the form of a higher return than on the comparative safety of lending abroad. Englishmen who were willing to own capital received, through the leverage of loans from the fainthearted, a return higher than the 10 percent return on real capital, while bondholders received a lower return. Some, and perhaps all, of the difference between the return on real capital at home and bond capital abroad, then, was a reward for assuming risk.

Nonetheless, some of the difference may have been the result of imperfections in the capital market. In an imperfect capital market Britain would have gained by bringing some of her capital home. The net gain to national income from eliminating the gap caused by imperfections is represented by the shaded area in Figure 5.1. The horizontal axis measures for 1911–13 capital at home, capital owned by citizens of the United Kingdom abroad and foreign capital abroad,[25] and the vertical axes the marginal products of capital at home and abroad. Income produced at home, since it is the total product of capital at home, is represented by the area under the solid curve of the marginal product of capital, while income from investments abroad, since it is the return on foreign bonds multiplied by the value of foreign bonds

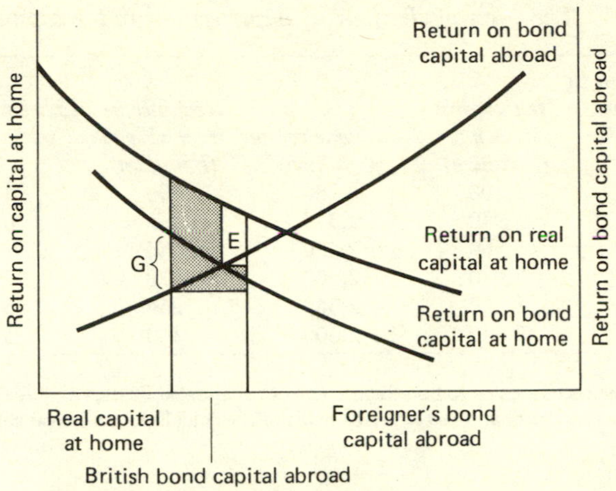

Figure 5.1 *The effect of eliminating imperfections in the capital market*

owned, is represented by the rectangle whose height is the return on foreign bonds.[26] The length G represents the gap between the return on domestic and foreign bonds and is the chief point at issue. A gap of 6 percent is an upper bound: it would be the true gap from imperfections only if none of the difference between the 10·7 percent return on physical capital at home and the 4·7 percent return on bond capital abroad was a premium for the risk of ownership. The gap, therefore, is taken to vary from 1 percent to 6 percent. Eliminating the gap would push the bond market to the equilibrium E, reducing the return on physical capital at home and raising the return on bonds abroad.[27] Subtracting the old income at home and abroad from the new leaves the shaded area as the net gain.

The gain is small, even assuming great imperfections in the capital market, as shown in Table 5.1.[28]

The elimination of the largest possible imperfection during the period 1870–1913, even though it would have required enormous capital *imports*, would have raised income by the end of the period by only 7·3 percent and would only have raised the rate of growth of income from 2·40 percent per year to 2·58 percent.

It has been argued that 'the City of London and its financial institutions . . . were the greatest single threat to the prosperity of England'.[29] The tiny increment to the growth of income from eliminating the threat suggests that this view is false. The United Kingdom exported a huge amount of capital in the period and it is tempting to believe that it could have drawn on this capital as a surplus for growth. In the light of the argument here, the temptation must be resisted.

The demand hypothesis of slower British growth, then, has a grave

Table 5.1 *The effect of eliminating imperfections in the capital market*

Excess of home interest rate over 4·7% (%)	*New capital at home (£ million)*	*New home income (£ million)*	*New income from abroad (£ million)*	*Additional income as % of old (%)*
1	2,100	2,180	95	4·5
2	3,940	2,310	nil	6·5
3	5,560	2,420	86	7·3
4	7,040	2,500	178	7·0
5	8,380	2,560	266	5·5
6	9,530	2,600	350	3·5

Source: The procedure was to find the increment to capital at home, using the given data, that equilibrates the bond market. The details of the calculations are available from the author.

defect. Meyer's test, though flawed, appears at first to lend it support. But the demand hypothesis, in any form, assumes elastic supplies of labor and capital and these were not available. In late Victorian England there was no reserve army of unemployed, no pool of underemployed agricultural labor, no excessive consumption at home and no profitless investment abroad. Had exports grown faster, output for domestic use would have grown slower: the total was fixed by the growth of resources and productivity.

III

The allegation of failure, therefore, must rest on slower-growing productivity. The measurement of how effectively an economy uses the resources available to it is a delicate matter with the best of information. With the poor quality of information available on the late Victorian economy, the task has seemed to some too difficult to attempt. They have passed on to reasons why Britain failed, taking as proven the fact of failure. It is not surprising that they have eschewed measurement, for the measures have given conflicting opinions on the course of productivity change. One group, using Prest's deflated national income data, places the climacteric of productivity in the 1890s while the other, using Hoffmann's index of industrial output, places it in the 1870s. D. J. Coppock was the first to notice the divergence between the measures of national income and of industrial output. Remarking that 'between 1875 and 1900 the two series are quite contradictory',[30] he chooses the industrial series and the earlier climacteric. C. Wilson leans the other way, but is disturbed by 'the gap between the *apparent* slackening of economic growth and the better substantiated estimates of rising aggregate national income, a conundrum to which no really satisfactory answer has been given'.[31]

The alleged conundrum is that industrial output grew slower than national income: Hoffmann's index grew at around 1·7 percent per year from 1872 to 1907, while real national income was growing at 2 percent or more per year. The coverage of the Hoffmann index, however, is surely smaller than the income estimates and the missing sectors may well have been growing faster.[32] Moreover, Hoffmann's index is essentially a gross output index. That is, although it uses value added weights the basic data are gross, not net, outputs of the commodities. Hoffmann's index is not an index of national income originating in industry, as those who are puzzled by its lack of identity with national income appear to believe. By the argument developed earlier, therefore, Hoffmann's index *must* grow slower than national income: gross output and final output can grow at the same rate only if productivity change in the sense of a fall in the interindustry coefficient is nil.[33] There is, in short, no conundrum: there is no clear contradiction between Hoffmann's index and real income.

Coppock attempted to explain the divergence between Hoffmann's index and the measures of real income of Phelps-Brown and Handfield-Jones[34] by arguing that the deflator of national income was too heavily weighted towards food and raw materials. Food and raw material prices were more volatile than more representative commodities, he said, falling faster before 1896 and rising faster after 1896, with the result that a change in trend of real national income appears in the 1890s.[35] This criticism rests on an inappropriate set of weights for a price index of output. Noting that the weight on food in the Phelps-Brown and Handfield-Jones price index is about 36 percent, for example, he remarks that 'it is obvious that the output of food bore no such relationship to national output'.[36] The evidence is the low share of income earned in agriculture. Income earned in an industry, however, is the sum of the rewards to labor, capital and land inputs and is not in general equal to the sum of final expenditures on the product of the industry. It is not necessarily true that 'what is relevant for a price index of final products is outputs not expenditures'.[37] It appears from the context that Coppock means value added when he speaks of 'outputs'. With perfect data, prices weighted by expenditures shares would give exactly the same income deflator as prices weighted by value added shares. There are no grounds for preferring one or the other, except when the data have been collected in one or the other fashion. In fact, because there are good indexes of final expenditure prices available (e.g. Bowley's cost of living index for consumption, Feinstein's gross investment deflator for investment, Imlah's export price index), it is convenient to construct a price index with final expenditure weights. It is the weight of each industry's product in final expenditure (gross national product) that the index of Phelps-Brown and Handfield-Jones aims to reflect. Ironically, when after 1900 consumption data by product become available, they show that food, drink and tobacco were almost exactly the 36 percent of gross national product that Coppock believed was obviously too high.[38]

It is entirely appropriate, then, to use national product estimates, with their heavy weight on food, for measuring productivity. Table 5.2 gives some estimates of the home-produced gross national product of the United Kingdom for ten-year intervals from 1860 to 1910. The estimates of real gross national product were made by adding together the expenditures in the prices of 1900 by consumers, investors, government and the rest of the world.

Table 5.2 *Real gross national product*

	Money GNP £ million	*Real GNP £ million 1900 prices*	*Implicit price index*	*Growth rate per year of real GNP (% in previous decade)*	*Hoffmann's index of industrial output*	*Growth rate per year of Hoffmann's index (%)*
1860	841	720	116·7		34·2	
1870	1,156	999	115·7	3·27	43·4	2·38
1880	1,349	1,233	101·3	2·11	54·2	2·21
1890	1,500	1,634	91·7	2·82	65·5	1·91
1900	2,037	2,037	100·0	2·19	77·1	1·62
1910	2,265	2,211	102·5	0·806	86·5	1·14

Source: Details of the estimating procedures available from the author on request. Consumption for 1860–90 is based on the series of J. B. Jeffreys and D. Walters (in S. Kuznets, ed., International Association for Research in Income and Wealth, *Income and Wealth, Series V* (1955), p. 27), deflated by Bowley's index of the cost of living. Consumption for 1900–10 is based on D. A. Rowe's series given in Mitchell, op. cit., p. 371. Gross investment in 1900 prices is Feinstein's series (ibid., p. 373) and government expenditure is the estimate given by A. T. Peacock and J. Wiseman, *The Growth of Public Expenditure in the United Kingdom* (Princeton, NJ, 1961) at pp. 37 and 42. Real exports of commodities and invisibles minus real imports are based on Imlah's estimates (Mitchell, op. cit., pp. 331–3).

The striking feature of the growth of real product is its rapid growth before 1900 and its sharp deceleration afterwards. Unless the pattern of growth of inputs explains this break, the climacteric should be placed not in the 1870s or 1890s but in the 1900s. The growth of the relevant inputs, labor and capital, is exhibited in Table 5.3.

Both inputs are necessary for a meaningful measure of productivity: it is not appropriate, for example, to use the growth of output per man to draw inferences about the performance of the economy or a sector of it. Not surprisingly, the growth of the inputs is relatively steady, labor

Table 5.3 *Capital, labor and productivity*

	Domestic capital value in 1900 prices (£ million)	*Capital growth rate per year (% in previous decade)*	*Labor (000s employed year after)*	*Labor growth rate per year (%)*	*Productivity growth rate per year (%)*
1860	3,732		11,678		
1870	4,316	1·44	13,064	1·115	2·160
1880	5,057	1·60	14,450	1·025	0·872
1890	5,708	1·24	16,020	1·025	1·750
1900	6,657	1·54	17,740	1·025	0·982
1910	7,713	1·47	19,700	1·045	−0·383

Source: Details available from the author on request. The capital estimate is a decumulation of J. C. Stamp's estimate of the domestic capital stock (*British Incomes and Property*, 1916, p. 404) by Feinstein's net fixed investment series (loc. cit.) and an estimate of inventory investment. Stamp's and Feinstein's estimates were adjusted for comparability. The labor series is an estimate given in Phelps-Brown and Handfield-Jones, op. cit., p. 298. For the method of estimating the shares of labor and capital in home-produced income see n. 12, p. 108.

growing at about 1·05 percent per year and capital at 1·45 percent per year during the period. The last column shows the resulting measure of productivity change, that is, the growth of real product not attributable to the growth of capital or labor. Once again, there is a sharp deceleration after the turn of the century.

More important, however, is the sustained growth of productivity in the 1870s, 1880s and 1890s, for it was during these years that the conviction grew in Englishmen that they were falling behind the technology of Germany and, especially, the United States. As far as can be ascertained, however, productivity growth in the United States was of the same order of magnitude as in the United Kingdom: rates of 1 or 1·5 percent per year are typical of the American as of the British economy at the time.[39] Given the uncertainties of the data for both countries, the most precise defensible statement is that there was little cause for alarm in the behavior of British productivity.

The case for a late Victorian failure in productivity, then, appears weak. Indeed the failure, to be precise, was Edwardian. Nor is there any evidence that productivity responded to the growth of exports: real exports grew faster in the decade and a half before World War I than they had since the 1860s, yet productivity declined. Moreover, the correlation between capital accumulation and productivity change on which the demand theory of British failure rests is poor: capital accumulation was low in the 1880s, for example, yet productivity growth was rapid.

A measure of productivity growth using national aggregates of output, labor and capital, however, is a fragile foundation on which to erect theories of British success or failure. This is not because of the large size of the uncertainties in the data, although those compound the problem. The difficulty is that even with very good data the range of doubt in the result is large. This is a general problem and applies to the measure of productivity change used here as well as to the conceptually less complete measures used elsewhere. For example, the measure of productivity grew at 1·2 percent per year from 1870 to 1900, a respectable pace. If the estimates in 1870 and 1900 of real gross national product, the stock of capital, the labor force and the shares of capital and labor in national product are incorrect by as little as ±3 percent, however, the resulting estimate of productivity change will range from 0·77 percent per year to 1·62 percent, that is, by comparison with the United States, from failure to success.

The case for failure or success in the growth of productivity must rest ultimately on international comparisons of productivity in specific industries, not on the aggregate measures about which the controversy on British economic performance has hitherto revolved. The measure for each industry, of course, will be open to the same criticism, but if the errors for each industry are independent, a set of many industry studies will constitute a sample of British behavior from which more reliable inferences can be drawn. For the present, it is enough to show that the aggregate measures are consistent with success.

IV

It is implausible, then, to draw the lines of causation in late Victorian England from export demand to the output of the economy. The thesis expressed here is that the resources available to the economy were not elastic in supply and reallocation of them (capital abroad, for example) would have brought little or no additional growth. The growth of output depended on how productively the available resources were used. The measure of productivity suggests no great failure of Britain on this score. There was a dip of productivity in the 1900s, but it was too short, too late and too uncertain to justify the dramatic description 'climacteric'. Nor does it support the notion that British businessmen were marking time from the 1870s onward.[40] There is, indeed, little left of the dismal picture of British failure painted by historians. The alternative is a picture of an economy not stagnating but growing as rapidly as permitted by the growth of its resources and the effective exploitation of the available technology.

NOTES

1 E.g. W. A. Lewis in *Economic Survey, 1919–1939* (1949), p. 74: 'There can be little doubt that the main cause of the relative British stagnation was to be found in the

export trade. In the first part of the nineteenth century the growth of British exports was astonishing'; D. J. Coppock, 'The climacteric of the 1890s: a critical note', *Manchester School*, XXIV (1956), p. 2: 'The low rate of capital accumulation is explained partly by an exogenous decline in the rate of export growth, which reduced the incentive to invest.'

2 *Explorations in Entrepreneurial History*, VIII (1955), pp. 12–34, reprinted with revisions as ch. 5 in A. H. Conrad and J. R. Meyer, *The Economics of Slavery and Other Studies in Econometric History* (Chicago, 1964), to which subsequent references are made.

3 ibid., pp. 184–92, *passim*.

4 Using Meyer's procedure, this is the rate of growth derived from increasing Hoffmann's index of industrial output including building in 1907 by the ratio of Meyer's hypothetical to actual industrial output in that year.

5 The Hoffmann index used here includes building (the results excluding building are virtually the same). Exports are Imlah's index, given in B. R. Mitchell, *Abstract of British Historical Statistics* (Cambridge, 1962), p. 328. National income is C. H. Feinstein's estimate (his net national income deflated by Bowley's retail price index), ibid., p. 367.

6 An improvement in the terms of trade arising from faster-growing export demand is not a part of the demand hypothesis as it is usually stated. The argument that follows, therefore, abstracts from it.

7 Since writing this I have discovered that D. H. Whitehead made essentially the same point about Meyer's argument in an interesting paper, 'The new economic history: counterfactuals and *ceteris paribus*', presented at the February 1968 Christchurch meeting of the Australian and New Zealand Association for the Advancement of Science.

8 The only detailed employment statistics are for Great Britain, not the United Kingdom. Agricultural employment was only 8·5 percent of the British work force in 1911 according to Mitchell, op. cit., p. 60. It is appropriate to take a year late in the period 1870–1914 because the proposition to be refuted asserts that there could have been substantially more reemployment of rural workers than was actually accomplished. Domestic service might have been another source of labor, although most of the workers were women with little alternative employment available (as their low wages suggest). In any case, in Great Britain the sum of employment in agriculture, domestic service and personal service was 22·6 percent of the labor force in 1911, contrasted with 41·5 percent in the United States in 1910. – US Bureau of the Census, *Historical Statistics of the United States, Colonial Times to 1957* (Washington, DC, 1960), p. 74.

9 The estimates of total employment in the United Kingdom are those of E. H. Phelps-Brown and S. J. Handfield-Jones in 'The climacteric of the 1890s: a study in the expanding economy', *Oxford Economic Papers*, N.S., IV (1952), p. 298. The emigration estimates are those of Ferenczi and Willcox, given in Mitchell, op. cit., p. 50.

10 Gross output in 1907 would have been twice what it actually was if it had grown at 3·71 percent from 1872. If technology and the amount of capital per man were independent of the growth of the labor force, the actual ratio of gross output to employment in 1911 will serve as the ratio under the hypothetical conditions. Applying this ratio to the actual labor force raises it to 39·5 million.

11 The constancy of the shares of labor, land and capital over the period 1870–1914 suggests that a unitary elasticity of substitution is a reasonable approximation. A production function for gross output can be written

$$Q_{go} = F(K, L, Q^i_{go}, T')$$

in which Q^i_{go} is the quantity of intermediate material input corresponding to the particular degree of interindustry detail chosen and T' is a parameter of technological change or time. The equation in the text can be derived from this production function. The shares attached to $\bar{K}$ and $\bar{L}$ are the shares in national income, not the shares in gross output. T' is about 0·005, using the data of the next two notes and the growth rate of the Hoffmann index (1·69 percent per year).

12 The growth rate of gross output is the hypothetical rate derived earlier. If the elasticity of substitution is 1 the shares of capital and labor will not change with different endowments. Consequently, the observed shares will be the shares under the hypothetical increase in the capital–labor ratio. The value 0·52 for labor is derived from the share of P. Deane and W. A. Cole's wages and salaries estimate in home-produced income (*British Economic Growth, 1688–1959*, Cambridge, 1964, p. 247) and the value 0·44 for capital is derived from the residual from 1·00 of land's share (based on Stamp's estimate of net property income) and labor's share. The rates of growth of labor (0·0102 each year) and productivity are also assumed to be the same under the new regime of rapid capital accumulation. The assumption that faster capital accumulation had little long-run effect on the rate of productivity change is justified by the pattern of productivity change reported below.

13 The estimate of the growth of domestic fixed capital is 1·43 percent per year, 1870–1910. Its derivation is explained below.

14 The capital output ratio, v, must have averaged about 4·9 in 1870–1910 because domestic fixed capital formation was about 7 percent of income (a low estimate) and the capital stock grew at about 1·43 percent (7/1·43=4·9). This agrees roughly with Deane and Cole's estimates (op. cit., p. 274). In 1870, therefore, a 6·09 percent growth of capital would require a savings ratio of (4·9) (6·09 percent)=30 percent. After 1870, with the capital stock growing at 6·09 percent and national income at 4·34 percent (the hypothetical growth rate of exports), v would rise from 4·9 at 6·09–4·34=1·75 percent each year. By 1910 it would be 9·95 (!) and the required savings ratio would be (9·95) (6·09)=60·5 percent. The geometric average of 30 and 60 is 42.

15 These years were chosen to include the years of very low saving in the 1890s and to cover one and a half business cycles (in order to ensure that the average approximates the underlying trend). Net investment in the United Kingdom is estimated as the sum of Feinstein's net fixed investment series (Mitchell, op. cit., p. 373), Imlah's overall balance on current account (ibid., p. 334), and 40 percent of the annual change in Feinstein's net national income (ibid., p. 367; this is the traditional way of estimating inventory investment). The ratio for the United States is S. Kuznets' estimate of net capital formation divided by his estimate of net national product for three quinquennia from 1887 to 1901 (US Department of Commerce, op. cit., p. 143). It is more comprehensive than the estimate for the United Kingdom.

16 Income growth rises less than in proportion to the rise in capital growth because there are other sources of growth, i.e. labor growth and technological change.

17 Strictly speaking, the assumption is false. National income would have been maximized if Britain had acted as a monopolist in the export of capital, as M. Kemp points out in the chapter 'Foreign lending and the national advantage – the lending country' in his book *The Pure Theory of International Trade* (Englewood Cliffs, NJ, 1964). The monopoly gain from restricting the export of capital, however, would have been trivial. A rough calculation using the assumptions described below suggests a gain of the order of one-tenth of 1 percent of national income.

18 J. M. Keynes, 'Foreign investment and national advantage', *Nation and Athenaeum*, XXXV (1924), pp. 584–7.

19 A. K. Cairncross, *Home and Foreign Investment, 1870–1913* (Cambridge, 1953), pp. 225–30.

20 ibid., p. 228. On p. 225 he remarks that 'there were constant defaults . . . but, for the most part, with the exception of those of the twenties and seventies, of a

comparatively minor character'. A complete case would require more definite information on defaults.

21 C. P. Kindleberger put it: 'Capital flows in channels, and these had been dug between London and the far reaches of the empire, but not between London and the industrial north' – *Economic Growth in France and Britain, 1851–1950* (Cambridge, Mass., 1964), p. 69. Cf. D. Landes, 'Technological change and industrial development in Western Europe, 1750–1914', in M. Postan and H. J. Habakkuk (eds.), *The Cambridge Economic History of Europe*, VI (Cambridge, 1965), p. 576. The belief in capital market imperfections is inconsistent with the conclusions of both Kindleberger and Landes that there was no shortage of capital to domestic industry. The imperfections, if effective, would have restricted the supply.

22 Keynes, op. cit., p. 586. All of his arguments have more force in the 1920s, when he formulated them, than in the decades before the war. On the other hand, he exaggerates the incentive given by the Trustees Acts to lending abroad. The Acts applied only to the minority of trust deeds that did not specify the form the lending was to take. Moreover, they permitted investment at home not only in consols but also in mortgages, railway bonds and issues of local authorities. cf. Cairncross, op. cit., pp. 89, 95, and C. K. Hobson, *The Export of Capital* (1914), p. 48.

23 Cf. Cairncross, op. cit., pp. 227–31.

24 These estimates are based on the home-produced income accruing to capitalists and foreign investment earnings. The return at home agrees with the estimate by E. H. Phelps Brown and B. Weber for the entire period 1870–1912 ('Accumulation, productivity, and distribution in the British economy, 1870–1938', *Economic Journal*, LXIII (1953), pp. 263–88). The underlying capital stock estimates are discussed below.

25 The domestic stock of capital in Great Britain was about £7,900 million in 1911–13, according to Deane and Cole, op. cit., p. 274 (based on H. Campion's income method estimate in *Public and Private Property in Great Britain*, 1939). To their estimate I have added £500 million for Ireland (based on the relation between the United Kingdom and Great Britain in 1885 for capital in farming, industry, commerce and finance: Deane and Cole, loc. cit.). A capital stock of £8,400 million agrees roughly with the estimate of £8,100 million by Phelps Brown and Handfield-Jones, op. cit., p. 302. The stock of capital abroad on which Englishmen had a claim was about £4,000 million. This figure can be reached by capitalizing Imlah's yearly overseas investment earnings for 1911–13 (£188 million, Mitchell, op. cit., p. 334) at the prevailing interest rate on bonds (e.g. R. A. Lehfeldt's 'The rate of interest on British and foreign investment', *Statistical Journal*, 1913, or American Railway bonds). Alternatively (and with the same result) Imlah's balance of payments on current account can be added year by year to the estimate of Cairncross for 1871 (op. cit., pp. 182–4). The relevant amount of foreign capital abroad can be taken at any reasonable magnitude, here £20,000 million, for it affects the results very little.

26 The average for 1911–13 of Imlah's foreign investment earnings was £188 million (Mitchell, op. cit., p. 274). Subtracting this from Feinstein's net national income estimate leaves £1,980 million home-produced income.

27 A reasonable estimate of the elasticity of the two curves involved, it can be shown, is the share of non-capital inputs in national income.

28 The fall in the net gain for a gap larger than 3 percent is not paradoxical. As more is borrowed abroad, the terms worsen.

29 P. Rosenstein-Rodan at the International Economic Association conference on *Capital Movements and Economic Development* (1967), p. 68. The rapporteur says that Rosenstein-Rodan 'drew attention to the major increase in the scale of British overseas investment during the few decades before World War I, and added that if this capital had been invested in England, England would have been much stronger'. In the discussion, G. Leduc makes the same point about France. One of the papers they are discussing, B. Thomas' 'The historical record of international

capital movements to 1913', concludes with a similar argument, but applies it, guardedly, only to the years 1900 to 1913.

30 Coppock, op. cit., p. 4.

31 C. Wilson, 'Economy and society in late Victorian Britain', *Economic History Review*, 2nd ser., XVIII (1965), p. 193 (italics his).

32 The coverage of the Hoffmann index is, of course, good. But a non-random sample, however large, yields biased estimates of the population characteristics. Wilson, op. cit., makes a convincing case that 'miscellaneous industries and incorporeal functions' (as Giffen called them) were growing rapidly in this period. He mentions soap, retailing and bicyles.

33 Coppock's assertion that 'a growth of some 0·5% or less per annum in industrial productivity [i.e. Hoffmann's index per man] cannot explain a growth of some 1·5% to 2·0% per annum in real income a head' (op. cit., p. 14) is, therefore, mistaken. There is no inconsistency between Hoffmann's index and the real national income estimates.

34 op. cit.

35 A similar point was made by J. F. Wright in his review article on Deane and Cole, 'British economic growth, 1688–1959', *Econ. Hist. Rev.*, 2nd ser., XVIII (1965), pp. 397–412. Their use of Rousseaux's price index to deflate national income, he argues, produced a false rejuvenation of real national income after 1870.

36 op. cit., p. 16.

37 Coppock, loc. cit.

38 The consumption data are D. A. Rowe's, in Mitchell, op. cit., p. 370. The estimates of gross national product are Deane and Cole's in op. cit., p. 332. They are the sum of Rowe's consumption estimates and estimates of domestic fixed investment, net foreign investment and public authorities expenditure. Food, drink and tobacco expenditures were 36·3 percent of gross national product from 1900 to 1909.

39 J. W. Kendrick, for example, finds that productivity change averaged about 1·5 percent per year from 1869 to 1909 in the United States. There are some difficulties with the data for 1869 and 1879. From 1889 to 1909 the measure averages about 1·3 percent per year. See *Productivity Trends in the United States* (Princeton, NJ, 1961), p. 331.

40 D. Landes, for example, asserts that 'There is no doubt, that British industry was not so vigorous and adaptable from the 1870s on as it could have been' – op. cit., p. 559.

6

Controversies

McCloskey on Victorian Growth: A Comment

DEREK H. ALDCROFT

Phelps-Brown and Handfield-Jones produced a veritable hare when in 1952 they put forward their climacteric thesis on Victorian growth.[1] Since then there has been the all-too-familiar flood of literature on the topic seeking either to explain the climacteric or to alter the temporal demarcation of it. Most commentators would probably accept that there was some degree of retardation in Britain's growth in the decade or more before 1914, and much of the controversy has centered around the explanations of it. A reaction was inevitable in time. It came with a blast in 1970 when McCloskey (in this *Journal*)[2] shattered all previous illusions about the performance of the Victorian economy. The climacteric or retardation thesis is virtually rejected, at least for the Victorian period. In fact, McCloskey concludes that: 'There is, indeed, little left of the dismal picture of British failure painted by historians. The alternative is a picture of an economy not stagnating but growing as rapidly as permitted by the growth of its resources and the effective exploitation of available technology.'

Basically his thesis falls into two parts. First, he regards the growth performance of the economy as reasonably satisfactory and argues that there was little potential for faster growth, through either home demand or exports, because of the inelastic supplies of labor and capital. Second, given the fact that total growth was fixed by the availability of resources and productivity gains, he then maintains that any allegation of failure must be attributed to a slowing down in productivity growth. He then proceeds to demonstrate that there was no significant failure on this score except for a check to productivity in the 1900s which was 'too short, too late, and too uncertain to justify the dramatic description "climacteric" '.

McCloskey's first proposition is only partly questioned here. He is substantially correct in claiming that there is no really sharp deceleration in industrial production and real product growth before the turn of the century, though before 1900 there were in both one or two awkward dips that require some explaining. However, these were not sufficient to warrant a break in trend. In fact, on a cyclical basis (that is, measuring from peak to peak of the cycle) there is no clearly defined break in trend in the growth of industrial production though GDP begins to tail off after 1890 (see Table 5.2). On the other hand, it is somewhat doubtful whether resource factors were as inelastic as he suggests (see below), while little concession is made to the possibilities of boosting growth through unrealized productivity gains. In short, he appears to assume that the economy is cast in a permanently rigid state with little or no leeway to maneuver. In defence he would no doubt argue that further productivity gains were very limited because the existing stock of technical resources was being fully exploited, and would then seek to confirm this by the fact that there is no evidence for a break in productivity before 1900. It is mainly the question of the productivity break which I wish to take up here.

Table 6.1 *Annual growth rates of output, labor, capital and productivity, 1860–1910*

	GDP at constant factor cost	*Labor in man-years*	*Capital stock*	*Output per worker*	*Growth due to total factor inputs*	*Residual*
1860–70	2·1	0·6	1·2	1·4	1·1	1·0
1870–80	1·9	0·6	1·6	1·2	1·0	0·9
1880–90	2·3	1·3	1·2	1·0	1·3	1·1
1890–1900	2·1	1·1	1·8	0·9	1·4	0·7
1900–10	1·1	0·7	2·0	0·5	1·2	−0·1

Quite rightly, McCloskey uses a measure of total productivity (output per unit of input – in this case capital and labor) rather than the partial indicators often employed in this type of exercise. Using a varied collection of data drawn from different sources, he calculates annual growth rates for labor, capital and productivity over decades starting with the year 1860. He finds that both labor and capital inputs grew fairly steadily from decade to decade but that total factor productivity fluctuated with a sharp break after 1900. However, from Table 5.3 there is more than an indication that the break came earlier, *c.*1890, and the use of some smoothing technique would certainly have demarcated the timing of the deceleration more clearly. Second, it might have been instructive to make the calculations on an intercyclical basis since the years chosen pay no special regard to variations in capacity utilization.

To begin with I calculated the relevant rates of growth for the same series using Feinstein's recent and more comprehensive estimates,[3] and adopting the same initial and terminal dates as McCloskey. These are presented in Table 6.1. They show a definite break in productivity growth before 1900. Output per worker, admittedly a partial indicator, fell steadily from a peak rate of 1·4 percent per annum between 1860 and 1870 to 0·5 percent in the 1900s, while total productivity (output per unit of input) grew fairly steadily until 1890 and then broke sharply. Furthermore, factor inputs did not grow steadily over each decade. There was a tendency for total factor inputs combined to increase down to 1900, but, as can be seen from the table, the growth of labor and capital inputs individually often varied considerably.

There may be some objection to the use of interdecennial points, since no account is taken of variations in capacity utilization. A far better approach would be to measure growth between dates on the same point of the cycle. In Table 6.2 the calculations have been repeated on the basis of cyclical peaks; a few of the dates might give rise to some dispute, but for the most part these were years of high capacity utilization. As it happens, the results do not differ markedly from those previously derived. Again output per worker shows a steady deceleration after the early 1870s and by the turn of the century it was only half as large as in the earlier years. Total productivity held up somewhat better, but by 1890 there is no doubt that deceleration had set in and again the rate of growth was down to one-half that recorded earlier.

Table 6.2 *Annual growth rates of output, labor, capital and productivity through intercyclical peaks, 1859–1913*

	GDP at constant factor cost	*Labor in man-years*	*Capital stock*	*Output per worker*	*Growth due to total factor inputs*	*Residual*
1859–65	2·1	0·9	1·2	1·2	1·0	1·1
1865–74	2·2	0·7	1·2	1·4	0·9	1·3
1874–83	1·8	0·7	1·6	1·3	1·1	0·7
1883–90	2·2	1·0	1·1	1·1	1·0	1·2
1890–1901	1·9	1·0	1·9	0·9	1·4	0·5
1901–7	1·7	0·8	1·9	0·7	1·2	0·5
1907–13	1·5	1·1	1·4	0·5	1·2	0·3

This raises several queries with regard to McCloskey's analysis. First, the productivity break, for both labor and total factor inputs, certainly occurred before the turn of the century. Even his own calculations are subject to reinterpretation in this respect. Second, the assumption that labor and capital inputs grew steadily through each decade is misleading. There were variations in both cases, a fact which calls in question his original contention that factor supplies were inelastic.[4] Indeed, it could be argued that it was the relatively *elastic* and increasing supplies of labor and capital which helped to maintain the growth of GDP down to 1900, and which in turn helped to depress the productivity performance. As long as capital and labor were easily available, businessmen accumulated factors of production to satisfy their requirements, and as a result there was no severe pressure on them to improve efficiency.

But could efficiency or productivity have been improved substantially at this time? This is a difficult question to answer briefly. I have some doubts on this score, though I cannot fully accept McCloskey's notion, based on the argument that available technology was being fully exploited, that it could not have been improved. This presupposes the widespread use of best-practice techniques, which was very unlikely, or alternatively the absence of large-scale innovations, which may give rise to significant productivity gains. Even in the absence of the latter there was still considerable scope for productivity improvement in this period through small incremental changes in technique over a wide area or by a fuller exploitation of existing resources.

However, small incremental gains in productivity are more difficult to achieve at certain stages of an economy's development unless subject to sudden shock treatment or cost pressures which force rapid advance along the technological front. In fact, given the structure of the economy at the time, it is possible to see the decline in productivity as being partly inevitable. In the first place there was a relative absence of new, high growth sectors with large innovations leading to interrelated productivity gains. Second, there was a large staple industrial sector, still growing steadily, plus a fairly buoyant service sector. Generally speaking, large-scale productivity-raising innovations were not a feature of either sector so that productivity growth had to come either from small incremental technical changes along the margin or through a thorough overhaul and rationalization of the use of existing resources. But both these sectors were still in a fairly strong 'factor accumulation stage'. Growth was being achieved largely by increasing the inputs of capital and labor with relatively scant regard to their utilization.[5] And in turn this was made possible by the elastic supplies of labor and capital. Thus from 1890 through to 1913 productivity accounted for less than one-half the growth derived from factor inputs, whereas previously it had been equal or slightly larger than the contribution from the latter.

It is easy to see this process at work in particular sectors. In coal mining and transport, especially the railways, for instance, large additions to the labor force were instrumental in producing additional output with productivity making little if any contribution. While, if the interwar experience is anything to go by, the service sector's growth was achieved largely by factor accumulation rather than by productivity change. A general comparison with the interwar period is instructive. In this period GDP grew at roughly the same rate as that of the late nineteenth and early twentieth centuries, at around 1·7 percent per annum. But total factor inputs contributed only 0·7 percentage points (that is, one-half prewar), whereas the productivity contribution was 1·0 percentage points, that is, a rate similar to that achieved in the third quarter of the nineteenth century. Two factors in particular were responsible for this change. First, a new, rapidly growing, industrial sector with a constant stream of innovations boosted productivity growth; second, the old staple industries, partly through cost and profit pressures, were forced to disgorge their overinflated labor supplies and innovate wherever possible. Neither of these forces was present before 1914.

The upshot of the argument is that one would have expected some productivity decline before 1914 and that is exactly what we have got. That it came before 1900 rather than after this date is almost certain and its causes are not hard to find. There was still scope for productivity improvements, but these were more difficult to exploit in conditions which facilitated growth through factor accumulation. Whether this be rated a failure or not is beside the point: the fact is that productivity did begin to decelerate in Victorian Britain.

NOTES

1 E. H. Phelps-Brown and S. J. Handfield-Jones, 'The climacteric of the 1890s: a study in the expanding economy', *Oxford Economic Papers*, IV (1952).
2 D. N. McCloskey, 'Did Victorian Britain fail?', *Economic History Review*, 2nd ser., XXIII (1970).
3 C. H. Feinstein, *National Income, Expenditure and Output of the United Kingdom, 1855–1965* (Cambridge, 1972).
4 McCloskey takes too rigid a line on the matter of supply constraints, especially with respect to labor, and this is partly conditioned by the fact that he has in mind a hypothetical growth rate objective based on exports. I am not suggesting that this rate could have been attained under the prevailing supply conditions, but I would suggest that there was sufficient elasticity in the manpower situation, e.g. via lower emigration, reduction in unemployment and a reduction on the degree of labor underutilization, to allow an increase in labor inputs had the need arisen.
5 The scope for productivity growth through more efficient utilization of existing resources, especially labor, was considerable. Far too little attention, for example, has been given to the potential economies which could have been derived from really efficient labor exploitation. See E. J. Hobsbawm, *Labouring Men: Studies in the History of Labour* (1964), p. 354, and L. Urwick, *The Making of Scientific Management*, Vol. II, *Management in British Industry* (1949).

Victorian Growth: A Rejoinder to Derek Aldcroft

I am glad that Dr Aldcroft and I agree on so many points of method and substance. We agree, for example, that one must inquire into the elasticity of aggregate factor supply before explaining Victorian growth in terms of aggregate demand; that total, not partial, productivity is the relevant measure of how well the Victorians used their factor supplies; and that the record of total productivity, pieced together in a rough way in my 1970 article and now calculable in greater detail from Charles Feinstein's pathbreaking work, belies any assertion of a mid-Victorian failure. Since these three points are the essence of my article and since, judging from his previous work on the subject, one could have expected Aldcroft to disagree with them, it would appear that I have little cause for complaint.

Still, there are some significant points of disagreement. The first is the timing of the break in the trend of productivity, an issue in descriptive statistics. If one accepts Aldcroft's reasonable procedure of dividing the period 1855–1913 into business cycles, there are four peaks in business cycles available to stand as 'the' date of the climacteric, 1873, 1883, 1890 and 1900. The averages of the annual rates of productivity change calculated from Feinstein's data are:[1]

1856–66	1·090	1884–90	1·090
1867–73	1·390	1891–1900	0·717
1874–83	0·693	1901–13	0·233

It should be noted that the pattern, allowing for the differences in dates chosen for comparison, is similar to that in my original calculation and in Aldcroft's calculations. We are not disagreeing about the evidence but about its interpretation. The issue can be put as follows: if for purposes of description one wishes to distinguish two periods within each of which a single rate of growth in total productivity is supposed to obtain, what year should be chosen to separate the two periods? That is, between which periods is the difference between the average rates of growth most significant, in the statistical sense of 'significant'? Aldcroft believes that it is 'almost certain' that the periods should break in 1890, whereas I believe, in the words of my article, that 'given the uncertainties of the data . . . the most precise defensible statement is that there was little cause for alarm in the behaviour of British productivity' down to 1900. A way to resolve this dispute is to examine the results of tests for the significance of difference between two means for each of the four alternative periodizations. The materials for these tests are given in Table 6.3.

The test discerns whether one can reject the null hypothesis of no significant difference between average rates of growth in the first compared with the second period, as compared with the alternative that the rate of growth in the first is larger than in the second period. The last column gives the level at which the difference is significant, that is, it gives the probability of making the error of accepting that there was in fact a deceleration in growth between the two periods when in fact it arose by chance. It is clear why no one has chosen 1883 as the climacteric year and equally clear why each of the remaining three dates has its enthusiasts. Of the three, as far as descriptive statistics on this aggregate level can distinguish them, 1900 is the appropriate choice for the climacteric.

Table 6.3 *Tests of the differences between mean annual rates of productivity growth for four alternative periodizations, 1856–1913*

Last year in the first period (date of climacteric)	*Difference between means of first and second periods*	*Variance of first period*	*Variance of second period*	*Student's t-statistic*	*Probability level at which difference is significant (one-tailed)*
1873	0·5865	2·410	2·329	1·347	0·10
1883	0·4277	2·117	2·770	1·039	0·15
1890	0·5931	1·868	3·076	1·444	0·08
1900	0·7322	2·465	1·848	1·522	0·06

The distinctions in significance among the three dates are not great, and this brings me to the second point of disagreement between us. In the article I emphasized that 'even with very good data the range of doubt in the results is large'. By contrast, Dr Aldcroft believes that the aggregate measures of productivity warrant assertions about when, 'certainly', productivity turned down. The tests reported in Table 6.3 bear out my original judgment, for they imply that, even if one believes that the measure of productivity change is exact, there is so much annual variation that the three potential climacterics are statistically speaking nearly indistinguishable. To take moving averages of the annual statistics ('some smoothing technique', Aldcroft suggests) would merely conceal the variability of the measure, not remove it. Although I did not, as Aldcroft believes, make 'the assumption that labor and capital inputs grew steadily through each decade', he himself apparently does: if this were the case there would be considerably less variability in the rate of productivity growth to disturb the certitude of comparisons between periods. But the uncertainty cannot be ignored. Indeed, as I emphasized in the article and as Feinstein emphasizes in his book, the uncertainty is deeper, in the statistics themselves. Measures of productivity are residuals and are therefore especially sensitive to errors in the series on which they are built. The appropriate inference, as I concluded in the article, is that 'the case for failure or success in the growth of productivity must rest ultimately on international comparisons of productivity in specific industries, not on the aggregate measures about which the controversy on British economic performance has hitherto revolved'.

The final, and most important, point of disagreement is a related one. Before turning to an explanation of a depressed productivity performance it is desirable to establish that it was in fact depressed by some relevant standard. Aldcroft, in common with many other writers on the Victorian economy, is vague on what standard he has in mind. My article, on the other hand, is explicitly comparative, adopting as the standard of comparison the performance of the most successful economy of the time, the economy of the United States. This is a stringent test: the United States was catching up to British standards of technology in many industries during the late nineteenth century, and its rate of productivity growth could be expected on this account to have been higher than the United Kingdom's. Yet their rates of productivity growth were roughly comparable down to 1900, and the Anglo-German comparison yields similar results.[2] The divergence after 1900 could be explained in terms of British exhaustion of a technology that Germany and the United States were still acquiring. This is true, or example, of the industry that has served most often as the worst case of slow British productivity growth, iron and steel.[3]

In any case, in the absence of comparative perspective and industrial detail it is exceedingly difficult to discover how the British economy performed and why. Aldcroft's hypothesis that 'productivity improvements . . . were more difficult to exploit in conditions which facilitated growth through factor accumulation' provides a case in point. In British shipbuilding, open-hearth steelmaking and retailing, for example, productivity growth was rapid after 1890 despite rapid factor accumulation. And factor accumulation was more rapid in the American and German economies than in the British, even though it is the allegedly superior performance of these economies that motivates the entire discussion. If coal and cotton in Britain awaited the interwar period to 'disgorge their overinflated labour supplies', agriculture in Germany and America did the same. And so forth. The discipline of a detailed comparative perspective is lacking in Aldcroft's argument.

The central message of my article, then, stands unrevised. To go beyond its purpose of casting reasonable doubt on the traditional tale of British economic failure after 1870 would have required a book, not an article. The book is in the process of being written, by many hands.

NOTES

1 The source for these figures, as for Aldcroft's Table 6.2, is app. Table 20 in C. H. Feinstein, *National Income, Expenditure and Output in the United Kingdom, 1855–1965* Cambridge, 1972). I have subtracted the annual rate of change of fixed reproducible capital per man, multiplied by capital's share in domestic product (assumed to be 0·4 throughout on the basis of a rough adjustment for the capital component of Feinstein's estimates of income from self-employment and income from land rents), from the annual rate of change of gross domestic product per man. The reported statistics are averages of these annual figures. The choice of peaks in the business cycle is W. W. Rostow's (his major peaks, in which 'conditions of virtually full employment were reached') in his *British Economy of the Nineteenth Century* (Oxford, 1948), p. 33.

2 From 1880 to 1910 the rate of growth of total factor productivity in Germany was 1·13 percent per annum (calculated from W. G. Hoffman, *Das Wachstum der deutschen Wirtschaft seit der Mitte des 19. Jagrhunderts* (Berlin, 1965), pp. 87, 204–6, 253–4, 507–9, 827ff.; I am indebted to Peter Lindert of the University of Wisconsin for pointing out to me the similarity of German and British rates of productivity

growth). This is comparable to the rate of 0·87 percent per annum for the United Kingdom, 1884–1900.

3 I refer the reader to my recent book, *Economic Maturity and Entrepreneurial Decline: British Iron and Steel, 1871–1913* (Cambridge, Mass., 1974), and, for a review of the relevant literature to, D. N. McCloskey and L. G. Sandberg, 'From damnation to redemption: judgments on the late Victorian entrepreneur', *Explorations in Economic History*, IX (1971), pp. 89–108.

A Counterfactual Dialogue with William Kennedy* on Late Victorian Failure or the Lack of It

Kennedy: I read your article and liked the way you set up the questions but not the way you answered them. You're right, I think, to emphasize that the elasticity of the supply of factors is important in assessing what it was possible for late Victorians to accomplish, that the arithmetic of savings rates and capital accumulation is a proper part of this assessment, and that the desirability of investment abroad is a central issue. But I would reverse each of your conclusions. And I do think that in one important respect you have set the question up incorrectly, by ignoring structural change. Firms adjust their decisions in response to changes in available technology. That adjustment, however, is influenced by a wide variety of factors. Hence it may not be sufficient simply to assume that the British economy, on the strength of private markets, was able to transform its structure before 1914 so rapidly as to take full advantage of evolving production possibilities.

McCloskey: Wait a minute: I didn't 'assume' that the British economy worked well; I tried to show that it in fact did by comparison with America, at least in terms of aggregate productivity. I do not suppose any economy has taken '*full* advantage of evolving production possibilities'. That is why it is important to have an explicit and reasonable standard of comparison in mind when assessing British performance. I agree with your implication that it would be more persuasive to look at productivity in individual industries – I suppose that's what you mean by 'structure' – and I say this towards the end. The paper was self-consciously crude in speaking in aggregates like national income and the rest. Other essays (including some of my own), such as Sandberg's on ring spinning, Saul's on engineering and Lindert and Trace's on the Solvay process, look behind the aggregates. What one is looking for behind the aggregates is evidence that there was some advantage to be had in specific industries from adopting new

*The opinions attributed to Dr Kennedy are those in a draft presented to the third Anglo-American conference on British economic history in September 1973 and printed in his 'Foreign investment, trade, and growth in the United Kingdom, 1870–1913', *Explorations in Economic History*, vol. XI, 1974, pp. 415–44.

production possibilities. If unusual profits could have been earned from, say, adopting basic steelmaking in the 1890s, this would be an indication that private markets were for some reason weak in allocating resources to the right processes, whether from the causes you list or from the cause I was chiefly concerned with in the paper, sloppy entrepreneurship. This is a good way to test for the adequacy with which Englishmen met new opportunities: could they make money by taking them? In the case of basic steelmaking (this is an advertisement for a chapter of my forthcoming book on the iron and steel industry) they could not. And so it has gone for the most part in the few other specific cases of alleged missed opportunities that have been examined recently.

K: Now *you* wait a minute. The missed opportunities were *structural* as well as technological. Isn't it obvious that Britain was overcommitted in the staple industries of the industrial revolution? After all, the new industries grew fastest after the war, while coal, cotton, shipbuilding and steel collapsed. Furthermore, in chemicals, electrical engineering and parts of mechanical engineering Britain before the war had not committed as much as had Germany or America. These were the industries of the future and of the nations with the most on the ball economically. You talk of comparative perspective! Use it!

M: I don't think that kind of international comparison is to the point. The US and Germany had enormous agricultural sectors: would you say, then, that Britain's should have been larger? Britain had little trouble moving capital out from agriculture faster than the US and Germany when agriculture was no longer profitable, which is at least some evidence that structural change (a quite large one at that) was possible in Britain when it was desirable. That America had, say, more telephones than Britain is not evidence that Britain should have had more, unless one wants to assume at the outset what is supposed to be the conclusion, namely, that America did everything better. The reasoning is circular.

K: But isn't it obvious from Britain's experience after the war that the failure to get out of textiles, coal and shipbuilding before 1914 made the British economy, as Austin Robinson put it, 'fragile'? These were the sectors that were large in Britain relative to the US, and each suffered heavy unemployment and a contracted labor force after the war. Even if you do not accept the structure of foreign countries as indicating a bad allocation of resources in Britain before the war, surely you'll concede that the structure that actually developed in Britain by 1939 is relevant.

M: No, I won't. The point is that you can't tell what was an appropriate structure for the British economy before the war – interpreting 'structure' to mean 'the pattern of allocation of resources among different activities, whether within individual industries or among them' – without looking into the profitability of the existing structure relative to alternatives *at the time.* I think that remarks about the 'fragility' of British industry on the eve of the war or its 'overcommitment' to old industries, when they are applied to the prewar period, express simply a feeling of irony, using the historian's most valuable but often most overused resource, hindsight. The writer is saying, 'Look at the irony: the very industries that proved so profitable for Britain in the nineteenth century turned out to be bad investments after the war. It is sad indeed that Britain was led down this garden path.' But this says nothing about the adequacy of the late Victorian (or Edwardian) response to opportunities as they could have been perceived by sensible men at the time. The reasoning involved is, once again, circular. One assumes that what eventually happened should have happened earlier and – presto! – one is able to indict the British capital market or British entrepreneurs for not leaping to the allocation of the future. The trouble, of course, is that one could on the same basis indict anyone. A small case in point (more advertising for my book, this) is by-product coking, which was used in Germany on a large scale long before it was used in the UK. By the retrospective identification of desirable changes that you are using the UK should have adopted it earlier. What is amusing about this case is that those paragons of technological progressiveness, the Americans, were even slower than the British to adopt it. The people who use the slow adoption as a club with which to beat late Victorian entrepreneurs in Britain seldom recognize this fact. It suggests that the adoption of the process was a response to relative factor prices (namely, the price of labor relative to the price of coal) rather than a quirk of national character.

K: Well, I don't know about coke ovens, but I do know that it was the industries in which British resources were concentrated that were vulnerable after the war.

M: True enough, but conditions changed after the war in a way that British entrepreneurs and investors could not have been expected to predict. Indeed, many informed prewar observers, among them Alfred Marshall, riveted their attention on the competition from America and Germany in the old industries. My working hypothesis is that the British were doing pretty well before the war adjusting to conditions that they then faced. That conditions turned against them later does not illuminate the working of the prewar economy. I don't like to keep throwing agriculture back in your face, since I think I can sustain this argument in industry alone, but look at the postwar depression in American agriculture. Are we to conclude that there was some failure on the part of American farmers and their bankers before the war?

K: But surely the British *could* have moved into the new industries. I've done some calculations, in a less offhand fashion than you did in one sentence and a footnote in your paper, that identify vast low-wage (and presumably low-productivity) areas of the British economy, a reserve of low-paid labor to meet the demands of expansion, if such a demand had ever been made.

M: Sure, they *could* have moved into the new industries faster, just as Americans *could* have moved out of agriculture before the war faster than they did. But the issue is, *should* they have done so? One way to answer the question is to calculate the gain to national income from the reallocation or, equivalently, to calculate the profitability of it. Look at this diagram:

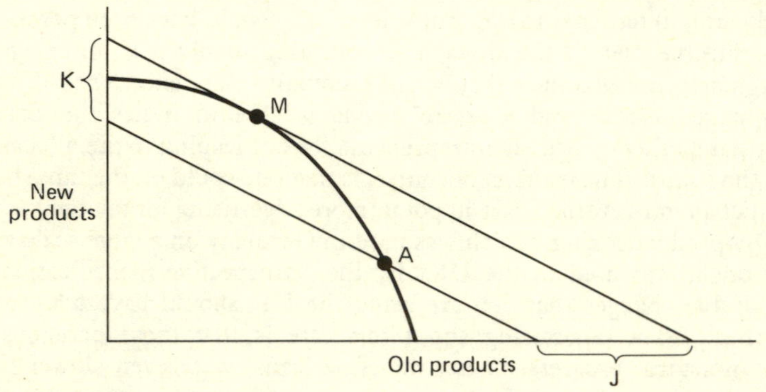

You're saying that the UK was at a point such as A and in view of the prices of the products should have been at a point like M. I'm saying that the way to find out is to measure the potential gain K (or, expressed in units of the old industry's output, J), not to look at allocations between the two sorts of industries at other times and in other places (although this might be a way of generating alternative allocations to examine for profitability). The measurement of the potential gain is what is involved in the papers I mentioned earlier looking at specific innovations; it is also involved in my crude calculations of the rate of productivity change compared with other countries.

K: You still haven't commented on my evidence of the reserve of low-paid labor, which you argued in your paper was small. But on productivity change: the American rate you report from 1869 to 1909, taken from Kendrick, was 1·5 percent, higher than the British, and this rate is a not unreasonable standard, for nineteenth-century technology was widely available. You use a lower rate.

M: I note in the paper, as does Kendrick, that there are serious deficiences in the American census for the earlier years. He himself gives annual estimates only after 1889. Since I wrote the paper I've calculated productivity change in Germany, using Hoffman's evidence, as 1·13 percent per year from 1880 to 1910. Anyway, the American or German rates, whatever they might be, are overly stringent standards against which to judge British performance, because Britain *started* with an advanced industrial technology and the others were catching up (I think most people would agree; I've shown it to be the case in the iron and steel industry). The underlying question is one about levels of productivity, not rates of change, although the latter might throw light on the former.

K: Well, what about the evidence of a reserve of low-paid labor?

M: I think you've got another piece of meaningless evidence. With it one could show that any economy with any dispersion in wages could grow indefinitely as demand increased, or nearly indefinitely. I admit that I started this hare in the paper, although I didn't use low relative wages as the criterion of 'underemployment'. It's no excuse, just an explanation, to say that I was momentarily adopting a popular view of economies with which I do not in fact agree for the purpose of arguing on the same grounds as my potential critics. They would say (with, I might say, very little supporting evidence, whether historical or current) that economies undergoing industrialization are 'dual economies', with sectors whose wage is higher than the true social opportunity cost of labor. Were this the case it would mean that markets would not yield maximum income and that income would grow as labor was transferred from agriculture (the usual sector chosen, except in Denmark and New Zealand) to industry. The limitation would then be the demand for industrial products, not their supply, and larger British exports of industrial products, as some have argued, could have increased national income. I take it you accept this view?

K: Yes, approximately, although I do concede that my calculation only counts heads and takes no account of skill requirements.

M: Precisely. If workers were homogeneous then any divergence in wages could indeed be attributable to disequilibrium, that is, to too many workers in, say, domestic service and too few in auto making. But workers are not homogeneous. When you switch a man from being a footman in m'lud's household to being a mechanic in an auto factory national income does not rise magically by the relabeling of the man. Skilled (or for that matter unskilled but disciplined) industrial workers are not free for the asking. That is why some of them earned high incomes. Your argument supposes that they were free. And the lowness of an industry's wages is no indication of its surplus or unprogressive character. Laborers in chemical factories and in electrical substations were no doubt poorly paid by comparison with weavers or coal miners and better paid by comparison with farm laborers and domestic servants. So what?

K: My calculations were only meant to be suggestive. Anyway, I've got some other calculations that nail you on a number of technical issues. Look at these. *(He shows McCloskey pages 419 and 420 of an essay.)* I think I've shown that the calculation of the limits to growth in your one-equation model is sensitive to the data and assumptions employed.

M: (after a long pause) No, I think you've shown that one can get any result if the evidence and the theory are used in an inconsistent way. For one thing you've missed the point of note 14 on page 108. The point was that if the capital stock were to grow much faster than it in fact did (holding other things constant, which was my experiment) it would be growing faster than income, and the capital–output ratio would be continuously rising. Since, in your notation, $\mathring{K}/K = s/k$ the higher k would require a higher and higher s to maintain the frenetic pace of growth. You've assumed that the capital–output ratio would be constant at the observed value 4·0, which is impossible under the hypothetical circumstances you set up. Further, you express surprise in your footnote 9 that I omit foreign capital. But the domestic capital stock and domestic output, which are measured in Feinstein's capital–output ratios (the ones you use and that I would have used, rather than being forced to estimate k from the identity just given), are just what I wanted to talk about. The are surely the correct concepts for assessing the efficiency of the British productive machine. Again, you use my estimate of 10·4 percent as though it were the rate of savings for *domestic* capital formation alone, which it is not (again, note 14 tells all), for it includes investment abroad. The roughly correct figure for the correct concept, savings for domestic investment, is 7 percent. You guessed it: it is given in note 14. You should have seen that something was wrong, for by the identity that you give (10·4)/(4) = 2·6 percent should have been the rate of growth of Feinstein's gross domestic reproducible capital stock at constant replacement cost from 1870 to 1910, which is far too high a figure (it is actually 1·6 percent; notice that the *net* capital stock grows slower, at 1·34 percent; I admit to some uncertainty as to which is the relevant concept).

Suppose that I accept 4 as the relevant capital–output ratio in 1870 and, with greater reluctance, accept your arguments that the rate of growth of the labor force could have been 1·6 percent and the rate of productivity growth 1·5 percent (I've already mentioned why I think the latter figure too high). And, to mend the gap in the argument left by the misinterpretation of the savings figures, suppose that the rate of savings out of income for domestic investment rose in proportion to the rise in all savings that you posit (namely, from 7 percent to

$$\frac{13 \cdot 7}{10 \cdot 4}(7) = 9 \cdot 22 \text{ percent}).$$

Then your calculation of the rate of growth would be in *1870*:

$$0 \cdot 44\left(\frac{9 \cdot 22}{4}\right) + 0 \cdot 52\,(1 \cdot 6) + 1 \cdot 5 = 3 \cdot 34 \text{ percent.}$$

The rate of growth of the capital stock that sustains this rate of growth is (9·22)/(4)=2·3 percent. This means that output is growing faster than the capital stock, and the capital–output ratio is *falling*, making it easier in terms of the savings effort to sustain this path of growth once it is started.

The reason we get different answers is *not* that my calculations are sensitive to the particular numbers I've chosen but that you are not making the same calculations. The article looks at each growth-inducing factor by itself, whereas you've put them all together. My procedure is relevant for examining arguments that posit simultaneous failure along a wide front. The latter class of arguments is harder to put in jeopardy by the sorts of calculations we are making here. In the limit it amounts to saying at the outset that anything that affects growth can be changed in any convenient way. Any growth rate will be achievable if every piece of behavior affecting the growth rate is freely altered. If, say, hours of work were included in the list of factors, income could be increased 50 percent by increasing hours 50 percent. To test a composite hypothesis (e.g. that there was a massive technological failure *and* low savings *and* income-responsive emigration and population growth) one must shift to examining the reasonableness of the growth-inducing changes contemplated. It is this, not a more disaggregated approach (as you put it), that would be necessary. Good luck.

K: But you yourself disaggregated to the extent of talking about the distribution of savings between home and foreign investment. And I've spotted holes. For one thing, you give a peculiar definition to the elasticity of demand for capital, name r^*/K^* (where asterisks signify proportional rates of change) rather than K^*/r^*, the usual definition, according to Samuelson.

M: It's the usual definition only if you want that definition, and I wanted the other.

K: Well, here's another point. Your analysis is insufficiently general. For example, as foreign investment was brought home, eliminating the differential return between home and foreign investment, the demand curve for goods would surely have shifted outwards. Therefore, whether the 'price' (and hence the marginal revenue) of the composite good would have risen or fallen depends on whether or not the shifts of the entire demand curve would have outweighed movements along the curve.

M: That strikes me as a meaningless assertion. Demand curves have *relative* prices in them, not absolute prices or aggregate price indexes. But I agree with your feeling that it would be good to look into second-order effects. Still, when you've shown that the first-order effects are small there is some warrant for ignoring the second-order effects on the first pass.

K: Be that as it may, I think the central issue here is the gap between foreign and domestic returns. Only a small portion, no more than a quarter, of total British foreign investments earned a yield as high as that which was earned on the average unit of domestic real capital (around 10 or 11 percent compared with 4 or 5 percent). The majority of British foreign investments were characterized by a pervasive conservatism which forsook considerably higher yields in the pursuit of safer yields. This is evidence of the conservatism of British investors and of the huge loss from not investing at home.

M: If that's your argument I think you've missed the boat. In the first place, that foreign investments were mostly in bonds rather than in equities says nothing about the conservatism of British investors as a group. It says that the conservative lenders invested abroad. Further, as I said in the paper, it is wrong to compare yields on foreign *bonds* with yields on domestic *real capital.* The total return to real capital is composed of a return to bondholders and a return to equityholders. Bonds are less risky, so the return to bonds at home is necessarily less than the 10 or 11 percent you use. In fact, as Cairncross showed (I cite him on this, on p. 109), interest rates for securities abroad were normally higher than securities at home with the same risk. Railroad bonds in India and in Lancashire earned about the same interest.

K: Hmm.

Victorian Britain Did Fail

by N. F. R. CRAFTS

In a recent extremely influential article Prof. McCloskey challenged central tenets of the conventional wisdom concerning the British economy of the late nineteenth century. He argued that significantly higher income growth could not have been obtained by a higher investment rate[1] and that growth was constrained by inelasticities on the supply side.[2] Instead of seeing the period as one of entrepreneurial failure he painted 'a picture of an economy not stagnating but growing as rapidly as permitted by the growth of its resources and the effective exploitation of the available technology'.[3]

These views were later criticized by Dr Kennedy who concluded 'not that British resources were incapable of sustaining more rapid growth, but rather that resources were not deployed to exploit opportunities which did exist'.[4] Kennedy reached his conclusion by maintaining that McCloskey's model was misspecified and thus the actual historical record had been compared with an inappropriate counterfactual situation.

This comment maintains that McCloskey's reinterpretation of the late nineteenth century should be rejected even on the basis of his own model. It is shown using this model that a higher domestic investment rate, entailing a higher capital-to-labour ratio, would have permitted a large increase in consumption per head. An investment rate similar to that of Germany would have given a 25 percent increase in consumption per head in 1911.

I

McCloskey used a neoclassical one-sector growth model in which the production function was Cobb-Douglas.

$$\Upsilon = Ae^{rt}K^{a}L^{\beta} \tag{1}$$

This particular form of the production function has the important attribute that the shares of profits and wages in national income will be constant for any capital-to-labour ratio. This is in accordance with the stylized facts of British economic growth in the late nineteenth century.[5] The sources of economic growth could be decomposed thus:

$$\triangle\Upsilon/\Upsilon = a.\triangle K/K + \beta.\triangle L/L + r \tag{2}$$

where a is the share of profits in national income, β is the share of wages and r (the residual) is the rate of growth of output per unit of total input.

This model is, of course, a familiar one whose properties have been extensively analysed in growth theory textbooks. It has an important property, on which McCloskey relied to develop his argument,[6] that raising the investment rate would not be a route to significantly higher income growth. The model will tend to a steady state in which the growth rates of capital, labor and income are at a constant, long-run equilibrium rate; the steady-state rate of growth of income is *independent* of the investment rate.

This result depends on the strong assumptions of the neoclassical model that there is no independent investment function, that there is a 'well-behaved' production function and an exogenously given rate of growth of the labor force.[7] The intuition behind the paradox is as follows. Given these assumptions it is easy to show that the rate of growth of the capital stock is equal to the net investment rate divided by the net capital to output ratio.[8] If capital is growing faster than output, then the capital-to-output ratio is rising and the rate of growth of the capital stock will be falling, and vice versa, given the level of the savings rate, whatever that may be. So the rates of growth of capital and output must be tending to the same rate eventually. In that case we could rewrite (2) as

$$\triangle\Upsilon/\Upsilon_{ss} = a.\triangle\Upsilon/\Upsilon_{ss} + \beta.\triangle L/L + r \tag{3}$$

using the subscript (*ss*) to denote steady state. Therefore the steady-state rate of growth of output is[9]

$$\triangle Y/Y_{ss} = \frac{\beta . \triangle L/L + r}{1 - \alpha} \tag{4}$$

The steady-state rate of growth of income is clearly independent of the investment rate. Given α and β, which are constant for the Cobb-Douglas case, the steady-state rate of growth of output and hence of capital is thus determined by the growth of the labor force and productivity, *not* by the investment rate.

Obviously, it could well be argued, as Kennedy did, that the assumptions of McCloskey's model are unhelpful for understanding the late Victorian economy. Whilst I sympathize with this point of view, given the impact of McCloskey's article, it seems worthwhile to explore the properties of his model a little further.

There are two particular points which need to be developed and are instrumental in creating doubts about McCloskey's conclusions, even supposing that one approved of his specification.

First, whilst it is true that in the long-run steady state the growth rate is independent of the investment rate, in the short and medium run this is not so and indeed economies are rarely, if ever, in a steady state. The basic point is that a higher investment rate will only *eventually* be offset by a rise in the capital-to-output ratio; during the interim (possibly quite lengthy) period there will be a rise in the growth rate of output and capital will grow faster than output.

Second, whilst the steady-state rate of growth is invariant with respect to the investment rate the capital intensivity of activity is not. Rises in the investment rate will tend to increase the capital-to-output ratio and the amount of capital per head. This last is in turn vital to the possible level of consumption per head. The basic point is straightforward. In the neoclassical model output per head is an increasing function of capital per head but a higher capital stock per person requires a higher savings rate. There are thus two offsetting effects on potential consumption standards, but in many cases it will be that raising the investment rate to obtain a higher capital-to-labor ratio will put the economy on a growth path with higher sustainable consumption per head.[10] An important question, prompted by McCloskey's model but ignored by him, is therefore, 'By undertaking lower domestic investment rates than other economies did Britain suffer reduced consumption levels?'

II

We can now investigate the possible importance of these two points.

Using Prof. Feinstein's recently published work, which was not available when McCloskey wrote his original article, but which has subsequently been accepted by him as authoritative,[11] we find that for 1872–1911 $\triangle \Upsilon/\Upsilon = 1{\cdot}73$ percent, $\triangle K/K = 1{\cdot}41$ percent, and $\triangle L/L = 0{\cdot}95$ percent.[12] From (2) we deduce a value of 0·6 percent for the residual, r, based on $\alpha = 0{\cdot}4$ and $\beta = 0{\cdot}6$; these values are those used by Matthews[13] and recently approved by McCloskey,[14] although not those used in his 1970 article.[15]

Let us then consider what would have been the effects of adopting a domestic net investment rate similar to that of the Americans or the Germans, still using McCloskey's model with its strong and restrictive assumptions. For the illustrative calculations below I chose a level of 12 percent[16] and suppose also that there was no foreign investment or property income from abroad.

Table 6.4 *Growth with a 12 percent net investment rate: a hypothetical calculation*

	Share of profits × growth rate of capital stock ($\alpha \times \triangle K/K$)	*Share of wages × growth rate of labor force* ($\beta \times \triangle L/L$)	*Growth rate of total factor productivity (r)*	*Growth rate of output* ($\triangle \Upsilon/\Upsilon$)
1872–82	0·4×3·75	0·6×0·95	0·6	2·67
1882–92	0·4×3·39	0·6×0·95	0·6	2·53
1892–1902	0·4×3·12	0·6×0·95	0·6	2·42
1902–11	0·4×2·91	0·6×0·95	0·6	2·29

	Net capital to output ratio	*Net capital*	*Output*
1872*	3·19	3,227	1,013
1882	3·54	4,667	1,318
1892	3·85	6,517	1,692
1902	4·12	8,861	2,149
1911	4·35	11,471	2,634

*Initial values from C. H. Feinstein, *National Income, Expenditure and Output of the United Kingdom, 1855–1965*, for the variables as defined in note 12 on p. 131.

The results are shown in Table 6.4.[17] Growth rates are calculated by the formula in equation (2) and $\triangle L/L$ and r are assumed constant at their average rates of 0·95 and 0·6 percent respectively.[18] The growth rate of the capital stock is the net investment rate divided by the net capital-to-output ratio. In 1872–82 this was $12/3{\cdot}19 = 3{\cdot}75$ percent and so $\triangle \Upsilon/\Upsilon = 2{\cdot}67$ percent. This implies, however, that capital is growing faster than output. We take account of this at the end of a decade and recompute $\triangle K/K$ on the basis of $12/3{\cdot}54 = 3{\cdot}39$ and so on. As a result of this rise in the investment rate the economy experiences growth which is faster than the steady-state rate but which is decreasing towards the steady-state rate as time passes and the capital-to-output ratio rises.

By 1911 net domestic output in this counterfactual is £2,634 million and after allowing for the investment rate of 12 percent and government spending at the actual rate, even with no net property income from abroad, this would have permitted consumption expenditure of £2,138 million (1900 factor cost), a rise of 25 percent.[19]

III

Used in this way the message of McCloskey's neoclassical model seems clear: Victorian Britain *did* fail! With the choice of an American or German net investment rate, by 1911 Britain could have enjoyed a 25 percent higher standard of consumption, even if she had forgone all property income from abroad.[20] This is not to claim any particular virtue for this model or these calculations, but rather to suggest that writers dealing with this period need not necessarily feel inhibited from arguing that British home investment was too low, even if they are of a neoclassical persuasion.

NOTES

1. D. N. McCloskey, 'Did Victorian Britain fail?', *Economic History Review*, 2nd ser., XXIII (1970), p. 451.
2. ibid.
3. ibid., p. 459.
4. W. P. Kennedy, 'Foreign investment, trade, and growth in the United Kingdom, 1870–1913', *Explorations in Economic History*, II (1973–4), p. 440.
5. P. Deane and W. A. Cole, *British Economic Growth, 1688–1959* (Cambridge, 1962), p. 247.
6. McCloskey also argued that a once-for-all repatriation of foreign investment back to Britain could not have raised output much. This argument was successfully challenged by Kennedy, loc. cit., pp. 422–4.
7. For an elementary exposition of the neoclassical one-sector growth model see H. G. Jones, *An Introducton to Modern Theories of Economic Growth* (1975), ch. 4.
8. Using the standard notation of macro-economics, let $\triangle K = I = sY$ and $K/Y = v$; then the rate of growth of the capital stock $= \triangle K/K = sY/vY = s/v$.
9. With constant returns to scale this simplifies to $\triangle L/L + r/(1 - \alpha)$ since in that case $\beta = 1 - \alpha$.
10. This problem was posed and solved by Phelps-Brown. He showed that the capital-to-labour ratio which maximizes sustained consumption per head in the long run will be achieved by a gross investment rate equal to the share of profits in national income; see Jones, op. cit., pp. 208–12. Britain in the late nineteenth century had a gross investment rate of about 8 percent according to Feinstein's data and a profit share of about 40 percent.
11. D. N. McCloskey, 'Victorian growth: a rejoinder', *Econ. Hist. Rev.* 2nd ser., XXVII (1974), p. 275. Prof. Feinstein is currently engaged in revising his figures for the growth of the capital stock and has indicated in private correspondence that he now believes that $\triangle K/K$ was at a higher value in this period. His preliminary figures

suggest a value of 2·1 percent. The implication of this revision would be to lower the residual to 0·3 percent. As it turns out this revision is unimportant for the thesis of this comment (calculations available from the author on request), although it would make a big difference to McCloskey's comparisons of productivity growth in Britain with that in Germany and the United States. – 'Victorian Britain', loc. cit., p. 458, and 'Rejoinder', loc. cit., p. 277.

12 All data are derived from C. H. Feinstein, *National Income, Expenditure and Output of the United Kingdom, 1855–1965* (Cambridge, 1972). $\triangle Y/Y$ is from net domestic output at 1900 factor cost (Table 5, cols 12–14); $\triangle L/L$ is from Table 57, col. 3; $\triangle K/K$ is from net capital stock at constant replacement cost plus stocks and work in progress (Table 43 and formula in Table 49). Initial and terminal values based on five-year averages.

13 R. C. O. Matthews, 'Some aspects of post-war growth in the British economy in relation to historical experience', *Transactions of the Manchester Statistical Society* (1964), p. 12.

14 McCloskey, 'Rejoinder', loc. cit., p. 275.

15 The differences are trivial, however.

16 Britain's net investment rate was generally about 3–4 percent, Feinstein op. cit., Table 5. Kuznets' data suggest that for Germany the net investment rate for 1881–1913 averaged 13·6 percent and for the United States for 1889–1908 13·4 percent – S. Kuznets, 'Long term trends in capital formation proportions', *Economic Development and Cultural Change*, IX, pt III (1961), pp. 64, 92.

17 The results are for a discrete approximation, within decades the effects of a rising capital-to-output ratio on $\triangle K/K$ are ignored. It should be noted that this counterfactual calculation rests heavily on two properties of McCloskey's original model and that a change in these assumptions could generate a different result. These properties are that the elasticity of substitution between factors is one and factor shares are constant, and that there is no additional mechanism operating to speed up the transition to the new steady-state growth path. Obviously a different result could be obtained if, for example, it were hypothesized that as the investment rate rose the share of profits fell dramatically. This is not, however, a characteristic of McCloskey's own model.

18 The calculation was redone with the actual values of r and $\triangle L/L$ in each decade and the result was virtually the same.

19 This would have been easily enough to avoid the overtaking of Britain by the United States in terms of real income per head; Maddison's figures suggest that in 1913 the United States enjoyed an 11 percent advantage. – A. Maddison, 'Comparative productivity levels in the developed countries', *Banca Nazionale del Lavoro Quarterly Review*, XX (1967), p. 308.

20 This does *not* mean that Britain should not have undertaken any foreign investment; presumably there would have been opportunities to increase still further her consumption possibilities by at least some foreign investment.

No It Did Not: A Reply to Crafts

The rewards of the scholarly life are usually like the rewards of abstention in Victorian Britain – small and tardy. Still, like the Victorians themselves (and unlike their critics), one must accept the vengeful god who arranges for 5 percent over twenty years to be a good return. At least in its size I have no cause for complaint in Mr Crafts' comment on my article published, it seems to me, so long ago. It is a comment on one paragraph.[1] Thus is my 300-word *torah* followed, after a suitable stay in oral tradition, by a 2,200-word *mishnah*. Moses himself did little better, and I accept with gratitude the implied compliment.

Two roads lie open in reply. The low road is through the brambles of Crafts' mismeasurement of British net domestic savings or of the share of income earned by capitalists, a sentence-by-sentence struggle over Errour. The reader will be relieved that I propose instead to take the high road, stopping briefly at the sights along the way worthy of note by other students of British history – even though the road not taken also held a few delights (for example, using the correct share of capital – defined conventionally, though as we shall see misleadingly, as the residual from the share of labor – rather than the 'stylized fact' reduces the fresh consumption from higher savings in Crafts' calculation by about 40 percent).

Before turning up the high road, however, I am compelled to mention a third, the Steady-state Turnpike, if only because Crafts spends most of his comment speeding along it. In fact, his discussion seems to me most bizarre. One might as well take the road to Scotland by way of Katmandu and Milwaukee with a stop in Wagga Wagga. I did not 'rely on' a steady-state model in my article, nor even did I use it. Indeed I have long maintained that such models are worthless for historical purposes, and have said so in print and correspondence. Our models are identical – namely, the idiot's friend, a production function with an identity about capital accumulation. Ruminations about the steady state keep mathematical economists off the street, but two economic historians can agree to stick to honest work.

All right, then: after getting down to business in the antepenultimate paragraph, what has Crafts tried to show? He has tried to show that had Britain invested at home as America did, Britain would have done much better. In particular, had Britain after 1871 matched American standards of 12 percent of domestic income invested at home it would have enjoyed consumption in 1911 a quarter higher than actual. Although he obscures the point in various ways, it must be made clear at once that he is not coming to a different answer to the question I posed in 1970: 'Whether the late Victorians were profligate in consumption compared with foreigners at the time or Englishmen before.' When investment abroad is added to investment at home and compared with income – that is, when all abstention from consumption is included – the British were only a little more profligate in consumption. This, then, is not the issue. Crafts means exactly *domestic* investment. He does not mean that in late Victorian Britain savings were very low in total, but that they were misdirected to Canadian railways and Italian mines. If Crafts had asked the British to emulate the standards of an industrializing country in domestic investment in addition to those of a mature economy in foreign investment he would be asking it to perform precisely the miracles of thrift I rejected in my article as unreasonable. But he in fact agrees with me in not imposing this burden of blame on his great-grandparents: according to him they were not profligate in their consumption, merely incredibly stupid in investing their savings.

For Crafts apparently knows better than his great-grandparents. They could have had a quarter more consumption in 1911 simply by passing a law in 1871 banning all investment abroad. What a marvel of ingenuity is such economics! How wonderful! By hobbling itself, Britain is made truly free. By offsetting the decisions of its businessmen, it is made rich. By a mere transfer of funds from one investment to another, its consumption is raised. The reader may notice a more than superficial resemblance to the marvellous and wonderful economics of certain Treasury advisers since Keynes. Good public policy can provide enormous free lunches to us all if only the dullards presently in power, or (if we are in power) in the City or the country or Zurich, will listen. Further, these policies are discoverable not by some tiresome empirical inquiry but by pure right reason unalloyed, possibly expressed in a few figures on the back of an envelope.

Such self-confidence in second guessing deserves a sterner test than mere comment-writing. It is always a serious point to ask the American Question of an economic historian who discerns some missed opportunity in the past, 'If you're so smart why aren't you rich?' Sometimes he can answer, 'I discerned the opportunity precisely because I am looking backward; I do not claim to have better powers of prediction than the businessmen I study.' But Crafts and many other critics of the late Victorians cannot answer this way, for they claim to have discerned missed opportunities of such magnitude and obviousness that anybody but a fool at the time would have seen them. This is why they so often conclude that the late Victorians were fools. Thorstein Veblen, for example, was scornful of the ridiculous little trucks on the British railways; Duncan Burn was shocked at the neglect of Lincolnshire ores; and Crafts, along with others, has found a way to wealth in redirecting investment abroad to home.

The astonishing magnitude of the new wealth is seen most easily by setting Crafts' world against the world that was. He emphasizes the increase in consumption by 1911 of a quarter. But it must be noted that this is achieved by an increase in net domestic income in 1900 prices of a third (comparing Crafts' £2,634 million with Feinstein, Table 5, cols 12 minus 14 for 1909–13), and this in turn by a net domestic capital stock in 1911 twice its actual size. By keeping savings at home the British people could have had two Forth Bridges, two Bakerloo Lines, two London housing stocks, two Port Sunlights. The common sense of this piece of political economy is, of course, that the rate of return would be driven down to nil. So deep is his fascination with the arithmetic of growth, however, that Crafts does not notice this problem.

Its centrepiece – and the source of the free lunch – is the assumption that foreign investment earning 5 percent could be brought home to earn much more than 5 percent (or the 1 percent to which Crafts' programme of investment would drive the economy), namely, 10 to 12 percent. The 5 percent (or less) we know from the return on foreign bonds. The 10 to 12 percent we believe we know by dividing the 'income of capitalists' (that is, 40 percent of income) by the value of the capital stock. That the 40 percent of income called the 'return to capital' contains incomes incomparable with the safe return on an Indian railway bond does not bother Crafts, or his predecessor in this error, Dr Kennedy. It contains, of course, the basic return to capital (5 percent), but also large incomes from accumulated depreciation funds, managing, self-employment, land and, most of all, risk. The identity between Crafts' magic and the assumption that these incomes would somehow accrue to funds kept at home is easily demonstrated. Crafts' world achieves high rates of growth of income (Υ) by way of the contribution of capital, that is, the high growth of the capital stock ($\triangle K/K$) multiplied by 'its' share in income (α). But this product can be shown to be equal to the rate of saving out of income (s, or 12 percent by assumption) multiplied by the pervailing interest rate in capital (i):

$$\alpha\left(\frac{\triangle K}{K}\right)=\left(\frac{iK}{\Upsilon}\right)\left(\frac{\triangle K}{K}\right)=\left(\frac{iK}{\Upsilon}\right)\left(\frac{s\Upsilon}{K}\right)=is.$$

There is no mystery here: if £10 out of £100 is saved and is put to work earning 10 percent, then income rises in the next and all future years by £1; and this £1 must be, arithmetically speaking, the 'contribution' of the rising capital stock to economic growth, which is to say that the left-hand side of the equation must equal the right. In Crafts' world we know α (=0·4), $\triangle K/K$ by decade (e.g. 3·75 percent per year during 1872–82), and s (=0·12). We therefore know the interest rate, i, that he is implicitly assuming could be earned on home investments. In the case of 1872–82 it is $\alpha(\triangle K/K)/(s)$=0·4 (0·0375)/0·12=0·125, which is to say that savings kept home could earn 12·5 percent (it falls gradually to 9·7 percent in 1902–11). But we know that this conclusion is somewhat deficient. We know that it is nonsense to suppose that Victorian investors would have foregone 12·5 percent at home in favor of 5 percent abroad. We know in fact that comparable assets earned comparable returns at home and abroad, with bonds earning around 5 percent and the right of ownership, with its risks and rewards, more. And we know the source of the nonsense, for Crafts has fallen headlong into a trap lying in wait in the national income statistics for economists who use arithmetic rather than behavior to guide their research – the trap of assigning to sleeping 'capital' all the incomes that cannot be assigned to labor. In the article I warned of the trap (pp. 100–1; Figure 5.1), but I should have warned louder, and shall do so here. There was no divergence of 7 percent between foreign investments earning 5 percent and domestic investments of the same sort earning 12. They were not of the same sort. Nor is the point at issue one of private versus social return: if the domestic return had been 12 percent it would have been a 12 percent available to any private holder of Indian government bonds, an unarbitraged divergence leaving him less than half as wealthy as he could have been. But there was in fact no such 12 percent available for being a domestic bondholder. He would have to have been as well a landlord, manager and risk-taker, selling tickets and doing the washing-up on the side. Had Victorians done more of these things Edwardians would have been richer – a remark that applies with equal force to Americans of the Gilded Age and Germans under Bismarck – but nothing in the record suggests that the British Victorians were by international standards unusually neglectful of their duty to their children.

The rebellion of children against their Victorian fathers is a stock description of British intellectual life between the wars. It should be recognized that the description applies to economic as well as to literary history. Keynes, the friend of Strachey and the rest, insisted throughout his career that the Victorians Did It To Us by sending their savings abroad. The anti-Victorian frame of mind dominated writings on British economic history for many a year. Perhaps it is time to stop looking for the Victorian failure that brought death into the world and all our woe with loss of Eden. Perhaps we should free ourselves from the preoccupations of Keynes and his intellectual brothers. And if we wish to criticize or defend the Victorian achievement we should certainly eschew blackboard history. Or at any rate we should do it right.

NOTES

1 'Did Victorian Britain fail?', *Economic History Review*, 2nd ser., XXIII (1970), pp. 450–1.

Part Three

Britain in the World Economy, 1846–1913

7

From Dependence to Autonomy: Judgments on Trade as an Engine of British Growth

From the perspective of earlier times the economic accomplishments of the United Kingdom in the nineteenth century are astonishing. Certainly it would have astonished Ricardo and Malthus, who agreed with each other on little but the dismal prospects for the years to come, to learn in 1820 that by 1913, in the face of a near doubling in the number of heads, real national income per head would more than triple.[1] Looking backwards over a century and a half of rapid economic growth spreading through Europe and its offshoots we are perhaps less inclined to be impressed with a growth rate in income per head of 1·3 percent per year, but this is because the successes of the United Kingdom then and the still greater successes of her imitators abroad now, for whom she prepared the way, have dulled our sense of wonder. This exceptional burst of economic growth requires explanation; that is, it requires the identification of a list of influences on the British economy in the nineteenth century that can distinguish it from the earlier and usual pattern of economic ebb and flow.

I THE ISSUE AND ITS SIGNIFICANCE

A handful of candidates for inclusion in the list have found special favor with students of the nineteenth century. The accumulation of capital and the growth of technology have figured in it, at any rate as proximate causes, although in which of their many incarnations and with what weights they should figure in a true list is uncertain. Was the rise in the savings rate or the uses to which the savings were put the critical feature of capital accumulation? Was the accumulation of mills and machinery as important as the accumulation of skills embodied in human beings? Is the history of technology best viewed as the triumph of great inventions – the steam engine, the railway, cheap steel – or as the quiet spread of ingenuity? Was technology extended and applied with equal vigor throughout the century? Historians inherited from the nineteenth century itself a set of answers to these questions, and have lately intensified their efforts to find what in this heritage survives criticism.

Some of it has not, and requires revision. One influence on the economy, however, foreign trade, is included in the list with capital accumulation and the growth of technology in much the same form and with much the same emphasis as it was by economists and politicians in the nineteenth century. Wherever one looks in the recent summaries of the issue by economic historians the nineteenth century speaks. John Stuart Mill would have found little with which to disagree in the assertion by Phyllis Deane and W. A. Cole, in their pioneering quantitative study of British growth, that 'from the beginning to the end of this story . . . the British people have depended for their standard of living largely on their ability to sell their products in overseas markets'; nor would Alfred Marshall in their parallel assertion that 'by the end of the nineteenth century the British economy was heavily dependent on world markets, and the rate and pattern of British economic growth was largely conditioned by the responses of producers and consumers in the rest of the world'.[2] Cobden or Peel might have used William Ashworth's words in proposing free trade on the floor of the House of Commons – 'Britain's livelihood depended on international trade and the performance of international services' – as Gladstone or Asquith might have used W. H. B. Court's in defending it – 'In a century in which economic growth depended very much on international commerce, no country's development had benefited more from world trade.'[3]

The verdict of the men of the nineteenth century on the role of Britain's economic dealings with the rest of the world in accelerating and decelerating her growth is reflected still more vividly in the writings of modern economists. Mill had said that the gains from trade through greater efficiency, however great, were supplemented by 'indirect effects, which must be accounted as benefits of a higher order'.[4] In 1937 Dennis Robertson echoed this sentiment, and coined a phrase embodying it that has reechoed through the postwar debate on the role of foreign trade in economic development: 'The specializations of the nineteenth century were not simply a device for using to the greatest effect the labors of a given number of human beings; they were above all an engine of *growth*.'[5] Most modern economists would agree with this historical assertion, disagreeing only on whether it is relevant to the twentieth century. Yet even in their disagreement they follow closely the self-perceptions of the nineteenth century. Just as there is a line of intellectual descent from Friedrich List and Henry Carey, with the economic successes in the nineteenth century of a protectionist Germany or America buttressing their theories with historical fact, to the belief of Raul Prebisch, Gunnar Myrdal, and others, that the prescription for growth in countries now underdeveloped is protection, there is one from John Stuart Mill, with the economic success of Britain, to the belief of Gottfried Haberler and others that it is free trade. Both sides believe that the medicine was strong historically and is strong now. Haberler has in mind the nineteenth century when he asserts that the 'international division of labor and international trade . . . have been and still are one of the basic factors . . . increasing the national income of every participating nation'.[6] A. K. Cairncross has in mind the British case in particular when he argues that 'in the nineteenth century foreign markets were growing faster than domestic markets and the external impulse to growth not only took causal priority over the domestic impulse, but was operating more powerfully'.[7] And Charles Kindleberger is explicit: 'There is no difficulty in illustrating the model of export-led growth. Great Britain furnishes the prime example, both in the way that exports of first textiles and then iron and coal stimulated the growth of income in Britain, and in the reflex action of British imports in spreading growth throughout the nineteenth century.'[8] So too are Gerald Meier and Robert Baldwin, who argue in their historically oriented summary of the postwar literature on economic development that 'its export sector was highly important in propelling the British economy forward'. They conclude by bringing together the promise and the threat of large dealings with the rest of the world (again, the medicine is strong, whether helpful or hurtful): 'the British case thus demonstrates how influential an expansion in exports may be in stimulating an economy's development, but at the same time it illustrates that . . . retardation in the growth of exports will have repercussions that slow down the rate of intensive development for the whole economy'.[9]

The orthodox position, then, has passed with little alteration from the writings of Victorian pamphleteers, journalists and scholars into the writings of modern economic historians and economists and thence into the minds of politicians and educated people generally. The British economy in the nineteenth century, it is said, depended on dealings with the rest of the world. As went the trade in commodities and the migration of factors, so went the nation. The move to free trade, therefore, was a great economic as well as political event, for it opened the throttle of the engine of growth in the middle of the nineteenth century, a lesson to be noted by currently developing countries with protectionist inclinations. And if the throttle could be opened, it could also be closed, as it was increasingly with the rise of foreign competition late in the century, another lesson for developing countries. This view of the reasons for British economic growth, in short, appears to be cogent, simple and relevant to the modern world.

A few have objected to the argument, but more to its generalization to Europe or the West as a whole than to its application to Britain by itself. In an important article reacting against the notion of trade as an engine of growth Irving Kravis, for example, argues that 'export expansion did not serve in the nineteenth century to differentiate successful from unsuccessful countries. Growth where it occurred was mainly a consequence of favorable internal factors, and external demand represented an added stimulus which varied in importance from country to country and period to period.'[10] He made the point by direct appeal to the facts: some economies grew when their exports increased, but others did not, and some grew with little foreign trade, the inference being that internal conditions, not exports, determined whether or not an economy would grow. This is reminiscent, again, of the point made by historically minded protectionists, a great comfort to them when free traders demolish their arguments on logical grounds: countries that restricted their trade (for example, Germany) or that both restricted it and had in proportion to national income little of it to begin with (for example, the United States or, latterly, the Soviet Union) nonetheless grew.

Although this line of reasoning undermines the argument for trade as a universal engine of growth, and might give pause to someone inclined to make flamboyant assertions about the power of the engine even in the British case, it leaves open the distinct possibility that Britain was an exception, that economic dealings with the rest of the world were crucial for her growth, if not for every country's growth. Britain was in the nineteenth century exceptionally open to the world economy. This openness is what leads economists and historians to believe that British growth was dominated by transactions with the rest of the world, and makes Britain a test case for the model of trade as an engine of growth: if the model fits anywhere it should fit the British economy in the nineteenth century.

II DIMENSIONS OF BRITISH INVOLVEMENT IN THE INTERNATIONAL ECONOMY

The most obvious measure of the openness of the British economy in the nineteenth century is the exceptionally high ratio of trade in commodities and services to national income. A satisfactory index is the ratio of the value of imports to national income. Commodity imports were larger than commodity exports in every year after 1822, but taking one year with the next Britain's exports of services filled the gap (her imports of services were probably negligible for the purpose at hand) bringing the balance of trade close to zero.[11] The net balance on commodity and service account, positive or negative, was usually in the neighborhood of 1 percent of gross national product, except in the late 1870s and in the 1890s and early 1900s, when the net balance (imports greater than exports) was usually just under 3 percent of national product. For years other than these, then, imports of commodities were close enough to exports of commodities and services to make it unimportant which one is used as the numerator of the ratio. At its peak in the early 1880s the ratio of net commodity imports to income was about 0·28, and persisted at nearly this level down to 1913.[12] This is very high for a country of Britain's size.

Among the twelve countries now developed for which Simon Kuznets was able to assemble historical statistics on imports as a percentage of income only four, Australia during the 1860s, Denmark, Norway and the Netherlands, ever have had higher ratios, and the largest of these in the nineteenth century, the Netherlands, had in 1900 a population only 13 percent as large as Britain's. The ratios in France and Germany, with comparable populations and land masses, were in the nineteenth century on the order of a fifth to a quarter lower.[13]

Furthermore, Britain bulked so large in the trade of the world that events in Britain affecting her trade, such as the move to free trade in the middle decades of the century, could be expected to react on the British economy for good or evil with special force. Britain was, of course, the pivot of international trade in the nineteenth century. Her pivotal position is apparent in the statistics of world trade in manufactures. In the decade 1876–85, the earliest dates for which usable statistics on the matter are available, Britain's exports of manufactured goods, her chief exports, were about 38 percent of the world's total, and in earlier years the share had no doubt been larger.[14] By 1899 her share had fallen, but according to Alfred Maizels' careful calculations was still about 33 percent of the exports of manufactured goods from the industrial countries (Western Europe, Canada, the United States and Japan) and India. [15] This position of dominance is unique in modern economic history, approached only by the United States, whose share in the manufactured exports of the industrial countries and India in the seven years of Maizels' statistics (1899, 1913, 1929, 1937, 1950, 1955 and 1957) reached its peak – only 27 percent – in 1950. Only after World War I did the United States exceed Britain in exports of all kinds (with American wheat and British coal included in the accounting) and only after World War II in total exports of manufactures.[16]

It was not only in the international movement of goods that Britain dominated and was dominated by the world economy in the nineteenth century: Britain participated to an unusual degree in the international movement of capital and men. During the years 1870–1913 Britain spent on average over 4 percent of her gross national product, a third of national savings, on foreign investment.[17] On the eve of World War I Britain was earning over 7 percent of her national income from foreign assets and these constituted a little under a third of the value of the nation's entire capital stock.[18]

Britain held two and a quarter times more foreign assets than did France, her nearest competitor, and three and a half times more than did Germany.[19] Once again, such deep involvement in the international capital market, as in the international market in goods and services, is remarkable in modern economic history. France under Napoleon III may have reached a comparable position, particularly in the share of national income invested abroad, but no other country has done so before or since over so long a period. The United States has taken over Britain's position as the world's chief creditor. American foreign investment as a percentage of gross national product peaked in the 1920s, and even at that time was exceeded by British investors carrying on the traditions of the nineteenth century into the twentieth. In the 1950s American foreign investment was a mere 0·5 percent of national income, and at the height of the Marshall Plan, in 1947, the United States and its government strained to achieve a level of foreign investment as a share of national income (something over 3 percent) that private British investors surpassed by a factor of two as a matter of routine in the decade before World War I.[20]

Britain sent men abroad as well. In the century of the great migrations few were more mobile across international boundaries than Englishmen – or, more accurately, Irishmen and Scots, it being important in this context to emphasize the inadequacy of the standard designation for citizens of the United Kingdom. The matter is usually viewed from the perspective of the New Worlds abroad, that is to say, with the volume of *intercontinental* emigration in mind. British intercontinental emigration was very large, accounting for over 40 percent of the European total from 1846 to 1910 of 36 million emigrants. Until the Italians took their place in the late 1890s and early 1900s, citizens of the United Kingdom were the largest national group of emigrants leaving Europe.[21] And from 1861 to 1910 on average only Norway had a higher proportion of its population leaving Europe.[22] From the perspective of the nations sending emigrants the rate of total emigration, whether intercontinental or intereuropean, is the more relevant statistic, and in this too citizens of the United Kingdom exhibited their unusual sensitivity to opportunities, or at any rate livings, abroad. This is apparent in the statistics of birth and death rates and rates of population growth, which in combination imply a rate of emigration. Before 1870 the statistics are spotty, and are especially unreliable for Ireland. There is little doubt, however, that the United Kingdom in the years after the potato famine of the late 1840s sent an unusually large share of its population abroad. In the 1870s, when the Irish statistics improve, out of the thirteen European countries for which the data are available only Norway and the Austro-Hungarian Empire had higher rates of emigration: Norway's was 5·2 per thousand of population, the Empire's 3·4 and the United Kingdom's 3·2. In the 1880s the picture is similar: Norway's rate was an astonishing 9·7 per thousand, Sweden's was an almost as astonishing 7·7 (these two are the highest rates observed over any of the decades from 1870 to 1910 for any country in Europe, and were probably matched only by Irish rates in the late 1840s and 1850s), and the United Kingdom's, the third highest among the fourteen countries for which the calculations are possible, was 3·6. In the 1890s British emigration fell off sharply, and all but the most stay-at-home nations of the fourteen (France, Belgium, Switzerland, Spain and Germany) had higher rates. In the early 1900s, however, only Norway, Sweden, Denmark and Italy had higher rates of emigration. During the nineteenth century, in short, the United Kingdom was closely tied to the international market in men as few other countries were then or have been since.[23]

III THE VOLATILITY OF THE INTERNATIONAL SECTOR

Britain, then, was unusually deeply involved in the international economy. If the depth of involvement had been unchanging in the nineteenth century the trade in goods, capital and men would hold less fascination than it does for historians and economists attempting to explain the course of British growth. But it was in fact changing rapidly throughout the century, deepening with each decade, and the international economy to which Britain was increasingly committed was changing as well. Commodity imports as a proportion of national income rose from around 0·12 in the early 1830s to, as we have seen, 0·28 in the early 1880s.[24] In other words, to look at the other side of the account, down to the last quarter of the century exports were growing much faster than national income. Furthermore, the terms on which Britain traded her commodity exports for imports fluctuated widely, moving unfavorably from the 1820s to the 1850s (falling to 56 percent of its 1820 value by 1857), and favorably, though irregularly, to 1913 (rising to 74 percent of its 1820 value).[25] The upshot is that real exports of commodities per head grew 4·4 percent per year from 1821 to 1873 (almost three times faster than the rate of growth in income per head of 1·53 percent per year over the same period) and 0·93 percent per year from 1873 to 1913 (12 percent *slower* than the rate of growth in income per head of 1·06 percent).[26] Little wonder, then, that foreign trade has been cast in the role of a 'leading sector' in British growth: as exports accelerated or decelerated, so also did income.

The economic world that Britain faced was changing as well, for reasons both beyond and within her control. The steady decline in Britain's share of world exports of manufactured goods noted above was to a large extent inevitable, a reflex of the industrialization of the rest of the world, especially Germany and America. By 1913 the share had fallen to 30 percent – still large, but well below the levels of midcentury, when Britain had been truly the workshop of the world.[27] And earlier Britain had quite deliberately changed her economic position in the world by leading the way to free trade, abandoning in the

1840s, 1850s and 1860s the tariff that had protected her agriculture, nurtured the more feeble of her manufacturing industries and discriminated in favor of her colonies.

The export of capital and men changed, too. Before the Irish famine of the 1840s it is unlikely that the rate of emigration was as high as it was to become later in the century, although in view of the deficiencies of the statistics it is difficult to be certain. The statistics on the export of capital are better, and reveal a sharp rise in investment abroad during the late 1850s. From 1845 to 1854 net foreign investment averaged 0·9 percent of national income and 10 percent of national savings, with no trend in earlier decades. From 1855 to 1864 it averaged 2·6 percent of income and 28 percent of savings, with an upward trend in later decades.[28]

These changes in Britain's economic dealings with the rest of the world can be made more vivid by considering how the economy might have looked in 1913 in their absence. A simple – not to say simple-minded – route to this perspective is to project the characteristics of the British economy before the rise in the import ratio, the move to free trade and the great migrations of capital and labor onto the data for 1913, making the naïve but useful assumption that the effects of the hypothetical alterations in the economy of 1913 extend no further than the arithmetic implies. The arithmetic is at any rate suggestive, and a presumption about its results, a presumption that it would imply an economy of a dramatically different description than the one that actually existed in 1913, underlies the conviction that Britain's fortunes were governed by her dealings with the rest of the world. Its implications are in fact less dramatic than one might expect.

Consider, for example, the experiment of reducing the ratio of net imports of commodities to national income from 0·26, its actual level in 1913, to 0·12, the ratio typical of the 1830s. In the minds of historians of Britain's trade in the nineteenth century, no doubt, the most significant result of such an enormous contraction of trade would be the disruption of Britain's beneficial specialization in manufacturing. Of Britain's £526 million-worth of domestic commodity exports in 1913, 78 percent were, in the language of the Trade and Navigation Accounts, 'Articles Wholly or Mainly Manufactures'. Of her £659 million-worth of net commodity imports, 25 percent were manufactured articles that she did not make as well as her competitors, 33 percent were raw materials to make still more, and the rest, 42 percent, were foods.[29] By means of foreign trade, in other words, Britain produced far more manufactured goods than she consumed and consumed far more food than she produced. As Sir John Clapham put it, 'The countries which fed, or nearly fed, themselves all had a much more even balance of agriculture with manufactures and commerce. A balance – or lack of balance – such as that in Britain had not been known before in the record of great nations.'[30] How far the scales were out of balance can be seen by comparing consumption and production, distinguishing manufactures, food and other (mainly nontraded) goods and services. The statistics of domestic expenditures on these categories are fairly reliable, as are the statistics of foreign trade, and from the two can be inferred the composition of final production in 1913 (see Table 7.1). Assuming that all the effects of a change would have been absorbed on the production rather than on the consumption side of the economy, if trade had been reduced in the proportion of 0·12 (the earlier ratio of all imports net of reexports to national income) to 0·28 (the actual ratio in 1913), the share of manufacturing in domestic product would have fallen from 0·38 to 0·31, the share of food would have risen from 0·16 to 0·22, and the share of services and nontraded goods would have fallen from 0·54 to 0·51.[31] Agriculture would have been nearly a third larger than it actually was in 1913, a substantial

Table 7.1 *Consumption and production of manufactures, food and other goods and services in 1913, and their shares in gross domestic expenditure and product at factor cost*
(£ million; shares of row sums given in brackets)

	Manufactures and coal	*Food*	*Services and nontraded goods*	*Imports (−) of raw materials*	*Row totals*
(1) Expenditure (consumption at factor cost)	560·1 (24%)	603·4 (26%)	1,139·4 (50%)		2,302·9
(2) Net exports (+) or imports (−), f.o.b.	+328·4	−218·6	+121	−191·7	39·1
(3) Production at factor cost (column totals)	888·5 (38%)	384·8 (16%)	1,260·4 (54%)	−191·7	2,342·0

Sources: The starting point is Feinstein's table of consumer expenditures (*National Income*, p. 285). Coal (that is, fuel and light, £76m.) was included in manufactures because of its close association with modern industry in the literature and its importance as an export. Alcoholic drink, it can be shown, was chiefly beer and beer was neither imported nor exported in any significant quantity. Therefore alcoholic drink (£175m.) was included in services and nontraded goods. Aside from these two items the allocation of consumer expenditures to the three categories was straightforward. All of government expenditure on goods and services (£203m., *National Income*, p. 232, col. 2) was added to services. The portion of gross domestic fixed capital formation that was ships, vehicles, plant and machinery (£88m.) was added to manufactures and the rest (£72m., chiefly dwellings) to services and nontraded goods (*National Income*, p. 308). Inventory investment (£45m., *National Income*, p. 232, col. 4) was allocated between manufactures and food (not services and nontraded goods, for most of which the notion of an inventory has no meaning) in proportion to their values of total realized (noninventory) expenditure at market prices. Taxes on expenditures (£175m., *National Income*, p. 232,

enough change, but manufacturing would have been less than a fifth smaller, no revolution in its size, or at any rate not a fall in size justifying without further inquiry a metaphor of British manufacturing's absolute 'dependence' on foreign markets.[32] And, to abandon the severely nonbehavioral method of the exercise for a moment, such reductions in trade would have produced or have been produced by rises in the domestic price of food relative to manufactures, throwing some of the burden of adjustment onto the consumption side of the economy and therefore reducing the extent of adjustment on the production side: in the absence of demand abroad, manufactures would have been cheaper at home and their consumption larger.

Table 7.1 can also be used to gauge the initial effects of another radical alteration of British trade in 1913, the absence of decline in Britain's share of world trade in manufactures. Had Britain's net exports of manufactures kept pace with, say, Germany's from the early 1880s down to 1913, they would have been almost three times higher in 1913 than they actually were.[33] Were the implied increase in the output of manufactured goods achievable, this hypothetical expansion would be relevant. Making the reasonable assumption that British exports of services (largely shipping and financial services tied to the volume of Britain's international trade) would, if anything, expand when exports of manufactures did, however, the expansion of exports would be limited by the resources available from eliminating the home production of food. That is to say, as a matter of arithmetic exports could expand no more than the complete specialization of Britain away from food production and towards manufacturing production implies.

Table 7.1 *Sources* contd:

col. 8) were subtracted from the values of total expenditure generated by the last step in proportion to each sector's share in total expenditure, yielding the first row of the table. The sum of this row is total domestic expenditure at factor cost.

The second row is derived from *Trade and Navigation Accounts of the U.K.*, as cited, adjusted in certain details to correspond with Feinstein's methods. The figures are net flows f.o.b. of the three sorts of goods and services out of (+) or into (−) the country. Gross imports (i.e. including goods for reexport) were converted to f.o.b. values by subtracting, as Feinstein does, 8 percent of the c.i.f. value. £12m. in diamond imports, implicit in Feinstein's procedure (see *National Income*, pp. 116–17, 262, col. 9), were added to raw material imports. The *Trade and Navigation Accounts* give all export, import and reexport statistics in three major categories, corresponding very well to food, manufacturing and raw materials as given here. The only exception is coal, which was transferred from raw materials to manufacturing in accord with the treatment of expenditure on fuel and light. There is a fourth, tiny 'Miscellaneous and unclassified' category of products which was distributed among the other three in proportion to their size. The estimate of exports minus imports of services is from *National Income*, p. 262, cols 2, 10.

The third row is the sum of the first and second. Its sum is gross domestic product at factor cost (equal, of course, to Feinstein's estimate, *National Income*, p. 234, col. 9). To this can be added £200m. net property income from abroad (*National Income*, p. 234, col. 6), yielding gross national product at factor cost (p. 232, col. 10).

The implied exports are 2·2, in contrast to almost three, times their actual level in 1913: the £384·8 million of resources used in British agriculture could be shifted to manufacturing and the increment to output exported (balanced by equal increase in imports of food), increasing exports by a factor of 2·2 and output of manufactures by 43 percent over its actual level in 1913.[34] This is a substantial change, although again not perhaps as large a one as might be expected from so massive a change in exports. And again the estimate is very much an upper bound on the resulting redistribution of national output, on two counts: the £384·8 million of resources in agriculture would be less valuable in manufacturing, probably considerably less so in view of the large component of economic rent on agricultural land in the total costs of agriculture; and the rising relative cost of manufactures as resources from agriculture were forced into less remunerative employment in manufacturing would lower consumption of manufactures, as above, and reduced the extent of adjustment on the production side of the economy.[35]

The arithmetic for the trade in capital and men is less involved. Had the £4 billion of investments abroad in 1913 not occurred, the British domestic capital stock in 1913 would have been, using the statistics on the domestic capital stock described above, some 48 percent higher than it was. Had population grown at the natural rate of growth experienced after 1870 (when the statistics become good enough to calculate it) from, say, 1850 onwards, population in 1913 would have been some 32 percent higher.[36] Once again, both figures can be shown to be overestimates when the analysis is taken beyond arithmetic. If one views each flow, of capital and of men, as unconnected with the other, it follows that bringing capital or men home would reduce their economic rewards and, if anything, reduce their total supply to the economy, yielding less of an increment in resources than the arithmetic implies. If one views the flows as causally connected – British capital moving abroad to fertilize the lands settled by British emigrants – it follows that the effect on the economy would be a mere expansion of its size, leaving the men who remained at home no better endowed with machines and the machines no better staffed with men. That the expansion of the size of the economy would have resulted in little change in the balance of factors of production, indeed, is implied by the arithmetic: according to it, had the emigration of both capital and men been closed off before becoming substantial in the middle of the nineteenth century, by 1913 the capital–labor ratio would have been only slightly altered, 12 percent higher.[37]

These arithmetic exercises are not to be taken overly seriously. Arithmetic is no substitute for properly framed historical questions and for full economic reasoning in answering them. To ask what would have happened to the British economy in the unlikely circumstances reflected in the exercises is not a burning historical question and in any case to make a serious attempt to answer it would push economic reasoning beyond its capacity. Still, it is useful to have them laid out in this bald manner. Exercises of this sort float half-consciously in the mind of anyone who contemplates Britain's unusual economic relations with the rest of the world in the nineteenth century and if not actually performed promise to support the belief that the relations were potent influences on the economy. It is useful to be told that they might not be as potent as one might suppose, even when replaced by utterly implausible alternatives, and it is also useful to know at the outset the crude outlines of a British economy without the influences of the trade in goods, capital and men. The economy would have been different, under some but not all circumstances quite different.

IV THE DIVIDE OF 1870: THE GOOD YEARS AND THE BAD

A different economy, however, is not necessarily a greatly richer or poorer one, and this is the question at issue: granted that with less involvement in the international economy and its vicissitudes Englishmen would have worked at different trades in different numbers, would their incomes have been greatly larger or smaller? What follows bears on this question.

The question has seldom been asked explicitly, but it has been answered implicitly in one or another of its forms many times. The character of the answer has depended on which part of the century is under discussion, for the narration of British foreign trade and economic growth in the nineteenth century breaks naturally into two parts around 1870. From 1820 to 1870 many historians have viewed British growth as depending on two unusually *favorable* events in Britain's economic dealings with the rest of the world, the spurt in exports as Britain's customers grew richer and more numerous and – the subject of the next chapter – Britain's removal of restrictions on trade. From 1870 to 1913 they have viewed it as depending on two unusually *unfavorable* events, the draining of labor and especially capital out of Britain (discussed briefly in Chapter 5 above) and – the subject of Chapter 9 below – the loss of monopoly in manufactured goods as the rest of the world industrialized. Whatever they feel about the emigration of factors of production from Britain that accompanied industrialization abroad, most observers have agreed that the resulting competition itself was hurtful to Britain, for it explains, they believe, the sluggish growth of exports and therefore of national income in the closing decades of the nineteenth century. In international monetary affairs alone – the subject of Chapter 10 below – is it believed that Britain retained the power to change the world economy. The belief appears to be false, and the lesson learned from close scrutiny of it is the same: domination of the world was not necessary for British prosperity.

The constraints on British growth were mostly internal matters, not matters of commercial policy, foreign competition, investment abroad or the rules of the gold standard game.

The distinction between a period in which Britain's involvement in the international economy was favorable to the growth of national income and a period in which it was unfavorable is traditional – the textbooks break the narrative at the 1870s, reflecting in large part the change in Britain's economic position in the world. Furthermore, it has the support of the crude characterization of the economy before and after 1870. Before, the United Kingdom had still an agricultural economy, although rapidly industrializing. Foreign trade was a small share of national income, although rising. Free trade was only gradually established, after a wrenching political debate. The export of capital and men, although accelerating around midcentury, was on the whole small in the period. The world at large, moving before 1870 in the direction of free trade along with Britain, was but slightly industrialized and offered little competition to British factories and forges. After 1870, in contrast, the economy was fully industrial, agriculture shrinking to the status of merely one major industry among others rather than the characteristic occupation of the people. Foreign trade was a large share of national income, with no trend in its share. Free trade was solidly established, so solidly that even the doubts expressed in the 'fair trade' movement could not shake it. The export of capital and men was enormous and routine. And the rest of the world, building up its own industries and reacting against its earlier flirtation with free trade, offered severe and growing competition to Britain's traditional exports.

The accuracy in detail of these two contrasting portraits of the British economy is not at issue. What is important is that in believing them historians have located what they consider to be the important historical issues. No one asks the question, Did free trade raise national income after 1870? Or, Would more foreign investment before 1870 have been desirable? One is free to ask these questions, but they are not the questions that have exercised historians of British trade and growth. Each of the two periods, in other words, has its characteristic set of historical questions, equivalent to a set of experiments in what might have been. To these we now turn.

NOTES

1 Income per head had increased in excess of 3·4 times its 1821 level by 1913. This estimate is constructed by splicing Charles H. Feinstein's estimate of gross domestic product per head in 1913 prices, 1855–1913 (in his *National Income Expenditure and Output of the United Kingdom, 1855–1965*, Cambridge: Cambridge University Press, 1971, Studies in the National Income and Expenditure of the U.K., #6, p. 266) to Phyllis Deane's estimate of gross national product at factor cost in 1900 prices (in her 'New estimates of gross national product for the United Kingdom,

1830–1914', *Review of Income and Wealth*, Series 14, pp. 95–112, June 1968, p. 106) by their ratio in 1855 in order to estimate a figure for 1831 comparable with Feinstein's series. This figure was then extrapolated back to 1821 on the basis of the estimates by Phyllis Deane and W. A. Cole of *British* national product per head deflated by an index of wholesale prices in 1821 and 1831 (in their *British Economic Growth, 1688–1959*, Cambridge: Cambridge University Press, 1962, p. 282). Irish income per head was no doubt growing slower than British from 1821 to 1831 and Ireland had about a third of the population of the United Kingdom at the time. But the figures will not bear a heavy weight of manipulation, and it is better therefore to keep the necessary manipulations simple.

2 Phyllis Deane and W. A. Cole, *British Economic Growth, 1688–1959* (Cambridge: Cambridge University Press, 1964), pp. 39, 28.

3 William Ashworth, *An Economic History of England, 1870–1939* (London: Methuen, 1960), p. 256; compare p. 138: 'foreign trade was throughout the nineteenth century one of the most powerful influences on the state of the British economy'. W. H. B. Court, *British Economic History, 1870–1914: Commentary and Documents* (Cambridge: Cambridge University Press, 1965), pp. 181–2.

4 J. S. Mill, *Principles of Political Economy*, 5th edn (New York, 1864), Vol. II, p. 134 (bk III, ch. XVII, sec. 5).

5 Dennis Robertson, in a lecture delivered to the Liverpool Economic and Statistical Society in 1937, published as 'The future of international trade', *Economic Journal*, 48 (March 1938), pp. 1–14, and reprinted as pp. 497–513 in American Economic Association, *Readings in the Theory of International Trade* (Homewood, Ill.: Irwin, 1950), from which the quotation is taken, p. 501 (italics in original).

6 Gottfried Haberler, *International Trade and Economic Development* (Cairo: National Bank of Egypt, 1959), p. 6.

7 A. K. Cairncross, 'International trade and economic development', *Economica*, N. S., 28 (August 1961), pp. 235–51, at p. 243. He asserts on p. 236 that 'no one doubts the propulsive rôle of foreign trade in the development of the countries that we now think of as advanced', giving the United Kingdom, the United States and Japan as cases in point.

8 Charles P. Kindleberger, *Foreign Trade and the National Economy* (New Haven: Yale University Press, 1962), p. 196.

9 Gerald M. Meier and Robert E. Baldwin, *Economic Development: Theory, History, Policy* (New York: Wiley, 1961), pp. 257, 228. Their Part 2 (of four parts), 'Historical outlines of economic development', is dominated by the case of the United Kingdom in the nineteenth century.

10 Irving B. Kravis, 'Trade as a handmaiden of growth: similarities between the nineteenth and twentieth centuries', *Economic Journal* , 80 (December 1970), pp. 850–72, at p. 872.

11 These assertions rest, as must any statistical assertion on the magnitudes of British trade in the nineteenth century, on Albert H. Imlah's seminal work, *Economic Elements in the Pax Britannica: Studies in British Foreign Trade in the Nineteenth Century* (Cambridge: Harvard University Press, 1958). Imlah gives figures for the balance of payments on pp. 70–5.

12 This is the value of imports c.i.f. net of reexported imports f.o.b. 1881–5 (given in Brian Mitchell, *Abstract of British Historical Statistics* (Cambridge: Cambridge University Press, 1962), p. 283, from the *Annual Statement of Trade of the U.K.*) divided by Feinstein's 'compromise estimate' of gross domestic product at factor cost plus his estimate of net property income from abroad (Feinstein, *National Income*, as cited, pp. 234, 236).

13 League of Nations, Economic, Financial and Transit Department (Folke Hilgerdt), *Industrialization and Foreign Trade* (League of Nations: no place of publication, 1945), pp. 157–8.

14 Simon Kuznets, *Modern Economic Growth* (New Haven: Yale University Press,

1966), pp. 312–13 for trade ratios for eleven of the countries; his *Six Lectures on Economic Growth* (Glencoe, Ill.: Free Press, 1959), p. 101 for the Netherlands' ratio; and D. V. Glass and E. Grebenik, 'World population, 1800–1950', in H. J. Habakkuk and M. Postan (eds), *The Cambridge Economic History of Europe*, Vol. VI, pt I, p. 61 for the populations.

15 Alfred Maizels, *Industrial Growth and World Trade* (Cambridge: Cambridge University Press, 1965), pp. 430–1.

16 Maizels, place cited, for exports of manufactures; and pp. 10–11 in his 'Corrections to industrial growth and world trade' (Cambridge: Cambridge University Press, 1969) for exports of all kinds.

17 These estimates are calculated from Feinstein's estimates of gross national product (*National Income . . . of U.K.*, as cited, p. 234), net foreign investment (p. 261), gross domestic fixed capital formation and net inventory investment (p. 232).

18 The share of income earned abroad is from Feinstein, work cited, p. 234 and the estimate for 1913 of gross domestic reproducible capital stock at constant replacement cost of 1900 from Feinstein, p. 319 (the estimate is £8·32 billion). The estimate of foreign assets owned by Englishmen of about £4 billion in 1913 is derived with confirming evidence in Imlah, *Economic Elements*, as cited, p. 79.

19 Based on Herbert Feis' estimates in his *Europe, The World's Banker 1870–1914* (New Haven: Yale University Press, 1930), pp. 47, 71, 74.

20 Kuznets, *Modern Economic Growth*, as cited, pp. 236–9, gives estimates of net foreign investment as a percentage of gross national product for eleven countries (unfortunately he was unable to include France) from the 1860s on. His estimate for the United States in the 1950s may be confirmed by adding together government long- and short-term outflows of capital and private direct and other long-term outflows (series U185, U186 and U187 in US Bureau of the Census, *Historical Statistics of the United States, Colonial Times to 1957* (Washington, DC, 1960), p. 564, and expressing the sum as a percentage of gross national product (work cited, series F1). This is the procedure for the 1947 estimate. If foreign aid (unilateral governmental transfers abroad, series U184) are added to the accounting, the share is still only 1·7 percent of income in the 1950s and 4·2 percent in 1947.

21 Imre Ferenczi and Walter F. Willcox, *International Migration* (New York: National Bureau of Economic Research, 1929), pp. 230–2.

22 Richard A. Easterlin, 'Influences in European overseas emigration before World War I', *Economic Development and Cultural Change*, 9 (April 1961), pp. 331–51, at p. 335.

23 The rates of births and deaths and rates of population growth for European nations are given in Glass and Grebenik, 'World population', as cited, pp. 61–2, 68–9. The birth and death rates relate to the second half of each of the four decades 1870–1910. Parallel statistics for the UK were calculated from Mitchell, *Abstract of British Historical Statistics*, as cited, pp. 8–9, 29–35.

24 The estimate for the 1830s is Imlah's estimate of gross inports (*Economic Elements*, p. 282) minus reexports (place cited) divided by Deane's estimate of GNP ('New estimates', as cited, p. 104).

25 This is Imlah's index of the net barter terms of trade, in Imlah, *Economic Elements*, as cited, pp. 94–8, column J.

26 Real exports (at 1880 prices) are given by Imlah in *Economic Elements*, as cited, pp. 94–8; population is given in Mitchell, *Abstract of British Historical Statistics*, pp. 8–10. The income estimates are described in the first note to this chapter.

27 Maizels, *Industrial Growth*, as cited, pp. 430–1.

28 These statistics are from Deane, 'New estimates', as cited, p. 99 (she used Imlah's estimates of net foreign investment), with her suggested '1 or 2 percent' (I have used 1·5 percent) of national income as a rough estimate of stock-building (to produce an estimate of total savings from her figures on foreign investment and gross domestic fixed capital formation).

29 *Trade and Navigation Accounts of the U.K.*, December 1913 (SP 1913, Vol. 66), pp. 4–7.

30 Sir John Clapham, *An Economic History of Modern Britain*, Vol. III, *Machines and National Rivalries (1887–1914)* (Cambridge: Cambridge University Press, 1938), p. 2.

31 The ratios add to more than 1·00 because of imports of raw materials, which are a debit against gross domestic product. Since total exports were £39·1 million greater than total imports in 1913 (that is to say, in another vocabulary, the balance of payments on current account was positive), an equal proportional change in all items of trade will reduce the trade surplus (£39 million) and reduce domestic product. To avoid this anomaly, the calculations reported here reduced net imports of food and raw materials by the full amount (0·12/0·28=0·429), but net exports of manufactures and services by an amount that yields a constant trade surplus (the proportion is 0·478). In fact this procedure yields results virtually identical with those from the procedure that shrinks all imports and exports in the same proportion (namely, 0·429).

32 These assertions use the £ figures implied by the experiment described in the previous note. The are: Manufactures and coal, £510 million; Food, £717 million; Services and nontraded goods, £1,197 million; and Imports of raw materials, £82 million. These sum to a domestic product of £2,342 million.

33 This estimate is achieved by subtracting imports of manufactures in Germany and Britain from exports, linking Maizels' estimates for 1899 and 1913 (*Industrial Growth*, as cited, pp. 430, 432 for exports in 1913 prices and pp. 431, 432, 446 and 452 for imports) with Hilgerdts' for 1881–5 and 1896–1900 (*Industrialization and Foreign Trade*, as cited, p. 160) by their ratio at 1899 and 1896–1900. Germany's real exports of manufactures net of exports increased on this basis by a factor of 3·73 from 1881–1885 to 1913, while Britain's increased by a factor of only 1·33. 3·73 divided by 1·33 is 2·8, or 'almost three'. There are some difficulties with Maizels' definition of 'imports', but for present purposes they can be neglected.

34 Shifting the £384·8 million from food production to manufactures and coal production in Table 7.1 increases output of manufactures and coal from £888·5 million to £1,273·3 million.

35 Some rough calculations will indicate the importance of these points. Rents of land in agriculture according to Feinstein (*National Income, op. cit.*, p. 284) were £43 million in 1913 (out of a factor income at the farm gate of £142 million: the rest of the £384·8 would be indirect use of resources to produce raw materials for agriculture – fertilizer, etc. – and to process and distribute agricultural outputs – bakeries, food retailing and transportation, etc.). If all this rent was economic rent, the real value of the transferred resources would be £43 million less, yielding an increase in output of manufactures of 38 rather than 43 percent. If the price of manufactures would have to have risen 50 percent relative to the price of food to achieve the redistribution of resources required and if the elasticity of demand for manufactures relative to food was as low as 0·5, consumption of manufactures would fall £140 million (i.e. (0·5) (0·5) (£560·1)=£140), and output of manufactures after exports had expanded would increase by only 23 rather than 43 percent over its actual level in 1913 (combining the effects of the loss of rent with that of the substitution in consumption).

36 The average rate of natural increase of UK population from 1870 to 1913 was 1·172 percent per year. Applying this rate (continuously compounded) to the 1850 population, 27·5 million, yields a population in 1913 of 60·3 million, compared with an actual population of 45·6 million.

37 Assuming that the labor force would have been the same proportion of the population, the calculations are: £8·32 million/45·6 million people=0·182, compared with the hypothetical ratio of £12·32 million/60·3 million people= 0·2043.

8

Magnanimous Albion: Free Trade and British National Income, 1841–1881

I FREE TRADE AND THE HISTORIANS

During the forty years from Peel's to Gladstone's second ministry, the commercial policy of the United Kingdom moved decisively from fettered to free trade. National income rose decisively as well, the income of labor with it. It was no surprise to free traders, of course, that the removal of a pernicious tax on enterprise, most particularly on the enterprise of industrial laborers and capitalists, brought with it greater wealth for all. They were even willing to concede that only a portion of the greater wealth, though a substantial portion, was attributable to free trade. After all, it was not the promise of material well-being alone that buoyed their spirits in the struggle against protection. Their spiritual leader, Cobden, saw far beyond cheaper corn and better markets for British cotton textiles; he saw, indeed, 'in the Free Trade principle that which shall act on the moral world as the principle of gravitation in the universe – drawing men together, thrusting aside the antagonism of race and creed, and language, and uniting us in the bonds of eternal peace'.[1] Such cosmopolitan visions dimmed in later controversy, for, unlike the material promise, they had all too plainly not been fulfilled. Later critics of free trade, such as the 'fair trade' historian, William Cunningham, could in the 1900s emphasize the more selfish motivation for free trade, namely, the fixing of Britain's monopoly of manufactures on the rest of the world for a few more decades than its natural term.[2] Free traders could (and did) respond, of course, that great benefit accrued to Britain's trading partners as well. And in their more pragmatic moods the free traders were willing to make the selfish

This essay was born in 1971 and has led since then a life of seminars and conferences, accumulating at them a long list of intellectual debts. The institutional debts are to the meetings of the Econometric Society in 1971, and to seminars at the Universities of Chicago, Illinois, Indiana, Michigan, North Carolina State University, Stanford University and the University of Wisconsin; the personal debts are to Geoffrey Andron, Michael Boskin, William Byerts, Rudiger Dornbusch, Steven Easton (for which, especially, the title), Stanley Engerman, Jacob Frenkel, Harry Johnson, Ronald Jones, Paul McGouldrick, and Michael Mussa.

argument. In his testimony to the Select Committee on Import Duties in 1840, J. D. Hume argued that discouraging foreigners from supplying Britain with agricultural products encouraged them to turn instead to manufacturing. In a passage that foreshadows the gloom of many Englishmen half a century later, when the German and American threat had become plain, he argues that by protecting agriculture 'we place ourselves at the risk of being surpassed by the manufactures of other countries; and . . . I can hardly doubt that [when that day arrives] the prosperity of this country will recede faster than it has gone forward' (*Report, Evidence*, Q. 1198, p. 98). But whether they believed free trade was a merely selfish policy or not, or as appropriate to the twentieth century as to the nineteenth, free trader and fair trader alike agreed that in the middle of the nineteenth century it could be justified if need be on selfish grounds alone: it had produced then, they believed, substantial material benefits for the nation.

Historians have adopted the contemporary view of the matter. The correlation between rising national income and the move to free trade, the apparent significance for the distribution of income of removing high duties on food and the intense involvement of Britain in the international economy have been the elements in a demonstration that commercial policy had a substantial effect on the size and distribution of British national income in the nineteenth century. The depth of analysis, to be sure, has left something to be desired, for free trade has not been isolated from other factors influencing national income, the effects on distribution have been treated in merely qualitative terms and the argument has been bound together by an unsupported conviction that foreign trade was crucial to Britain's economic welfare. Of course, free trade had ideological and political effects, and it would be idle to deny that these in turn may have had large effects on the economy: the constitution, for example, might not have survived the European revolutions of 1848 without the repeal of the Corn Laws in 1846. The direct economic effects, however, have been exaggerated. Historians have naturally if not always correctly assumed that it matters economically how a great issue of economic policy such as this is resolved, the more so as the historical study of the issue has been left largely to political rather than economic historians. The history of economics itself has lent credence to this view of the importance of British commercial policy: since the inception of the discipline its best minds (many of them British) have put commercial policy at the center of their thinking. The most impressive intellectual tools developed by Smith, Ricardo, Mill and Marshall were developed precisely for the examination of the effect of international trade and of government policy towards that trade on national income, and their practical motive was in large part the early encouragement and late defense of Britain's policy of free trade. The sheer weight of the intellectual achievement would incline an economist, like the historians, towards attributing great significance to free trade in the nineteenth century.

The theory of international trade has been considerably refined since then, to the point where it can be applied with suitable modifications to fit the circumstances of the time to the question of whether this root event deserves the attention it naturally attracts. What follows is a preliminary assault on that question.

II THE MOVE TO FREE TRADE

The first step in assessing the economic effects of the change in British commercial policy is to discover what it was and how it changed. The free trade movement began in earnest in the 1840s, the most dramatic event in its beginnings (although, despite its symbolic importance, not by itself constituting free trade) being the repeal of the Corn Laws on 26 June 1846. The 1840s are no exception to the historiographic lemma that it is always possible to smooth the discontinuities of events by examining their preparations in the past. One can date the beginning of the ideological preparation, of course, at the appearance of *The Wealth of Nations* and the administrative preparation in the 1780s, with some tentative simplifications of a complex tariff inherited from an age in which, as Maitland put it, 'the British parliament seems rarely to rise to the dignity of a general proposition'.[3] The Napoleonic Wars interrupted many trends in the British economy, among them these stirrings of a rational tariff policy. Every commodity or transaction within reach of the government was taxed and retaxed to fight the French, from dogs and attorneys to incomes and imports. One major tax alone, that on incomes – 'the oppressive and inquisitorial tax' as contemporaries knew it – was repealed with the peace, reducing the government to a policy of continuing other war taxes to meet payments on the national debt (over half of the budget down to the 1850s) and irreducible expenditures on the civil service. In 1820, Sydney Smith could write, after five years of peace, that 'the dying Englishman, pouring his medicine, which has paid 7 percent, into a spoon that has paid 15 percent, flings himself back upon his chintz bed which has paid 22 percent, and expires in the arms of an apothecary who has paid a license of a hundred pounds for the privilege of putting him to death'.[4]

What few changes were made during the next twenty years in the role of customs revenues in this mélange of taxes were accomplished largely by Huskisson's budgets of 1824 and 1825: obsolete duties were repealed on imports of manufactured commodities such as cotton textiles and iron (for which Britain had in any case a crushing comparative advantage), some duties on raw materials were reduced, many export bounties were abolished, and most prohibitions, except those on certain agricultural products, were abolished as well. The goal was rationalization more than reduction – who, after all, could quarrel with a program of removing contradictory or inoperative duties? – and even this modest program was far from complete in 1840. The Select Committee on Import Duties (filled with free traders, who had of late become a formidable political force) reported that in 1839 seventeen of 721 articles in the tariff schedule produced 94·5 percent of the tariff revenue.[5] This was a Benthamite calculation: the tariff revenue, it argued, could be collected more efficiently even without a fundamental change in commercial policy. By 1840 the hard political decision to move to lower rather than merely simpler duties – involving as it did the reimposition of the income tax, the removal of duties discriminating in favor of the colonies and, hardest of all, the abandonment of protection to agriculture – had yet to be made. Even with these rationalizations the tariff on the eve of the move to free trade was complex. It contained prohibitions of imports of live or dead meat, duties on 'slave-grown' sugar two or more times higher than those on sugar from British colonies, drawbacks on timber for use in the mines of Cornwall or in churches, eighty-odd different specifications of skins, from badger to weasel, with associated duties, export duties on coal and wool, and over 2,000 import duties on items ranging from agates to zebra wood.[6]

Despite the bewildering detail, however, the thrust of the tariff is relatively clear. Its protective effect was felt primarily in land-intensive products, these being in any case the dominant products of importation: late in the nineteenth century, under a regime of free trade and of increasing foreign competition in manufactures, nearly four-fifths by value of British net imports were land-intensive raw materials and food.[7] In other words, the categories of the simple theory of trade – importables, exportables and nontraded goods – correspond well in Victorian Britain with agriculture (including some mining), manufacturing and the residual sector, services. The Navigation Acts (repealed in 1849) protected shipping services, to be sure, but it is doubtful whether the protection was by this time important for the industry, particularly for its more modern branches. A few manufacturing industries, notably silk manufacturing, received substantial protection in the tariff, but for most protection would have been superfluous. Indeed, by 1840 the effective rate of protection for factors of production specialized in manufacturing was slightly negative: as free traders pointed out, Britain's exports of manufactures contained raw materials made more expensive by tariffs, whether for revenue on warm-climate raw materials such as raw cotton, for the good of the empire and its landowners on cold-climate materials such as Canadian timber, or for the protection of British rents on metals such as copper and tin ore. The British tariff in the early 1840s, then, raised the price of land-intensive raw materials and food relative to manufactures

Table 8.1 *Net imports, tariff collected and tariff rates, 1841, 1854 and 1881 (£ thousand)*

Commodity	*1841* *Imports value before tariff*	*Tariff revenue*	*Rate (proportion)*	*1854* *Imports value before tariff*	*Tariff revenue*	*Rate (proportion)*	*1881* *Imports value before tariff*	*Tariff revenue*	*Rate (proportion)*
Coffee	925	888	0·96	887	468	0·53	1,081	195	0·18
Wheat	6,950	386	0·056	11,800	173	0·015	31,000	0	0
Other grain	1,040	135	0·13	10,100	242	0·024	19,800	0	0
Cotton	10,400	528	0·051	17,900	0	0	38,800	0	0
Rum	738	1,060	1·4	558	1,280	2·3	462	2,358	5·1
Brandy	419	1,330	3·2	770	1,400	1·8	1,396	1,613	1·2
Sugar	7,630	5,110	0·67	8,550	4,490	0·53	23,800	0	0
Tea	3,480	3,970	1·1	4,000	4,780	1·2	8,560	4,000	0·47
Staves	472	40·6	0·086	666	0	0	567	0	0
Unsawn fir	4,060	568	0·14	5,260	253	0·048	3,470	0	0
Tobacco	402	3,390	8·4	998	4,780	4·8	1,369	8,380	6·1
Wine	1,510	1,720	1·1	2,250	1,910	0·85	5,426	1,380	0·25
Sum:	38,000	19,000	0·50	64,000	20,000	0·31	136,000	17,900	0·13
All other	30,000	4,700	0·16	70,000	5,000	0·07	198,000	1,300	0·01
Total	68,000	23,700	0·35	134,000	25,000	0·19	334,000	19,200	0·06

Sources: After 1854 it is no great trick to acquire the statistics from the Annual Statement of Trade and Navigation (S.P. 1854–5, Vol. LI for 1854; S.P. 1882, Vol. LXVIII for 1881). As was pointed out above, before 1854 the Board of Trade did not give values of British imports. Porter's Tables for 1841 (S.P. 1843, Vol. LVI, pp. 17–27) contain physical volumes of net imports and the tariffs paid for these dozen commodities. Gayer, Rostow and Schwartz, in Part III of the microfilm supplement to *The Growth and Fluctuation of the British Economy, 1790–1850* (Oxford, 1953), give their prices (or for certain varieties of them) in 1841 before and after tariffs. The two methods of conflating these data to arrive at figures for imports are: (1) to apply the before-tariff prices to the (known) quantities of imports; (2) to apply the rates of tariff implied by the two sets of prices (before and after tariff) to the (known) tariff revenues. The second is chosen here because it involves a more plausible (and more testable) assumption than the first: that the rate of tariff is roughly the same across varieties of, say, rum rather than that the Gayer – Rostow – Schwartz variety of rum is roughly the average variety. The two methods, in any case, give much the same result.

and services. A tariff designed by committees of landlords in Parliament and imposed on the imports of a nation that required from the rest of the world little but raw materials and food could hardly be expected to achieve any other result.

The tariff in the early 1840s, furthermore, bulked large in British economic and political life: it was high and, as we shall see in a moment, imports were substantial in relation to national income and the revenues from taxing them were a significant fraction of the revenues of the central government. The height of the tariff and the changes in its height may be measured by the ratio of tariff revenues to the value of imports. Changes in the ratio, of course, reflect not only changes in tariffs but also changes in the composition of imports. For example, we know that tariff rates changed little from the budget of 1825 to 1840, yet the ratio fell from 47 percent in 1826–30 to 31 percent in 1836–40. As Albert Imlah, who made these calculations, observed, this was a result of 'a rise in the rate of flow of goods bearing low duties', principally raw cotton.[8] The solution is to calculate tariff rates weighted by shares of imports before and after the move to free trade. For a dozen items making up 56 percent of the value of imports in 1841 and 41 percent in 1881, and paying always over 80 percent of tariff revenues, Table 8.1 gives the materials of such a calculation.

The average tariff rates using the weights (the shares of commodities in the total value of imports) for various years are shown in Table 8.2.

Table 8.2 *Alternative calculations of the tariff rate, 1841, 1854 and 1881*

The average rate of year:	*Weighted by each commodity's share of imports in the year:* 1841	1854	1881
1841	0·35	0·30	0·27
1854	0·25	0·18	0·16
1881	0·13	0·10	0·06
Total decline, 1841–81	0·22	0·21	0·21

Notice the uniformity of result in the critical figure, the absolute change in the tariff rate from 1841 to 1881. From whatever perspective it is viewed, the move to free trade consisted in a narrowing of the wedge between world and British prices of imports by about 21 percent of the world price.

III EXPLAINING FREE TRADE

If a policy of free trade consisted simply of the reduction of the wedge, the explanation of the policy would present fewer difficulties. But such a view ignores the revenue function of tariffs: the British government needed revenue, and tariffs were one important way of getting it. Tariff policy, in other words, operated under a constraint of a given size of government revenues, a constraint which contemporaries felt binding. The rate of fall in tariffs was in fact held back in each budget by the demand for revenue and by opposition to increases in alternative taxes, notably the income tax. If the size of the government budget fell relative to the yield of other taxes or if the yield from the tariff itself rose in an import boom, the tariff rate could be reduced. From the perspective of tariff policy these would be favorable accidents resulting from other, independent policies – such as retrenchment in government expenditure – or other, independent events – such as a boom in imports. The pure case of a policy of free trade would be the replacement of the tariff by other taxes. By virtue of two fortunate accidents, in fact, British commitment to free trade was not put to this stringent test: the ratio of imports to national income rose, bringing a larger share of taxable transactions under the eye of the customs officer and making it possible, therefore, to collect the same revenue at lower rates; and the required government revenue fell in relation to national income.

These accidents can be measured as follows. The ratio of all tax revenue to national income (t) was determined by the desirability of governmental expenditures and was to a first approximation independent of how the revenue was raised: there is no reason to believe that Britain would have spent less on servicing the government debt and maintaining its armed forces (which together were two-thirds of the total even in 1881) had some method of taxation been eliminated. The rallying cry of free traders was 'Retrenchment and Reform', the one an appeal for lower taxes in total (lower t), the other for a different set of taxes. The taxes to be reformed were of three sorts, customs, excise and income taxes. The taxable transactions for excise and income taxes may be taken to be income as a whole, and public policy here may be summarized, therefore, in terms of ratios of excise and income tax revenues to national income (r_e and r_i). The taxable transactions for customs taxes were, of course, imports, and the rate of tax a ratio of customs revenues to imports (r_c). The magnitudes in 1841 and 1881, and in 1861 for comparison, are exhibited in Table 8.3.

The ratio of imports to national income (m) was determined in part by tariff policy. What part depends on the elasticity of demand for imports. Measured at current values (necessary to preserve the identity to follow in a moment), the fall in the tariff rate from 1841 to 1881 was equivalent by itself to a 29 percent fall in the price of imports, or a fall of 0·84 percent per year. Imports increased about 3·98 percent per year over the forty years, and national income 1·84 percent per year. The higher the price elasticity of demand the more of this high rate of growth of imports can be attributed to the effect of tariff reductions

Table 8.3 *Tax revenues, national income and imports, UK 1841, 1861 and 1881 (£ million)*

		1841	*1861*	*1881*
(1)	Revenue from taxes	£49·9	£67·5	£69·0
(2)	Gross National Product of UK	548·0	744·0	1,145·0
(3)	Excise (indirect domestic) taxes	24·3	30·8	32·4
(4)	Income (direct domestic) taxes	2·2	13·4	17·4
(5)	Customs taxes	23·4	23·3	19·2
(6)	Net imports	68·0	183·0	334·0

Notes and Sources

Row (1): Tax revenues of UK central government = Rows (3)+(4)+(5). This excludes income from the post office and telegraph, as well as other nontax revenues (fees for other services and some interest income on government loans). Nontax revenues were £12·9m in 1881. B. R. Mitchell, with Phyllis Deane, *Abstract of British Historical Statistics* (Cambridge, 1962) (henceforth 'Mitchell'), pp. 393ff.

Row (2): Gross National Product of United Kingdom. For 1841 this is an extrapolation from an estimate of gross national income of Great Britain alone by Phyllis Deane and W. A. Cole in their *British Economic Growth, 1688–1959* (Cambridge, 1964) (henceforth 'Deane and Cole'), p. 166, on the basis of their estimate (p. 168) that Irish gross national income was 15 to 20 percent of the income of the United Kingdom before the potato famine. The midpoint (17·5 percent) was used, yielding a range of error in the extrapolation alone of ±£17m. The figures for 1861 and 1881 are C. H. Feinstein's estimates of net national income of the United Kingdom (given in Mitchell, p. 367) plus his implied estimates of £17m and £28m for depreciation investment (gross investment minus net investment, given in Mitchell, p. 373).

Row (3): Excise (indirect domestic) taxes are approximately the sum of the categories in the official Finance Accounts entitled 'Excise', 'Stamps' and 'Land and Assessed Taxes' given in Mitchell, pp. 393ff. An attempt was made to distinguish indirect taxes (in economic terms, taxes that primarily distort the marginal rates of substitution among commodities alone) from direct taxes (that distort the marginal rate of substitution between leisure and all commodities). Clearly, an excise tax on goods complementary with leisure (beer, playing cards) will affect the choice between leisure and commodities: the distinction is not, in other words, a sharp one. On the basis of Buxton's explication of the Finance Accounts in 1886 (*Finance and Politics*, Vol. II, pp. 382ff., from Finance Accounts, P.P. 204 of 1887), Death Duties were shifted out of Stamps (where they were placed entirely before 1870 in the official accounts and partly – in the form in 1886 of £2m of stamps on deeds, legacies and other instruments – thereafter) into Income Taxes (Row (4)). In 1841, according to G. R. Porter, *The Progress of the Nation* (London, 1851), p. 495, stamp duties on legacies, probates, etc. were £2·12m: these were taken to be the total of Death Duties in this year. Land and Assessed Taxes (consisting in 1886 of £2·0m on house duty and £1·1m on land tax: from 1871 the assessed taxes – a miscellany of excises on horses, dogs, armorial bearings, wig-powder, etc. – were placed under Excises; they were about £1m) are taken to be taxes on housing services, with no effect on the choice between effort and leisure, and are included here.

Row (4): Income (direct domestic) taxes are the sum of 'Property and Income Taxes' and 'Death Duties' (Mitchell, pp. 393ff.), the latter defined as explained in the previous note to include the Death Duties placed in the Stamp account.

Row (5): Customs taxes are the category of Customs in the official accounts (Mitchell, place cited), apparently net of drawbacks.

Row (6): Value of imports net of reexports (no correction is made for divergence between c.i.f. and f.o.b. values) are Imlah's estimates for 1841 and official statistics for 1861 and 1881 (both given in Mitchell, pp. 282ff.).

alone: with a price elasticity of 2·55 and an income elasticity of 1·0, for example, the entire rise in the ratio of imports to national income can be attributed to it, for in this case 1·84 percentage points of the total 3·98 percent growth of imports per year can be attributed to the effects of rising income and 2·5 (0·84)=2·14 (that is, the entire residual) to the effects of the tariff reductions. The elasticities are not known. The subsequent argument, therefore, will allow for the possibility that part, at least, of the rise in *m* is attributable to tariff policy itself.

It is true by definition, in any case, that total tax revenue is equal to the sum of the various sources of revenue (*Y* is national income, the other variables are as defined above and in Table 8.4):

$$tY = r_e Y + r_i Y + r_c m Y$$

Solving for r, the tariff rate must be:

$$r_c = \frac{1}{m}(t - r_e - r_i)$$

Since this is identically true, the change in the tariff rate (call it $\triangle r_c$) can be expressed as:

$$\triangle r_c = (t - r_e - r_i)\triangle(\frac{1}{m}) + \frac{1}{m}(\triangle t - \triangle r_e - \triangle r_i) + \triangle(\frac{1}{m})(\triangle t - \triangle r_e - \triangle r_i)$$

The total change in r_c, therefore, can be decomposed into the effects of the retrenchment in government expenditures (the fall in *t*), the rise in the ratio of imports to national income, *m* (itself partly, but only partly, a result of tariff reductions), and pure reform, the rise in excise, r_e, and income taxes, r_i, to replace revenue lost from the customs. The values of r_c, *m*, *t*, r_e and r_i were as shown in Table 8.4.

Table 8.4 *Tax rates and the ratio of imports to national income, UK 1841, 1861 and 1881*

		1841	*1861*	*1881*
r_c,	Rate of import duties	0·344	0·127	0·058
m,	Ratio of imports to national income	0·124	0·246	0·292
t,	Ratio of all tax revenues to income	0·091	0·091	0·060
r_e,	Rate of excise taxation	0·044	0·042	0·028
r_i,	Rate of income taxation	0·004	0·018	0·015

Source: Table 8.3.

There are two ways of calculating the effect of each variable by itself:

one can either ask how much the tariff rate would have changed if only the variable in question was allowed to change, leaving the others at their initial values; or how much it would have changed if only that variable was *not* allowed to change, allowing the others to vary as they in fact did and subtracting the result from the actual change. The choice between these two is arbitrary, but the ranking and relative magnitude of factors is the same for both (see Table 8.5).

Table 8.5 *The amount of reduction in the tariff rate, 1841–81, attributable to certain sets of determinants when:*

	Only these determinants change, 1841–81 (1)	*Only these determinants do not change, 1841–81* (2)
(1) t	0·25	0·10
(2) m	0·20	0·076
(3) r_e	−0·13	−0·058
(4) r_i	0·089	0·035
	Σ=0·41	Σ=0·15
(5) m and t	0·31	0·33
(6) r_e and r_i	−0·040	−0·020
(7) r_e, r_i and m	0·18	0·04

Notes: Differences from Table 8.4. The formula in the text can be expanded as follows (below each term is its value):

$$\Delta r_c = [(t-r_e-r_i)(\Delta\frac{1}{m})] + [\frac{1}{m}\Delta t] - [\frac{1}{m}\Delta r_e] - [\frac{1}{m}\Delta r_i] + [(\Delta\frac{1}{m})\Delta t] - [(\Delta\frac{1}{m})\Delta r_e] - [(\Delta\frac{1}{m})\Delta r_i]$$

−0·200 −0·250 +0·129 −0·089 +0·144 −0·074 +0·051

These terms sum to the total change in r_c of −0·286, as required. Each experiment becomes, then, a problem in addition: add together the terms that are not zero under each specification. For the second column, subtract the result (with its sign changed) from the actual Δr_c(0·286), the difference being the contribution of the factor in question.

The first four rows of the table give the reductions in tariff attributable to each factor in isolation. The reduction attributable to the fall in the rate of excise taxation is negative because excise taxes fell despite a relative decline in revenues from tariffs: had other events not offset the effect of excise policy, tariffs would have had to rise. The actual fall in the tariff rate was 0·286. The sum of the four isolated factors in the first column exceeds this figure and the sum in the second falls short of it because of the way the two techniques treat interactions among the factors. The significant point is that for either technique retrenchment (the fall in t) and the rise of imports relative to national income (the rise in m) accounts each by itself for around half of the sum, and the variables describing pure reform (r_e and r_i) for nearly none. The fifth and sixth rows confirm this impression: the changes in m and t together more than explain the 0·286 fall in the tariff from 1841 to 1881, while those in r_e and r_i together would have yielded a slight rise, not a fall, in the tariff.

As was noted above, of course, some of the rise in the import ratio is itself attributable to the fall in the tariff. But allowing for the endogeneity of the import ratio would merely reinforce the results: because the variables describing pure reform would imply a rise in the tariff, they evidently cannot account for a rise in the ratio of imports to national income (and even if they somehow could, their combined impact, including all the impact of the change in m, is considerably smaller than retrenchment alone, as line 7 of Table 8.5 shows). The fall in the ratio of all taxes to income, on the other hand, can account for the rise in m. Were the income elasticity of demand for imports about 1·0 and the price elasticity in or around the range 3 to 8 (depending on the experiment in Table 8.5 chosen as relevant) – not an impossibly high elasticity considering that many imports had close domestic substitutes and were a fairly small percentage of total domestic supply (wheat, for example, satisfies these conditions) – the fall in tariff permitted by retrenchment alone could explain, if necessary, all the rise in imports relative to income.

A deliberate policy of freer international trade, in short, was responsible for only a part – a small part, indeed – of the reduction in tariff rates. The accident of a higher ratio of imports to national income, itself only partly a consequence of British financial reform, accounts for much of the reduction, the triumph of the ideology of free trade for very little of it. The related ideology of retrenchment, expressed in a lower ratio of government expenditure to national income, appears at first to account for still more than the rise in imports, but even here historical accident, on closer examination, dominates the result. In 1841 56 percent of the government budget was spent in servicing the government debt accumulated from the struggle with Bonaparte; in 1881, despite the addition of debts from the Crimean War, only 36 percent. Government expenditures on goods and services, on the other hand, rose in step with national income. It was the success of a policy of balanced budgets – that is, the absence of British involvement in major wars, itself an accident from the point of view of financial policy – not a reduction of expenditure on collectively consumed goods in relation to national income that permitted the government to reduce taxes.

Keynes had in mind the doctrines of free traders, among others, when he wrote: 'the ideas of economists and political philosophers, both when they are right and when they are wrong, are more powerful than is commonly understood. Indeed the world is ruled by little else.' It is possible, however, to make the opposite error, and attribute to an idea such as Retrenchment and Reform results that are more properly attributed to the momentum of events. If free trade had substantial effects on the British economy, it was not so much by policy that it did, but by inadvertence.

IV THE EFFECTS ON INCOME

The effects on the British economy of the move to free trade from 1841 to 1881 can be divided into changes in the size of national income and changes in its distribution. Contemporary observers, and historians after them, have considered these to be the important issues: the one an issue of how much free trade increased British income as a whole, the other of how much it helped or hurt specific groups, landlords and laborers in particular. Both depend on how free trade affected the British terms of trade, for the only effect of altering a tariff is to alter the equilibrium terms of trade. The effect of the terms of trade on the distribution of national income will be considered briefly later; here the question is one of their effect on its size.

The simplest way to frame an answer to the question is to view the sector of an economy in which trade with other economies takes place as an industry gaining importable goods through the sacrifice of the resources embodied in exportable goods, just as the steel or clothing industries gain goods through the sacrifice of resources which could be employed elsewhere to produce other goods. The terms of trade are the productivity of this industry: if some external event such as an increase in foreign demand for British goods or the manipulation of a British tariff increases the terms of trade, more importables can be gained from any given sacrifice of exportables, just as technological improvement in steel allows more to be gained from any given sacrifice of alternative uses of the resources to make steel. Clearly, the more important the industry is in the economy, the more significant for the size of national income is a given increase in productivity. Because the increase saves resources whose value in alternative uses is the value of output, the relevant definition of an industry's 'importance' is the ratio of the value of its output to national income (and not, for example, the ratio of its value added to national income, or the strength of its links with the rest of the economy). In consequence, with imports at a quarter of British national income, a 10 percent improvement in the terms of trade through a change in the tariff would increase British national income by (¼) (10), or 2·5 percent.

An alternative way of looking at the effect of free trade on national income which has been popular among free traders and their historians is to focus not on improved British terms of trade but on larger British exports. Lower tariffs, it is argued, permitted more imports and therefore, from either the accounting identity between the two or from the rise in foreign incomes with greater purchases by Britain, more exports. And (although this step in the argument is seldom made explicit) more exports are desirable. As Peter Mathias puts it, summarizing a long tradition of reasoning on the issue (which may fairly be described, with no intent to belittle such reasoning in more appropriate contexts, as mercantilist):

> The great gains of free trade came from stabilizing wheat prices and developing steadier, rising food-import trades which . . . create[d] purchasing power abroad for British exports and fed a great increase in international trade in a generation when Britain was the pivot of the international economy. The main immediate gain from free trade thus became the increase in exports markets as imports to Britain expanded, not a fall in food prices.[9]

On one interpretation of this argument it confuses movements along a given demand curve with movements of the curve itself. Britain, to be sure, chose to trade at another point on the rest of the world's demand curve by abandoning tariffs. But the rest of the world's demand curve – or, to state the argument more completely, its offer curve – did not on this account move. On another interpretation of the argument it equates exports with income, which is legitimate only if British and other economies were operating always at less than full employment to the full extent of the increased exports. Since exports grew considerably faster than national income and unemployment was surely not increasing in the period (and was in any case low) this position is difficult to maintain. The neomercantilist approach to the issue, in short, is misleading.

The alternative, and sharper, weapon in the intellectual armory of the free traders was an appeal to the logic of comparative advantage. In 1820 Thomas Tooke, in his so-called 'Petition of the Merchants' to Parliament, the opening shot in the long postwar campaign to make free trade the policy of the nation, wrote: '[F]reedom from restraint is calculated to give the utmost extension to foreign trade, and the best direction to the capital and industry of the country . . . [A] policy founded on these principles would render the commerce of the world an interchange of mutual advantages.'[10] This passage and the many others like it in the subsequent outpouring of pamphlets and books on free trade contains an error in economic reasoning, the significance of which was not fully realized by economists until long after the debate on free trade closed. Tooke's argument is that free foreign trade is better than no trade at all, which is certainly correct. The argument is irrelevant, however, to the point at issue, namely, whether Britain was made better off by moving from *some* trade to *more* trade. The elimination of duties increased British demand for importables by enabling British consumers to buy at the true, low world price of importables in terms of other commodities. If British demand for importables was a nonnegligible portion of the world's demand (as, in fact, it was) the increase would raise the world price to a nonnegligible extent. That is to say, the terms of trade would turn against Britain. The deterioration of the terms of trade from the lowering of duties could be large enough to offset the advantage of more trade. In other words, it is not self-evident that it was wise policy to permit British consumers to buy or sell in foreign markets free of all encumbrances: free trade, by way of its adverse effect on the terms on which imports were purchased with exports, may have reduced British national income.

Economists will recognize this as the argument for an 'optimal tariff'. By analogy with the optimal behavior of a monopolist, a nation whose purchases and sales abroad have a discernible effect on world prices is well advised to restrict its purchases and sales to some degree. And, just as one can deduce from the elasticity of demand facing a monopolist the optimal extent of divergence between his marginal cost and the price he charges, one can deduce from the elasticities of British export demand and import supply the optimal British tariff, compare it with the tariffs actually in force and gauge the consequent loss, if any, of British income.

It is possible to create a presumption that British tariffs by 1881 were less than optimal and that, therefore, welfare was reduced by the move to free trade. A full demonstration would require an estimate of the elasticity of the foreign offer curve. Lacking such an estimate, one can nonetheless infer that it was low from the sheer bulk of British trade. By a familiar line of reasoning, for given elasticities of world demand for British exportables and of world supply of importables, the elasticities of excess demand and supply facing Britain would be lower the higher was the British share in world production of exportables and consumption of importables. In the limit, infinitesimal shares yield infinite elasticities, that is, given prices of imports and exports over which the country – a 'small country' in the jargon of trade theory – has no influence. The critical point is that nineteenth-century Britain was not in this sense a small country: in 1870, for example, when German and American industrialization was already well advanced, British exporters supplied about a ninth of the rest of the world's demand for manufactures.[11] The elasticity of demand facing British exporters, therefore, was likely to be low. With world elasticities of manufacturing demand and supply on the order of 1, to be sure, the implied elasticity is rather high: 17.[12] But in view of Britain's far larger shares of world output in the particular products in which she specialized – cotton textiles and iron, for example – this is surely an extreme upper bound. The elasticity of supply of imports into Britain was probably low, on the same grounds: for many imports – raw cotton, for example – the British share was high and the elasticity of world supply low.

The implication is that the optimal tariff was high. The standard formula for an optimal tariff is:

$$t = \frac{\frac{1}{\epsilon_m} + \frac{1}{\eta_x}}{1 - \frac{1}{\eta_x}}$$

in which t is the optimal tariff on imports, ϵ_m the elasticity of foreign supply of British importables (i.e. food and raw materials) and η_x the elasticity of foreign demand for British exportables (i.e. manufactures and mercantile services). The tariff of 0·058 in 1881 would be optimal only if the elasticities were impossibly higher than they in fact were. If ϵ_m and η_x were equal, for example, they would each have to be in excess of 35 (in absolute values, of course) to make the optimal tariff as low as 0·058. Britain, in other words, magnanimous in her midcentury conquest of the world's markets, gave back some portion of her booty by moving this far towards free trade.[13]

The conclusion is that free trade caused the British terms of trade to deteriorate, reducing national income. It might seem possible to rescue the prevalent notion that free trade was a Good Thing for Britain by pointing out that other countries followed the British example. As more countries become convinced (from a selfish point of view, irrationally) that tariffs should be reduced the demand and supply curves facing Britain would move out, improving the terms on which Britain exchanged cotton textiles for wheat. This pleasing prospect, however, has historical flaws. Well before free trade became the ruling ideology in Britain, Alexander Hamilton and Friedrich List had provided an opposing rationale for high duties, which their countrymen and others adopted with enthusiasm. The French and Prussian enchantment with free trade in midcentury was brief, and some important trading partners of Britain – most notably the United States – never came under the spell. If the British example was followed briefly, it was soon abandoned, leaving Britain in 1881, if not before, with the lowest duties in the world. In the 1930s Britain herself finally did abandon free trade, but by then, alas, the dominant position that would have enabled her over the preceding century to exploit the rest of the world was gone.

It must be understood, however, that to say that British income was reduced by the move to free trade is not to say that the reduction was large. The worst that the 0·21 fall in the rate of tariff could do would be to reduce the terms of trade by 21 percent. This is because at best (for Britain) foreigners would pay all the tariff imposed on British imports, accepting a 21 percent lower price for, say, wheat and timber in exchange for Britain's cloth and iron; the world price of Britain's imports would be 21 percent lower than it would be without the tariff; that is, the price of her exports relative to her imports would be 21 percent higher. Reverting to an earlier line of argument, then, the maximum percentage reduction in national income was the maximum percentage deterioration in the terms of trade occasioned by abandoning high tariffs (21 percent) multiplied by the share of the foreign trade 'industry' in national income (a fifth would here be a high estimate of the share, given the dependence of the share on the tariff), or 21 (1/5) = 4 percent of national income at most. This is not a trivial fall in national income, but neither is it a disaster. Neither the negative sign nor the small size of the result will be surprising to students of the theory of international trade. This, however, is the point: thinking in simple economic terms, one cannot attribute great significance to free trade as a cause of economic growth. It accompanied a political and intellectual upheaval in mid-Victorian Britain, but did not itself determine the wealth of Victoria's subjects.

V EXTENSIONS

Thinking in simple economic terms is not an infallible route to historical truth. Free trade had other, more complex economic effects, and these in turn could have been important in raising national income. For the present it will suffice to name them and to encourage others to give them deeper thought.

At bottom most of the secondary effects of free trade depend on induced changes in the composition of British output. There is little doubt that free trade reinforced a specialization in manufacturing at the expense of agriculture, although it may be surprising to learn that from 1841 to 1881 the share of domestic trade and transport in British production rose as much as did manufacturing, and that manufacturing itself rose only from 35 to 40 percent of production.[14] Whatever the magnitudes, in qualitative terms the changes in composition have potential effects on income as a whole. One could attempt to assemble evidence, for example, that manufacturing exhibited economies of scale that agriculture did not; or that the rate of technological advance in manufacturing was faster than in agriculture. Either of these would present the British economy with a gain in efficiency unattainable without a shift in the composition of output. But it would be necessary to show that the effects were in fact asymmetric between the export and import industries. Again, one could attempt to measure the extent of disequilibria in the British labor market at midcentury, locating pools of badly employed labor ready to move to higher wages in industries connected with exports. This, too, would raise efficiency. One would have to recognize, of course, that the pools might exist in export industries as well (coal comes to mind): again, asymmetry is essential to the argument. Or, still again, one could attempt to show that free trade altered the distribution of income in a way that raised the savings rate, and therefore the rate of growth of income. Here the chief difficulty would be that the savings rate did not rise; and a subsidiary one would be that it is at least uncertain that the distribution of income between savers and nonsavers changed in the four decades after 1841.

Such ruminations are enough, perhaps, to illustrate the difficulties in placing free trade at the center of mid-Victorian growth. In any case, the purpose here has been to loosen free trade from its traditional historical moorings. Its moorings to the ideology of Reform has been shown to be weak: reductions in tariffs were in good part due to a shrinking government budget and to an expanding volume of trade, not merely to the powerful arguments of Cobden, Bright and their manufacturing allies. Its moorings to the mid-Victorian boom is weaker still:[15] free trade did not cause British growth; indeed, it may have retarded it. The moorings loosened, then, let the ship set sail.

NOTES

1 Speech of 15 January 1846 in Free Trade Hall, Manchester, printed in F. W. Hirst, *Free Trade and Other Fundamental Doctrines of the Manchester School* (London, 1903), p. 229.

2 'Free Trade', *Encyclopedia Britannica*, 11th edn (New York, 1910–11).

3 F. W. Maitland, 'English Law', *Encyclopedia Britannica*, 11th edn (New York, 1910–11).

4 In the *Edinburgh Review*, January 1820, p. 77, quoted in Sydney Buxton, *Finance and Politics; An Historical Study* (London, 1888), Vol. 1, p. 20.

5 S. C. on Import Duties (1840), *Report*, p. iv. Sir Henry Parnell (Lord Congleton), a member of the committee of 1840, had made a similar calculation ten years before in his influential book, *Financial Reform* (London, 1830, p. 114 of 3rd edition of 1831), with similar results: in 1827 eighteen of 566 articles produced 89 percent of the revenue. He argued that 'The effect . . . is to render the accounts complex, and to generate smugglers. Prices are enhanced with little or no advantage to the revenue . . . [T]he saving of expense in management would, in all probability, be greater than the revenue . . . which would be lost by repealing [the 510 duties with low yields]' (p. 115).

6 The retrospective study of *Customs Tariffs of the United Kingdom from 1800 to 1897*, S.P. 1898 LXXXV (c. 8706) gives the complete tariff schedule. The schedule in effect from 1833–4 to 1841–2 takes up 100 large pages in this volume, that from 1876–7 to 1885–6 ten pages.

7 Calculated from the Trade and Navigation Accounts for 1891, S.P. 1890–1 LXXXI. Corn of all sorts was 14 percent of the value of imports – this after the disasters that befell British agriculture in the 1870s and 1880s: it is not wise to construe 'Free Trade' as 'the fall of the Corn Laws'.

8 *Economic Elements in the 'Pax Britannica'* (Cambridge, Mass., 1958), p. 121.

9 P. Mathias, *The First Industrial Nation: An Economic History of Britain 1700–1914* (London, 1969), pp. 302ff. Compare Imlah, *Economic Elements*, p. 144, where the assumption of less-than-full employment lies just below the surface. It is made explicit in R. C. O. Matthews, *A Study in Trade Cycle-History: Economic Fluctuations in Great Britain, 1833–1842* (Cambridge, 1954), *passim*; p. 78, for example. But his is a study of trade cycles, not of secular trends, and for his purposes the neomercantilist reasoning has the usual Keynesian justification. It is startling to find free traders in the early nineteenth century, sworn foes of

mercantilism, putting forward with no sense of the incongruity involved mercantilists' arguments for free trade.

10 Hirst, *Free Trade*, p. 118.

11 Britain produced a third of world manufacturing output in 1870 (inferred from League of Nations Secretariat, Economic, Financial and Transit Department [Folke Hilgerdt], *Industrialization and Foreign Trade*, Geneva, 1945, pp. 128, 138–40). She regularly exported a quarter of her manufacturing output (inferred from the ratio of W. Schlote's estimate of manufacturing exports, *British Overseas Trade from 1700 to the 1930s*, trans. from 1938 German edition by W. O. Henderson and W. H. Chaloner, Oxford, 1952, to manufacturing output at the time of the first British census of industry (1907) checked against the Hoffmann index of industrial output and the Imlah index of commodity exports). Thus, Britain consumed herself 3/12 (=(3/4) (1/3)) of total world demand for manufactures, and supplied one-ninth of the rest of the world's demand ((1 − 3/12)÷(1/4) (1/3)). By similar reasoning, British exports were an eighth of the rest of the world's supply of manufactures.

12 The excess demand for British exportables by the rest of the world (ED_B: that is, British exports) is equal to the demand in the rest of the world (D_R) minus the supply (S_R). Therefore, by the usual argument,

$$\frac{D_R}{ED_B}\epsilon^{D}_{R} - \frac{S_R}{ED_B}\epsilon^{S}_{R} = \epsilon^{ED}_{B}$$

Inserting the shares developed in the previous footnote,

$$\epsilon^{D}_{R} = 1, \text{ and } \epsilon^{S}_{R} = 1$$

yields $9(-1) - 8(1) = -17$.

13 The tariff Britain should have imposed, on this reasoning, is not the issue here, though interesting in itself. The 34 percent tariff of 1841 is not impossibly high: with equal elasticities the elasticities would need only to be as low as 6·8, well above levels estimated recently for countries with a much looser grip on their markets than Britain had in 1881, not to speak of 1841.

14 Phyllis Deane and W. A. Cole, *British Economic Growth 1688–1959* (Cambridge, 1964), p. 166, removing income from foreign investment.

15 A perspicacious discussion with a similar theme but from another perspective is contained in R. A. Church, *The Great Victorian Boom 1850–1873* (London, 1975), pp. 59–65.

9

Britain's Loss from Foreign Industrialization: A Provisional Estimate

It is pardonable to use an occasional metaphorical flourish to elevate the commonplaces and simplify the complexities of economic history. The danger, however, is that the flourish will become an obstruction rather than an aid to thought. A case in point is the set of assertions made explicitly by many scholars and reaffirmed by the very mass of the literature on Britain's international economic relations in the nineteenth century, that British income 'depended' on foreign trade, that trade was 'crucial', or that it was 'of central importance' to the economy. William Ashworth, for example, asserts that 'Britain's livelihood depended on international trade and the performance of international services',[1] and Phyllis Deane and W. A. Cole state that 'by the end of the nineteenth century the British economy was heavily dependent on world markets, and the rate and pattern of British economic growth was largely conditioned by the response of producers and consumers in the rest of the world'.[2] The difficulty is that these metaphors of dependence have attached to them no clear literal meaning, or at best none that does justice to their connotations. The primary piece of evidence for the importance of trade, for example, is the high ratio of exports to national income – typically 0·20 from 1870 to 1913 for domestic commodity exports alone and 0·27 including net exports of invisibles – and the ratio is often used as an implicit definition of importance. This somewhat casual attempt at giving concrete meaning to the metaphor of 'dependence', however, is not very successful. It cannot mean that income falls in proportion as exports fall, for this is unlikely to be the case, except in the very short run. Nor can it mean that any sector of this size is considered to be just as important. Domestic service employed many more men and women than all textiles and mining combined in the late nineteenth century and

I should like to thank Stanley Engerman of the University of Rochester and the members of seminars at McGill University and the University of Illinois, for their helpful comments on earlier drafts of this paper.

its gross value of output was probably larger than the value of exports of textiles and coal, yet few would say that it was 'crucial' or that with a decline in the demand for butlers and nannies 'Britain could no longer hope to depend on the demand for domestic service as she had in the past.'

The natural response to this criticism is that great changes were occurring in the export markets for textiles and coal in the late nineteenth century, but not in the markets for domestic service; it is the combination of these changes with the export sector's large size that make it important. Again, however, the discussion has been dominated by metaphor. The most significant of the changes, it is said, was the rise of new industrial powers, especially Germany and the United States, who broke the British monopoly of trade in manufactures. In response to the apparent failure of free trade to meet the new challenge to Britain, there arose a body of fair trade opinion, with a bellicose vocabulary of commercial 'peril', 'struggle', 'invasion' and 'conquest'. The issue of what policy to take towards the new industrial competition was one of the most heated in British politics, and the violence of the metaphors is therefore not surprising. Edwin Cannan, a partisan in the debate, expressed his scorn for the violent fair trade vocabulary in the following violent words:

> In regard to international relations, the first business of the teacher of economic theory is to tear to pieces and trample upon the misleading military metaphors which have been applied by sciolists to the peaceful exchange of commodities. We hear much, for example, in these days of 'England's commercial supremacy', and of other nations 'challenging' it, and how it is our duty to 'repel the attack', and so on. The economist asks 'what is commercial supremacy?' and there is no answer.[3]

Notwithstanding Cannan's just rage, however, the military metaphors of the fair traders have been adopted by many historians, among them R. J. S. Hoffman in his pioneering study *Great Britain and the German Trade Rivalry, 1875–1914.* He describes the 1870s, for example, in the following terms:

> Competition of a threatening character from the European Continent and America had not yet begun to make itself felt, for the new industrialism beyond England was still in comparative infancy [and tariffs were low]. . . . Great Britain stood out in the early seventies, perhaps more conspicuously than ever before, as the supreme commerial power of the world. Never again was this position to be so removed from challenge, for [by the end of the seventies] . . . there were clearly in operation all of the great factors which ultimately

pulled Britain down from her high estate of trade supremacy and forced her to fight for her life in a new economic world.[4]

Hoffman's belief in the foreign threat to Britain's welfare is not peculiar to him: in less emphatic form, it has become part of the accepted view of Britain's prospects in the late nineteenth century.

If the metaphors of Britain being 'defeated' in a trade on which she was 'dependent' are taken seriously, the deduction is that Britain should have collapsed, which she did not. To resolve this contradiction, which is inherent in the prevailing interpretation of Britain's mid-century monopoly of manufacturing trade and its subsequent dissolution, it appears that one or both of the metaphors must be abandoned.

The meaning of Britain's 'defeat' in international trade seems plain enough: Britain's share in world manufacturing exports fell dramatically from 1870 to 1913, as first Germany and then the United States expanded into markets beyond their borders. According to Folke Hilgerdt's *Industrialization and Foreign Trade*, the first comprehensive work on the statistics of world trade and manufacturing, Britain's share of trade in manufactures fell from about 38 percent in the late 1870s to about 27 percent in 1913.[5] A. Maizels and H. Tyszynski tell the same story and make the further point that this loss of trade was primarily a fall in Britain's share of each market rather than an unfavorable shift of the composition of markets by location or product. Maizels, for example, estimates that from 1899 to 1914 Britain lost £360 million in annual manufacturing exports on account of competition in each market, a loss of about 18 percent of the actual value of her manufacturing exports in 1913, while Germany gained £330 million.[6] The economic meaning of this arithmetic is that the supply curve of manufactures in the rest of the world was moving out faster than in Great Britain during the late nineteenth century. That is, the fall in Britain's share of exports was indeed a result of the industrialization of other countries: larger output of manufactures elsewhere – a loss of manufacturing 'supremacy' – reduced British exports below what they would otherwise have been.

Giving a precise meaning to Britain's defeat in exports, then, requires an estimate of 'what they would otherwise have been'. Industrialization of Britain's competitors amounted to an increase in their supply of manufactures, so that removing the effect of industrialization on Britain's export trade in 1913 would require a hypothetical reduction in the supply of the rest of the world. If the demand for manufactures by the rest of the world, to take one extreme, was in no way related to its supply, the excess demand for manufactures by the rest of the world – that is, the rest of the world's imports of manufactures from Britain – would increase by the full amount of the hypothetical decrease in the rest of the world's supply. A diagram putting the demand and supply systems of Britain and the rest of the world in 1913 back to back illustrates this case (see Figure 9.1). The supply curve of

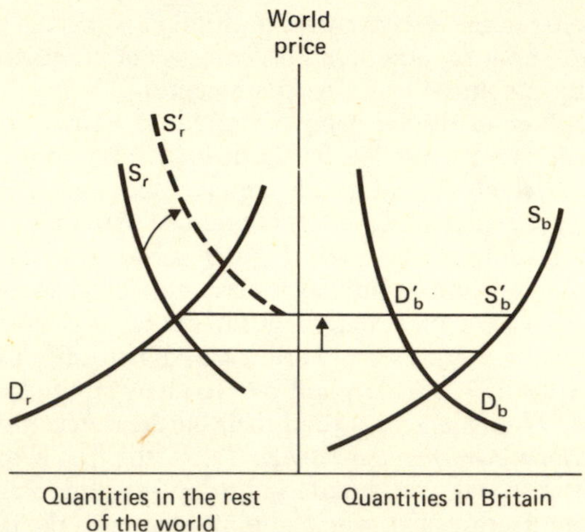

Figure 9.1 *Deindustrialization without an induced change in demand*

the rest of the world is reduced without industrialization, but the demand curve is taken to be unchanged. Given constant and known elasticities for the curves, the new equilibrium exports from Britain, $D'_bS'_b$, can be estimated by reducing the rest of the world's supply curve until it yields the share of total output of 1870. The essential feature of the solution at this extreme is that Britain's share of manufacturing output, not exports, is increased to its level of 1870 to find the hypothetical exports in 1913.

The demand for manufactures, of course, would not be as high without as it was with industrialization in the rest of the world, both because a substantial portion of the demand for manufactures is for manufactured investment and intermediate goods and because the lower level of income without industrialization would reduce the demand for manufactured consumers' goods. Assuming that *all* the increase in the demand for manufactures in industrializing countries was a result of industrialization, Britain's hypothetical exports in 1913 could be estimated by extrapolating her 1870 share of *exports* (rather than output, as above) to 1913. If demand as well as supply is presumed to grow more slowly without industrialization, in other words, the excess supply (exports) rather than the total supply (output) of Britain will remain in its 1870 relation to the rest of the world. In terms of the diagram, in this case the demand curve as well as the supply curve is reduced (see Figure 9.2). The measure of export losses from industrialization based on the British share of world *exports* assumes

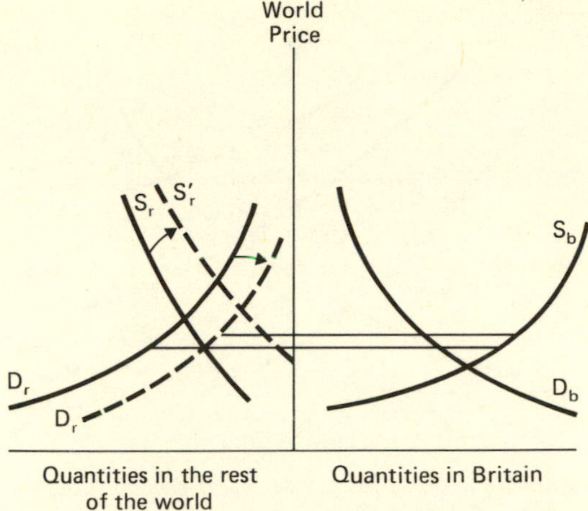

Figure 9.2 *Deindustrialization with an induced change in demand*

that all the growth in demand was induced, and the measure based on the share in world *output* assumes that none of it was induced. In short, the fall in Britain's share of world exports and world output of manufactures – the statistical counterparts of her 'defeat' in exports and her 'loss of supremacy' in output – yields bounds on the loss of manufacturing exports due to competing industrialization.

It is less easy to give a concrete interpretation of the metaphor of Britain's 'dependence' on these manufacturing exports. The extensive literature on industrialization and manufacturing trade has astonishingly little to say about the significance to the countries involved of the quantities of exports lost or gained. The sheer size of Britain's lost exports, which range from 35 to 350 percent of actual exports in 1913 depending on which method of estimation is used, might seem to be sufficient evidence that competing industrialization was an important influence on British welfare. Only if the resources used in making exports have no alternative employment, however, would the full value of the lost exports have been equal to the lost national income. That is, the lost exports would have been the lost income only if the British economy from 1870 to 1913 was always far below full employment, which is very difficult to believe.[7]

Given full employment, a fall in the demand for exports would have reduced national income by the fall in British producers' surplus, that is, by the loss in total export revenue minus the sum of the value in alternative uses of the freed resources and the value of consumers' surplus gained from the lower price of exportables (which is merely a transfer from British producers to British consumers). In other words, the rent that Britain could extract from the rest of the world would have

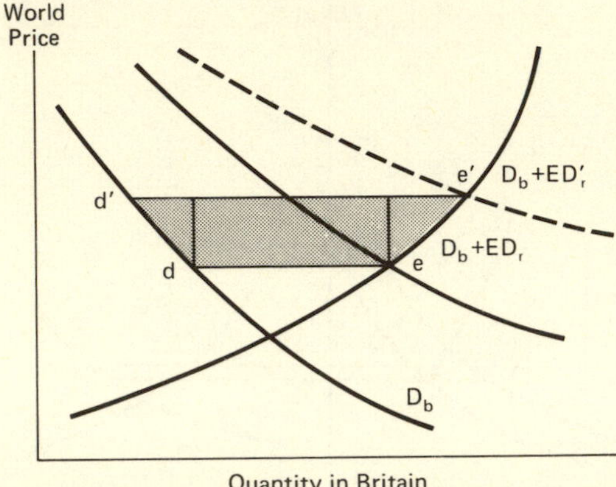

Figure 9.3 *Britain's loss from the fall in export demand from industrialization elsewhere*

fallen. In Figure 9.3, the sum of the British demand for her own exportables (D_b) and the rest of the world's excess demand (ED_r) is reduced by industrialization from its hypothetical position ($D_b + ED'_r$) to its actual position ($D_b + ED_r$), reducing British national income by the area dd′ee′. That area measures the loss to Britain from the industrialization of the rest of the world.

The question, then, is how large this loss was to Britain. The striking feature of the answer – striking in view of the widespread belief that Britain's welfare depended critically on foreign trade – is that the loss appears to have been small. To show that Britain's national income was on all accounts little affected by the industrialization of the rest of the world would be a formidable task, and it would be unwise to make sweeping statements about the results of such a rearrangement of the world as the nonindustrialization of the United States and Germany. For the limited range of connections between industrialization and Britain's income considered here, however, the results do appear to have been surprisingly small.

To show this it is convenient to recast the geometry of the above model in algebra. There are two equations, one summarizing the normative argument of how the rent lost is related to the income lost and the second the behavioral argument of how the new equilibrium is related to the old. The first gives the approximately trapezoidal area of loss dd′ee′ in Figure 9.3 above as a function of the elasticities of demand and supply in Britain, the quantities of exportables demanded and supplied in 1913, and the percentage change in the world price resulting from a hypothetical deindustrialization of the rest of the world in 1913 (a bar over a variable, as over *P* here, will signify the percentage change in the variable between its actual and hypothetical value):

$$(1)\quad dd'ee' = \tfrac{1}{2}\bar{P}(D_d\epsilon\bar{P}) + \bar{P}(S_b - D_b) + \tfrac{1}{2}\bar{P}(S_b\eta\bar{P})$$

It is assumed here that the demand for manufactured exportables can be represented by the constant-elasticity form $Q_d = D_b P^{-\epsilon}$, where ϵ is the elasticity of demand, and the supply by $Q_s = S_b P^{\eta}$, where η is the elasticity of supply. One million pounds worth of exportables in 1913 is taken as the unit, so that its price in 1913 is 1 and the parameters D_b and S_b are simply the values of exportables consumed and produced in 1913. The equation breaks the trapezoid into a middle rectangle $\bar{P}(S_b - D_b)$, representing the increased value of the old excess supply (that is, old exports) and two side triangles representing the increased value of the new exports. Its substance is merely that the increase in rents accruing to Britain will be larger the larger is the increase in price from the hypothetical deindustrialization elsewhere.

The second equation, giving the increase in price sufficient to reestablish equilibrium after deindustrialization, is derived from the equilibrium condition in the world market for manufactures that the excess supply of the manufacturing nations other than Britain $(S_g P^{\eta'} - D_g P^{-\epsilon'})$ plus Britain's excess supply must equal the demand of the rest of the world $(D_r P^{-\epsilon''})$:

$$(S_g P^{\eta'} - D_g P^{-\epsilon'}) = D_r P^{-\epsilon''}$$

The other manufacturing countries (primarily Germany and the United States) are separated from world demand for British exports in order to exhibit the effects of their deindustrialization on the export transactions of the world. For the purposes of the rough approximations desired here, the elasticities may be assumed to be the same in each part of the world. In that case, the equation can be rewritten:

$$P = \left(\frac{S_b + S_g}{D_b + D_g + D_r}\right)^{-[1/(\epsilon+\eta)]}$$

As was argued earlier, the hypothetical deindustrialization involves a reduction in the foreigners' supply curve of manufactures and, to some extent, an induced reduction in their demand curve. If the percentage reduction of the demand curve, $\bar{D}_g$, is a certain proportion, δ, of the percentage reduction of the supply curve, S_g, then the rate of change of price necessary to reestablish equilibrium will be, taking the proportional derivative of the last expression:

$$(2)\quad \bar{P} = -\left(\frac{1}{\epsilon+\eta}\right)\left[\frac{S_g - \delta D_g}{S_b - S_g}\right]\bar{S}_g$$

The elasticities ϵ and η appear because the higher they are, the less need the world price change to reestablish equilibrium after a disturbance to supply. The term in square brackets merely shows the weight with which the reduction of supply in the industrializing countries ($\overline{S}_g$) affects supply as a whole. If none of the demand for manufactures would have been reduced along with the supply, then δ equals zero and the weight is the share of these countries in world manufacturing output; if the demand would have been reduced in proportion, δ equals one and the weight is the share of their exports alone in output.

Equations (1) and (2) depend on the following variables, arranged in increasing difficulty of empirical estimation:

- S_b Britain's output of manufactures in 1913 (£1,520 million)
- D_b Britain's consumption of home-produced manufactures in 1913 (£1,120 million)
- S_g Other manufacturing countries' output of manufactures in 1913 (£9,300 million)
- D_g Other manufacturing countries' consumption of home-produced manufactures in 1913 (£8,200 million)
- $\overline{S}_g$ Proportional change of S_g necessary to reduce its share in world output to its level in 1870 (100 percent)
- ϵ Elasticity of demand for manufactures with respect to price
- η Elasticity of supply of manufactures with respect to price
- δ Elasticity of D_g with respect to S_g

The estimation of the British supply of manufactures in 1913 (S_b) presents no serious problems, since the results of Britain's Census of Production in 1907 can be extrapolated with little danger of error to 1913. The appropriate definition of 'output' is output with the same degree of duplication by stages of production as in the export statistics. For most industries the estimate made by the census of gross output excluding sales within the industry itself is appropriate, yielding a total of £1,140 million for the manufacturing portion of industry as a whole.[8] Making an ample allowance of £100 million for the output of semifinished items that were important exports, such as cotton yarn, and extrapolating the result to 1913 gives a value of S_b in 1913 of £1,520 million.[9] The corresponding value of consumption of home-produced manufacturing output, D_b, is simply output minus exports of £397 million,[10] or £1,120 million.

For the rest of the world's output of manufactures (S_g) one must rely on Hilgerdt's index. Representing world output in 1925–9 (the base years for the index) by 100 units, his index implies that British output in 1913 was 10·4 units and the rest of the world's output 63·5.[11] Consequently, the value of the rest of the world's output in British prices (S_g), given that 10·4 units correspond to an S_b of £1,520 million, was £9,300 million. The exports of the rest of the world were £1,100 million in 1913,[12] leaving consumption of home-produced manufactures in the industrializing countries (D_g) of £8,200 million.

One need go only this far in the exercise to see that the impact of the industrialization of Germany alone was very small, a notable result in view of the contemporary alarm over Germany's rise. The reason is that Germany produced only 12·5 percent of world manufacturing output in 1913: reducing Germany's share to its level before she industrialized – a retrospective Morgenthau plan, as it were – would reduce world supply very little and therefore raise British export prices very little. Had German manufacturing output per capita remained at its level of 1870, the percentage reduction in the non-British output in 1913 ($\overline{S}_g$) would have been about 13 percent[13] and, making strong assumptions to bias the estimate upward that ϵ and η were 1 and δ was 0, the rise in world prices would have been only 0·8 percent. National income would have been only £4 million above its actual level of £2,260 million in 1913. The threat of German industrialization was apparently political, not economic.

To make a similar argument about the industrialization of other countries in addition to Germany, especially the United States, requires stronger yet plausible assumptions about the parameters ϵ, η and δ. The elasticity of demand, ϵ, was probably greater than 1 in absolute value in view of the high income elasticity and importance in total consumption of manufactured goods. The elasticity of supply is less certain, but some crude visual estimates, in lieu of a full econometric study of the matter, suggest that it was high. This is reasonable because throughout the period well over half of manufacturing exports were textiles, which used imported raw materials and ubiquitous skills: the very fact that Britain's competitors found her textile production easy to imitate suggests that there were few limitations of supply on its long-term expansion. In these circumstances, an elasticity of 3 is probably low. The last parameter, the elasticity of manufacturing demand with respect to a shift in supply (δ), surely lies between zero and one, but where exactly is difficult to say. It is probably much above zero, for both higher income and derived demand would raise demand as supply rose; indeed, the work of Hilgerdt and Maizels can be interpreted as an attempt to show that δ was high. A value of δ above 0·5 is perhaps reasonable.

Using these rough estimates of lower bounds on the elasticities in the price equation gives an estimate of $\overline{P}$ of about 12 percent and an estimate of the increase in 1913 income of about £88 million, or 3·9 percent of national income. In view of the uncertainty surrounding the value of η and δ it is useful to consider a range of both, as in Table 9.1 (assuming ϵ equals 1·0). For reasonable values of η and δ, the result is

Table 9.1 *Percentage of British national income gained in 1913*

		δ, Elasticity of non-British demand for manufactures with respect to non-British supply				
		0	*0·1*	*0·5*	*0·7*	*1·0*
η,	1	19	16	7·6	4·4	1·0
Elasticity	2	13	11	5·2	3·0	0·7
of supply	3	9·5	8·2	3·9	2·3	0·5
of British	4	7·8	6·5	3·1	1·8	0·4
manufactures	5	6·4	5·6	2·7	1·5	0·3

Source: Equations (1) and (2), with values discussed in text.

the same: the gain of income from deindustrializing the rest of the world in 1913 would have been remarkably small.

The limitations on the result are clear enough that there is no need to examine them in detail on this occasion. The model is a partial equilibrium one; Britain's gain in the alternative world from cheaper imports of agricultural goods, as well as her loss from more expensive manufactured imports and cheaper coal exports, is suppressed; the estimates of the elasticities could be much improved; and redistributive and transitional effects are ignored. Nonetheless, the exercise points to an important moral, namely, that the attention lavished on the trade sector and especially on foreign competition in that sector as a 'determinant' of British income does not appear to be warranted by the facts. The late nineteenth century was the time of the greatest development of the international economy, with Britain – the world's banker, the world's shipper and, less than before, the world's manufacturer – at its center. The inference that Britain was therefore dependent on even substantial changes in the character of the international economy, however, is doubtful. If the argument made here is even approximately true, another view is more tenable: if we must use metaphors, Britain's income 'depended' not on the great changes in the international economy of the late nineteenth century, but on the pace of technological change and enterprise at home.

NOTES

1 *An Economic History of England, 1870–1939* (London: Methuen, 1960), p. 256.
2 *British Economic Growth, 1688–1959* (Cambridge: Cambridge University Press, 1962), p. 28.
3 'The practical utility of economic science', *Economic Journal*, 12 (1902), p. 470.
4 *Great Britain and the German Trade Rivalry* (Philadelphia: University of Pennsylvania Press, 1933), pp. 5ff.
5 *Industrialization and Foreign Trade* (Geneva: League of Nations Secretariat, Economic, Financial and Transit Department, 1945), pp. 157ff.
6 A. Maizels, *Industrial Growth and World Trade* (Cambridge: Cambridge University

Press, 1963), p. 200. Cf. H. Tyszynski, 'World trade in manufactured commodities, 1899–1950', *Manchester School,* 19 (September 1951), pp. 272–304.

7 I have examined this question more closely in another paper, 'Did Victorian Britain fail?' *Economic History Review,* forthcoming, December 1970.

8 The *Final Report* of the census gives an estimate of these nonduplicative outputs in the introduction to each industry's statistics. I have added them together, excluding the Mining, Utilities, Building and Gas Industries (UK Board of Trade, *Final Report on the First Census of Production of the U.K.* [*1907*], London: HMSO, 1912, *passim*). The classification of industries, by the way, was chosen by the designers of the census to reflect the export list. W. Schlote, however, whose estimates of exports are used here, used the Brussels Register classification (*British Overseas Trade from 1700 to the 1930s,* trans. W. O. Henderson and W. H. Chaloner, Oxford: Oxford University Press, 1952).

9 The extrapolation uses the Hoffman index of industrial production excluding building and Schlote's price index of exports of manufactured goods (Schlote, p. 177) to estimate the 1913 value of output from 1907.

10 From Schlote, p. 126. Hilgerdt's estimate is £417 million, *Industrialization and Foreign Trade,* p. 158.

11 Hilgerdt, pp. 128, 140. His weights for 1925–9 are, unfortunately, value added weights.

12 Hilgerdt, pp. 157ff.: world exports minus UK exports.

13 This is a percentage change which uses the midpoint of the new and old value as the base, as will all subsequent percentage changes. The 1870 and 1913 German outputs are derived from Hilgerdt, pp. 128, 138ff.

10

How the Gold Standard Worked, 1880–1913

DONALD N. McCLOSKEY
and J. RICHARD ZECHER

I THE MONETARY THEORY AND ITS IMPLICATIONS FOR THE GOLD STANDARD

Each intellectual generation since the mercantilists has revised or refined the understanding of how the balance of payments is kept in equilibrium under a system of fixed exchange rates, and all these understandings find a place in the historical literature on the gold standard of the late nineteenth century. It is difficult, therefore, to locate the orthodox view on how the gold standard worked, for it is many views. If one can find historical and economic writings describing the gold standard (and other systems of fixed exchange rates) in the manner of Hume, as a price–specie–flow mechanism, involving changes in the level of prices, one can also find writings describing it in the manner of Marshall, involving changes in the interest rate, or of Taussig, involving changes in the relative price of exportables and importables, or of Ohlin, involving changes in income. The theoretical jumble is made still more confusing by a number of factual anomalies uncovered lately.[1] Among other difficulties with the orthodox views, it has been found that the gold standard, even in its heyday, was a standard involving the major currencies as well as gold itself, and that few, if any, central banks followed the putative 'rules of the game'.

This essay reinterprets the gold standard by applying the monetary theory of the balance of payments to the experience of the two most important countries on it, America and Britain. Before explaining, testing and using the theory in detail, it will be useful to indicate a few of the ways in which accepting it will change the interpretation of the

An earlier and longer version of this essay (available on request) was presented to the Workshop in Economic History at the University of Chicago and to the Cliometrics Conference at the University of Wisconsin. We wish to thank the participants in these meetings for their comments. The friendly skepticism of Moses Abramovitz, C. K. Harley, Hugh Rockoff, Jeffrey Williamson and our colleagues at the University of Chicago, among them Stanley Fischer, Robert J. Gordon, A. C. Harberger, Harry G. Johnson, Arthur Laffer and H. Gregg Lewis, contributed to a sharpening of the argument.

gold standard of the late nineteenth century. The most direct implication is that central bankers did not have control over the variables over which they and their historians have believed they had control. The theory assumes that interest rates and prices are determined on world markets, and therefore that the central bank of a small country has little influence over them and the central bank of a large country has influence over them only by way of its influence over the world as a whole.

A case in point is the Bank of England. It is often asserted, as Keynes put it, that 'During the latter half of the nineteenth century the influence of London on credit conditions throughout the world was so predominant that the Bank of England could almost have claimed to be the conductor of the international orchestra. By modifying the terms on which she was prepared to lend, aided by her own readiness to vary the volume of her gold reserves and the unreadiness of other central banks to vary the volumes of theirs, she could to a large extent determine the credit conditions prevailing elsewhere.'[2] When this musical metaphor is examined in the light of the monetary theory it loses much of its charm. If it is supposed, as in the monetary theory, that the world's economy was unified by arbitrage, and if it is supposed further that the level of prices in the world market was determined, other things equal, by the amount of money existing in the world, it follows that the Bank's potential influence on prices (and perhaps through prices on interest rates) depended simply on its power to accumulate or disburse gold and other reserves available to support the world's supply of money. By raising the interest rate (the bank rate) at which it would lend to brokers of commercial bills, the Bank could induce the brokers or whoever else in the British capital market was caught short of funds to seek loans abroad, bringing gold into the country and eventually into the vaults of the Bank. If it merely issued bank notes to pay for the gold the reserves available to support the supply of money would be unchanged, for Bank of England notes were used both at home and abroad as reserves. Only by decreasing the securities and increasing the gold, it held – an automatic result when it discouraged brokers from selling more bills to the Bank and allowed the bills it already held to come to maturity – could the Bank exert a net effect on the world's reserves. In other words, a rise in the bank rate was effective only to the extent that it was accompanied by an open market operation, that is, by a shift in the assets of the Bank of England out of securities and into gold. The amounts of these two assets held by the Bank, then, provide extreme limits on the influence of the Bank on the world's money supply. Had the Bank in 1913 sold off all the securities held in its banking department it would have decreased world reserves by only 0·6 percent; had it sold off all the gold in its issue department, it would have increased world reserves by only 0·5 percent.[3] Apparently the

Bank was no more than the second violinist, not to say the triangle player, in the world's orchestra. The result hinges on the assumption of the monetary theory that the world's economy was unified, much as each nation's economy is assumed to be in any theory of the gold standard. If the assumption is correct the historical inference is that the Bank of England had no more independent influence over the prices and interest rates it faced than, say, the First National Bank of Chicago has over the prices and interest rates it faces, and for the same reason.

A related inference from the monetary theory is that the United Kingdom, the United States, and other countries on the gold standard had little influence over their money supplies. Since money, like other commodities, could be imported and exported, the supply of money in a country could adjust to its demand and the demand would depend on the country's income and on prices and interest rates determined in the world market. The creation of money in a little country would have little influence on these determinants of demand and in consequence little influence over the amount actually supplied. How 'little' America and Britain were depends on how large they were relative to the world market, and in a world of full employment and well-functioning markets the relevant magnitude is simply the share of the nation's supply of money in the world's supply. One must depend on an assumption that the money owned by citizens of a country was in rough proportion to its income, for the historical study of the world's money supply is still in its infancy.[4] In 1913 America and Britain together earned about 40 percent of the world's income, America alone 27 percent.[5] A rise in the American money supply of 10 percent, then, would raise the world's money supply on the order of 2·7 percent; the comparable British figure is half the American. Clearly, in the jargon of international economics, America and Britain were not literally 'small countries'. Yet 2·7 percent is far from the 10 percent implied by the usual model, that of a closed monetary system, and the British figure is far enough from it to make it unnecessary for most purposes in dealing with the British experience to look closely into the worldwide impact of British policy.

Finally, the monetary theory implies that it matters little whether or not central banks under the gold standard played conscientiously the 'rules of the game', that is, the rule that a deficit in the balance of payments should be accompanied be domestic policies to deflate the economy. The theory argues that neither gold flows nor domestic deflation have effects on prevailing prices, interest rates and incomes. The inconsequentiality of the rules of the game may perhaps explain why they were ignored by most central bankers in the period of the gold standard, in deed if not in words, with no dire effects on the stability of the system.

II EMPIRICAL ANOMALIES IN THE LITERATURE ON THE GOLD STANDARD

If the orthodox theories of the gold standard are incorrect, it should be possible to observe signs of strain in the literature when they are applied to the experience of the late nineteenth century. This is the case. Indeed, in the midst of their difficulties in applying the theories earlier observers have anticipated most of the elements of the alternative theory proposed here.

On the broadest level it has always been puzzling that the gold standard in its prime worked so smoothly. After all, the mechanism described by Hume, in which an initial divergence in price levels was to be corrected by flows of gold inducing a return to parity, might be expected to work fairly slowly, requiring alterations in the money supply and, more important, in expectations concerning the level and rate of change of prices which would have been difficult to achieve. The actual flows of gold in the late nineteenth century, furthermore, appear to be too small to play the large role assigned to them.[6] Of course, one should ask, 'Too small relative to what?' Gold was a substantial part of the monetary base, and one could rescue the argument by positing, as Milton Friedman and Anna Schwartz have done in their classic study of American monetary history, a close causal connection between the monetary base ('high-powered money' in their terminology) on the one hand and money and the price level on the other. This is an attractive argument for the United Kingdom, as might be expected for a country with nearly 100 percent gold reserves against its currency and with no gold mines. For the United States, however, it is considerably less attractive. Only half of the variations in the American stock of high-powered money from 1880 to 1913 can be explained directly by gold flows, and other national moneys with a less mechanical connection to external flows of gold than the British, such as the French and German, could be expected to have a similar record.[7] Most observers, perhaps anticipating these results, have emphasised the function of gold flows as a mere signal to central bankers to contract or expand their economies. If central bankers did play the rules of the game, reacting to a small outflow of gold by reducing the monetary base still further, a small flow of gold could, of course, have large effects, at any rate if one believes the orthodox theories. To repeat, however, central bankers often did not play the rules: the Bank of France and the National Bank of Belgium, for example, kept their discount rates low regardless of gold flows.[8] An alternative indicator of the extent to which central bankers played the rules is the extent to which the relationship between inflows of gold and increases in domestic credit (that is, increases in the portion of the money supply determined by factors other than the inflow of gold) was positive. Once again, the indications are that in the late nineteenth century the monetary authorities, in this case American and British, cheated: the correlation between gold flows and annual changes in domestic credit was −0·07 in the United States and −0·74 in the United Kingdom.[9]

Yet the gold standard, it is said, worked quickly and well. The exchange rate between sterling and dollars, among many other rates, remained virtually unchanged from January 1879, when the United States put itself back on gold, to August 1914, when the war put the United Kingdom effectively off it. Nobody ran out of gold. And over this third of a century the restrictions on flows of gold, commodities, immigrants and capital that were in the eighteenth century and have become again in the twentieth such popular instruments of government policy either were not used (for gold, immigrants and capital) or were used for purposes other than correcting deficits in the balance of payments (for commodities). In view of its strange efficacy central bankers may be forgiven for looking back on the gold standard of the late nineteenth century with the pious awe usually reserved for religious mysteries.

The mystery of the smooth working of the gold standard fades if the central postulate of the monetary theory, the unity of commodity and capital markets, is an adequate characterisation of the world's economy in the late nineteenth century. If the postulate is accepted, it implies that the wrenching adjustments of prices, interest rates and incomes that the orthodox theory in its many forms holds necessary for reestablishing equilibrium in the balance of payments were in fact not necessary. The world's economy determined the prices and interest rates prevailing in each nation's economy and it was the flow of gold itself that reestablished equilibrium in the money market by satisfying the demand for money that prompted the flow in the first place.

Whether the postulate of unified markets is acceptable or not is an empirical matter to be examined below. What is relevant here is that writers on the history of the gold standard, even as they have passed by its implications, have accepted it in part. The postulate is most easily defended (in fact, nearly universally accepted) for goods that enter international trade. Hume himself emphasised that the prices of such goods could differ only by transport or tariff costs, and Jacob Viner, in his survey in 1937 of the development of the theory of the gold standard, quoting Hume to this effect, was emphatic that all important subsequent writers agreed.[10] Frank Taussig certainly did. He wrote in 1906: 'Those commodities that enter into international trade have a common price the world over. The extraordinary cheapening of transportation during the last half-century, the perfected organisation of markets and exchanges, contribute to make this assumption a safe one for all the great staples.'[11] Taussig, like many others before and since, went on to emphasise that nontraded goods existed, arguing that the gold standard reestablished equilibrium in a nation's balance of payments by altering the price of nontraded relative to traded goods. It is worth remarking here that it is not enough to reject the postulate of unified markets that nontraded goods merely exist: as will be argued in detail below, there must be low substitutability between traded and nontraded goods in both consumption and production. In any case, later writers have made larger concessions to the force of arbitrage in commodity markets. In his massive study of the interwar gold standard published in 1940, W. A. Brown, for example, asserted that 'the international influence of the London or Liverpool price of many important commodities was a factor tending to prevent substantial divergence in the movements of *general* prices of countries adhering to the international gold standard'.[12] And in 1964, Robert Triffin, in an important piece of iconoclasm on the gold standard, was still more explicit:

> Under these conditions, national price and wage levels remained closely linked together internationally, even in the face of divergent rates of monetary and credit expansion, as import and export competition constituted a powerful brake on the emergence of any large disparity between internal and external price and cost levels. Inflationary pressures could not be contained within the domestic market, but spilled out *directly* to a considerable extent, into balance-of-payments deficits rather than into uncontrolled rises of internal prices, costs, and wage levels.[13]

A flow of gold is by no means a necessary part of this process of arbitrage. In fact, the mere *threat* of arbitrage may be sufficient to bring a nation's prices and interest rates into line with the world's, without flows of anything. The usual justification for seizing on the flow of gold as the central mechanism of adjustment in prices and interest rates among countries on the gold standard is that gold is cheap to ship: slight variations in the exchange rate between two currencies caused by disturbances in the balance of payments and correctable by changes in prices and interest rates will cause gold to flow if the two currencies are both attached to gold at fixed rates. As Marshall put it in the early 1920s, when the exchange rate between French and Belgian money is favorable to France, 'really it is favorable to those who bring goods to France from Belgium and it is unfavorable to all who send goods in the opposite direction. *One* of the goods, which may be sent, is gold.'[14] Marshall was choosing his words carefully, as he usually did, for he realized that other commodities could and did serve this function as well. Gold, being cheap to transport, was always close to the price at which it would be exported (if foreign means of payments were especially desired by, say, Englishmen) or imported (if English means of payment were especially desired by foreigners); but a large number of commodities or securities would also at any one time be at their export or import price if arbitrage, allowing for transport costs and tariffs, were effective. At the end of the same chapter, in a section entitled, in Marshall's descriptive manner, 'So long as national currencies are effectively based on gold, the wholesale price of each commodity tends to equality everywhere', he agrees, speaking by analogy with the gold points of the 'leadpoint' and the 'Egyptian bond-point' without drawing explicitly the inference that gold does not in that case play the central role in forcing parallel movements of prices and interest rates in different nations assigned to it in the orthodox theories.[15] The firm belief of the classical and neo-classical economists in the unity of world markets under modern conditions did not fit well with their views on the gold standard.

The behavior of prices in the late nineteenth century has suggested to some observers that the view that it was gold flows that were transmitting price changes from one country to another is indeed flawed. Over a short period, perhaps a year or so, the simple price–specie–flow mechanism predicts an inverse correlation in the price levels of two countries interacting with each other on the gold standard. A monetary expansion in Britain, the story goes, would raise the British price level, making British exports less competitive. This would produce a deficit in Britain's payments, equivalent to an outflow of gold. The outflow of gold would reduce the supply of money in Britain and raise it elsewhere, driving prices in Britain down and prices in, say, America up. Yet, as Triffin has noted and as we shall demonstrate presently, even over a period as brief as a single year, what is impressive is 'the overall parallelism – rather than divergence – of price movements, expressed in the same unit of measurement, between the various trading countries maintaining a minimum degree of freedom of trade and exchange in their international transactions'.[16]

Over a longer period of time, of course, the parallelism is consistent with the theory of price–specie–flow. In fact, one is free to assume that the lags in its mechanism are shorter than a year, attributing the close correlations among national price levels within the same year to a speedy flow of gold and a speedy price change resulting from the flow rather than to direct and rapid arbitrage. One is not free, however, to assume that there were no lags at all; in the price–specie–flow theory inflows of gold must precede increases in prices by at least the number of months necessary for the money supply to adjust to the new gold and for the increased amount of money to have its inflationary effect. The American inflation following the resumption of specie payments in January 1879 is a good example. After examining the annual statistics on gold flows and price levels for the period, Friedman and Schwartz concluded that 'It would be hard to find a much neater example in history of the classical gold-standard mechanism in operation.'[17] Gold flowed in during 1879, 1880 and 1881 and American prices rose each year. Yet the monthly statistics on American gold flows and price changes tell a very different story. Changes in the Warren and Pearson wholesale price index during 1879–81 run closely parallel month by month with gold flows, rising prices corresponding to net inflows of gold. There is no tendency for prices to lag behind a gold flow and some tendency for them to lead it, suggesting not only that the episode is an especially poor example of the price–specie–flow theory in operation, but also that it might well be a reasonably good one of the monetary theory.[18]

The strain of interpreting the gold standard of the late nineteenth century in terms of the available theories shows most clearly in the relations uncovered in empirical work between gold flows and income. After World War I economists put increasing emphasis on variations in income induced by deficits or surpluses in the balance of payments as the critical element in reestablishing equilibrium. As the matter was put in one historical survey of the gold standard, 'What is important to note . . . is that the adjustment attributed to price changes and gold flows in the nineteenth century was swift and smooth, not because of the power of price changes to effect adjustment, but because income changes were always acting in the same direction to reinforce the price change.'[19] Yet the negative correlation between income and gold inflows over the course of the business cycle predicted by such assertions did not hold, at any rate not during the late nineteenth century in the United Kingdom and the United States, and this uncomfortable fact has long been known. To a first approximation (the succeeding approximations will be presented in section IV below), the monetary theory predicts the opposite correlation, which is the correlation in fact observed: as incomes rise in a country the demand for money of its citizens will rise as well, and the demand can be satisfied, if it is not satisfied by the domestic monetary authorities, by an importation of gold, that is to say, by a surplus – not a deficit – in the balance of payments.[20]

A. P. Andrew observed as early as 1907 that this was the case for the United States in the late nineteenth century, and W. E. Beach in 1935 and Alec Ford in 1962 that it was the case for the United Kingdom as well.[21] In a book on the American balance of payments during the nineteenth century published in 1964, and in a set of related articles, Jeffrey Williamson went further, arguing explicitly that a rise in income in the United States, when not accompanied by a rise in the internal supply of money (as it was, for example, during the period of intensive exploitation of the Californian gold discoveries), produced an excess demand for real money balances and, therefore, a surplus in the balance of payments.[22] And an article by P. B. Whale in 1937 is a still earlier anticipation of this point in the monetary theory. Citing Andrew and Beach, he wrote:

> [T]he suggestion is that in a regime of fixed exchange rates the monetary requirements of a particular country may be altered by changes in prices or trade activity independent of any prior change in the supply of money . . . evidence of concomitant [domestic] movements of gold into and out of circulation [concomitant, that is, with evidence of inward and outward movements of gold internationally, which was correlated positively with the business cycle] confirms the view that it was the monetary requirements determined by a given price level which provided the underlying cause of the international gold movements.[23]

At another point he refers approvingly to a contemporary German writer who treated 'gold flows somewhat similarly as a result of an excess of money balances at the equilibrium level of incomes', that is to say, in precisely the manner of the monetary theory.[24] Evidently, it would be grossly unfair to earlier work on the gold standard of the nineteenth century to claim that the elements drawn together in this essay are novel with us. They are all in the earlier work, however uncomfortably they fit with the successive versions of the orthodox theory.

III DID INTERNATIONAL MARKETS WORK WELL?

If arbitrage – or, more precisely, a close correlation among national price levels brought about by the ordinary working of markets – can be shown to characterize the international economy of the late nineteenth century, many of the conclusions of the monetary theory will follow directly and the rest will gain in plausibility. In the monetary theory, the international market short-circuits the effects of domestic policy on American prices, and the expansion of the domestic supply of money spills directly into a deficit in the balance of payments.

It is essential, therefore, to examine the evidence for this short-circuiting. As a criterion of its effectiveness, we use the size of the contemporaneous correlations among changes in the prices of the same commodities in different countries. We have chosen a sample of the voluminous information on prices for examination here.[25] The statistical power of the tests is not as high as one might wish, for even if two nations shared no markets they could nonetheless exhibit common movements in prices if they shared similar experiences of climate, technological change, income growth or any of the other determinants of prices. In the long run, indeed, the other theories of the balance of payments imply some degree of correlation among national prices. For this reason we have resisted the temptation to improve the correlations by elaborate experimentation with lags and have concentrated on contemporaneous correlations, that is, on correlations among prices in the same year. If international markets worked as sluggishly as the other theories assume, there would be little reason to expect contemporaneous correlations to be high.

The simplest way to think about arbitrage is in terms of a single market. Given fixed exchange rates and the vigorous pursuit of profit through arbitrage, the correlation between price changes for a homogeneous commodity in two countries, say America and Britain, separated by transportation costs and tariffs, would be zero within the limits of the export and import points and unity at those points. A regression of British on American prices would test simultaneously for the lowness of the commodity's cost of transportation, including tariffs, relative to its price and the vigor with which prices were arbitraged. The good would not actually have to be traded between the two countries for the correlation to be high: the mere threat of arbitrage, or a common source of supply or demand, would be sufficient for goods with low transport costs. For goods actually flowing in trade in a uniform direction over the period 1880 to 1913, such as wheat from America to Britain, one would expect the correlation to be perfect and the slope of the corresponding regression to be unity, no matter what the cost of transport or the level of tariffs, so long as these did not change. They both did change, of course, as exemplified by the failure of the German price of wheat to fall as far as the British or American during the 1880s, as the Germans imposed protective duties on wheat imports.[26] Nonetheless, the average correlation among the changes in American, British and German prices of wheat is high, about 0·78. A regression of the annual change in British prices on the change in American prices (Britain had no tariffs on wheat, but the cost of ocean transport was falling sharply in the period) yields the following result (all the variables here and elsewhere in this section are measured as annual absolute changes; the figures below the coefficients in parentheses are standard errors; the levels of the variables have been converted to an index in which the average levels are equal to one).[27]

$$BWT = \underset{(0\cdot 0012)}{0\cdot 0076} + \underset{(0\cdot 102)}{0\cdot 646}\,AWT \qquad R^2 = 0\cdot 58 \quad D.-W. = 2\cdot 02$$

One would expect errors in the independent variable to affect this and the later regressions, biasing the slope towards zero (there were changes in the source of the American wheat price, for example, and after 1890 it is a New York price alone). The value of 0·646 would be a lower bound on the true slope and the value implied by a regression of the American on the British price (1·124) an upper bound. The two bounds bracket reasonably closely the value to be expected theoretically, namely, 1·0, and the constants in both regressions (which represent the trend in the dependent price over time) are insignificantly different from zero. Not surprisingly, in short, wheat appears to have had a unified world market in the late nineteenth century; *a fortiori*, so did gold, silver, copper, diamonds, racehorses and fine art.

This conclusion can be reinforced from another direction. For wheat the reinforcement is unnecessary, for few would doubt the international character of the wheat market, but it is useful to develop here the line of argument. Because of transport costs, information costs and other impediments to a perfect correlation among changes in national prices, any use of the notion of a perfectly unified market must be an approximation, within one country as well as between two countries. For purposes of explaining the balance of payments economists have been willing to accept the approximation that within each country there is one price for each product, setting aside as a second-order matter the indisputable lack of perfect correlation between price changes in California and Massachusetts or between price changes in Cornwall and Midlothian. It is reasonable, therefore, to use the level of the contemporaneous correlation between the prices of a good in different regions within a country as a standard against which to judge the unity of the market for that good between different countries. If the correlations between the prices of wheat in America, Britain and Germany were no lower than those between the prices of wheat in, say, different parts of Germany, there would be no grounds for distinguishing between the degree of unity in the national German market and in the international market for wheat. This was in fact the case. The average correlation between changes in the prices of wheat in pairs of German cities (Berlin, Breslau, Frankfurt, Konigsberg, Leipzig, Lindau and Mannheim) from 1881 to 1912 was 0·85, quite close to the average correlation for the three countries over the same period of 0·78.

One could proceed in this fashion through all individual prices, but a shorter route to the same objective is to examine correlations across countries between pairs of aggregate price indexes. Contrary to the intuition embodied in this thought, however, there is no guarantee, at any rate none that we have been able to discover, that the correlation of the indexes is an unbiased estimator of the average degree of correlation among the individual prices or, for that matter, that it is biased in any particular direction.[28] In other words, barriers to trade could be high or low in each individual market without the aggregate correlation necessarily registering these truths. Nonetheless, putting these doubts to one side, we will trust henceforth to the intuition.

The pioneers of the method of index numbers, Laspeyres, Jevons and others writing in the middle of the nineteenth century, produced indexes of wholesale prices – believable indexes of retail prices began to be produced only in the 1890s and implicit GNP deflators, of course, much later – and in consequence wholesale price indexes dominated empirical work on the balance of payments in the formative years of the theory. The contemporaneous correlation between annual changes in British and American wholesale prices 1880–1913 is 0·66, high enough in view of the differences in weights in the indexes and in view of the low correlation of annual changes implied by the lags operating in the orthodox theories to lend support to the postulate of a unified world market.

It is at this point, however, that supporters of the orthodox theory begin to quarrel with the argument, as did Taussig with those bold enough to suggest that world markets in more than merely traded goods were integrated in the late nineteenth century, or as did the many doubters of the theory of purchasing power parity with those who used wholesale prices to indicate the appropriate rates of exchange after World War I. The standard objection has been that wholesale price indexes are biased samples from the distribution of correlations because they consist largely of easily traded goods, ignoring nontraded services and underrepresenting nontraded goods. A large lower tail of the distribution, it is said, is left off, leading to a false impression that national price levels are closely correlated.

A point that must be made at once, however, is that traded goods, in the sense of goods actually traded and goods identical to those actually traded, were not a small proportion of national income. Historians and economists have usually thought of the openness of economies in terms of the ratio of actual exports or imports to national income, and have inferred that the United States, with a ratio of exports to national income of about 0·07 in the late nineteenth century, was relatively isolated from the influence of international prices and that the United Kingdom, with a ratio of 0·28, was relatively open to it. Yet in both countries consumption of tradable goods, defined as all goods that figured in the import and export lists, was on the order of half of national income.[29] If any substantial part of the national consumption or production of wheat, coal or cloth entered international markets in which the country in question was a small supplier or demander, the prices of these items at home would be determined exogenously by prices abroad. Wholesale indexes, if they do indeed consist chiefly of traded goods, are not so unrepresentative of all of national income as might be supposed.

But what of the other, nontradable half of national income? Surely, as James Angell wrote in 1926, 'for non-traded articles there is of course no direct equalisation [of price] at all'.[30] The operative word in this assertion is 'direct', for without it the assertion is incorrect. The price of a good in one country is constrained not only by the direct limits of transport costs to and from world markets but by the indirect constraints arising from the good's substitutability for other goods in consumption or production. This was clear to Bertil Ohlin, who asked, 'To what extent are interregional discrepancies in home market prices kept within narrow limits not only through the potential trade in these goods that would come into existence if interregional price differences exceeded the costs of transfer, but also through the actual trade in *other* goods?'[31] It is not surprising to find Ohlin asking such a question, for the analytical issue is identical to the one that gave birth to that errant child of the Heckscher–Ohlin theory, factor–price equalisation. The price of the milk used as much as the wage of the labor used is affected by the international price of butter and cheese. A rise in the price of a traded good will cause substitutions in production and consumption that will raise the prices of nontraded goods. To put the point more extremely than is necessary for present purposes, in a general equilibrium of prices the fixing of any one price by trade determines all the rest. The adjustment to the real equilibrium of relative prices, which must be achieved eventually, can be slow or quick. The monetary theory assumes that it is quick.

If it were in fact slow, one would expect the contemporaneous correlation between prices for countries on the gold standard to fall sharply as more comprehensive price indexes, embodying nontraded goods, are compared. This is not the case. The correlation between the annual changes in the GNP deflators 1880–1912 for America and Britain is 0·60, to be compared with the correlation for wholesale prices alone of 0·66. The regressions of the annual changes of American on British deflators and British on American were (standard errors in parentheses; levels of the price variables converted to indexes with their averages as the base):

$$AP = 0{\cdot}0002 + 0{\cdot}961\,BP \qquad R^2 = 0{\cdot}35,\quad D.-W. = 1{\cdot}98$$
$$\quad (0{\cdot}0050)\quad (0{\cdot}266)$$

Standard error of the regression as a percentage of the average level of the American price = 2·5%

$$BP = 0{\cdot}0017 + 0{\cdot}33\,AP \qquad R^2 = 0{\cdot}34,\quad D.-W. = 1{\cdot}92$$
$$\quad (0{\cdot}0028)\quad (0{\cdot}089)$$

Standard error of the regression as a percentage of the average level of the British price = 1·4%

The correlations of the German GNP deflator with the American

(0·40) and the British (0·45) are considerably lower, but this may be simply a reflection of the inevitable frailties of Walther Hoffman's pioneering effort to produce such a deflator, or, perhaps, a reflection of the sharp rises in German tariffs. More countries have retail price indexes (generally with weights from working-class budgets) than have reliable GNP deflators, and these statistics tell a story that is equally encouraging for the postulate of arbitrage. The correlation matrix of annual changes in retail prices for the United States, the United Kingdom, Germany, France and Sweden is shown in Table 10.1. The British–American correlation (0·57) is again not markedly below the correlation of the wholesale indexes, despite the importance of such nontraded goods as housing in the retail indexes.[32]

Table 10.1 *Simple correlations between annual changes in retail prices, 1880–1912*

	USA	*UK*	*Germany*	*France*	*Sweden*
USA	1·00	0·57	0·28	0·24	0·38
UK		1·00	0·53	0·42	0·57
Germany			1·00	0·45	0·62
France				1·00	0·32
Sweden					1·00

The correlation of American with British retail prices is probably not attributable to the trade in food offsetting a lower correlation between nontraded goods, for the simple correlation between American and British food prices in the years for which it is available (1894–1913) is lower, 0·49 compared with 0·57. Against this encouraging finding, however, must be put a less encouraging one. The average correlation between the changes in food prices in five regions of the United States (North Atlantic, South Atlantic, North Central, South Central and the West) for 1891–1913 is very high, 0·87, contrasted with the British–American correlation of only 0·49. If food prices were as well arbitraged between as inside countries the British–American correlation would have to be much higher than it is. Still, even with perfect unity in the market for each item of food, one would not expect countries with substantially different budget shares to exhibit close correlations in the aggregate indexes. The lower correlation between Britain and the United States than between regions of the United States, then, may well reflect international differences of tastes and income rather than lower arbitrage.

If one proceeds in this fashion further in the direction of less traded goods the results continue to be mixed, although on balance giving support to the postulate of unity in world markets. The most obvious nontraded good is labor. The correlation between changes in wages of British and American coal miners 1891–1913 is 0·42 but the correlation between those of British and American farm laborers is only 0·26. Both are lower than the correlations between changes in the wages of the two employments in each country, 0·65 in Britain and 0·53 in America. The correlation between the annual changes in Paul Douglas' index of hourly earnings of union men in American building and the changes in A. L. Bowley's index of wages in British building from 1891 to 1901 is negligible, only 0·10. On the other hand, the average correlation among bricklayers' hourly wages in four cities (Boston, Cincinnati, Cleveland and Philadelphia) selected from the mass of data for 1890–1903 in the 19th Annual Report of the US Commissioner of Labor is only 0·14. The correlations for changes in wages between countries are low, in other words, but there is reason to believe that they are nearly as low within a geographically large country like the United States as well.

The same is true for an unambiguously nontraded commodity, common brick. That it is nontraded, that is, a poor substitute for traded goods, and that it enters into the production of nontraded commodities is evident from the negligible correlation between changes in its average price in Britain and America. Yet from 1894, when the statistics first become available, to 1913, the average correlation between prices of common brick at the plant in seven scattered states of the United States (California, Georgia, Illinois, New York, Ohio, Pennsylvania and Texas) was only 0·11, and even between three states in the same region (New York, Ohio and Pennsylvania) it was only 0·13. This degree of correlation may be taken as an indicator of the correlation between regions of the United States attributable to a common experience of general inflation, technological change and growth of income rather than to the unity of markets. It is small. In any case, common brick is a good at the lower end of the distribution of goods by their correlations, and there is little evidence of greater integration of markets within than between countries.

All these tests can be much expanded and improved, and we plan to do so in later work.[33] What has been established here is that there is a reasonable case, if not at this stage an overwhelming one, for the postulate of integrated commodity markets between the British and American economies in the late nineteenth century, vindicating the monetary theory. There appears to be little reason to treat these two countries on the gold standard differently in their monetary transactions from any two regions within each country.

IV MONEY, GOLD AND THE BALANCE OF PAYMENTS

If international arbitrage of prices and interest rates was thoroughgoing and if the growth of real income in a country was exogenous to its supply of money, then the country's demand for money can be estimated by relatively straightforward econometric techniques. The balance of payments – identified here with flows of gold – predicted by the monetary theory can then be estimated as the difference between the growth in the country's total predicted demand for money and the growth in its actual domestic supply. If, further, the actual flow of gold closely approximates the flow implied by the estimated change in the demand for money minus the actual change in the domestic supply of money, the monetary theory of the gold standard warrants serious consideration. In fact, to a remarkable degree the monetary theory for the United States and the United Kingdom from 1880 to 1913 passes this final test.

In Table 10.2 are presented the average movements of the British and

Table 10.2 *Average annual rates of change 1882–1913 of American and British money supplies (domestic and international), incomes, prices and interest rates (percentages; standard errors in parentheses)*

	United Kingdom	*United States*
1 Money supply attributable to gold flows	2·22 (2·41)	−0·09 (2·89)
2 Money supply attributable to other influences	0·12 (2·51)	5·77 4·56
3 Total money supply	2·35 (1·78)	5·68 (5·21)
4 Real income	1·84 (2·33)	3·69 (5·35)
5 Implicit price deflator	0·24 (1·75)	0·23 (3·09)
6 Long-term interest rates (absolute change in basis points)	2·9 (2·0)	−2·3 (15·0)

Sources:

Line 1. The rate of change of the money supply attributable to gold flows was calculated as:

$$100\left[\log\left(M_{t-1}+\frac{M_t}{H_t}R_t\right)-\log M_{t-1}\right]$$

where M is the total money supply, H is 'high-powered money' (M_t/H_t, therefore, is the so-called 'money multiplier') and R is the annual net flow of gold. The figures on money supply and high-powered money for the United Kingdom were taken from D. K. Sheppard, 'Asset preferences and the money supply in the United Kingdom 1880–1962', University of Birmingham Discussion Papers, Ser. A, no. 111 (November 1969), p. 16; and for the United States from Friedman and Schwartz, op. cit., pp. 704–7. The figures on gold flows for the United Kingdom were compiled from Beach, op. cit., pp. 46ff. These are for England alone, excluding Scotland and Ireland, but there is little doubt that they cover the great bulk of flows into and out of the United Kingdom. Gold

American variables to be explained (the movements, that is, in money supplies and in that part of the money supply attributable to international flows of gold) and the average movements of the variables with which the monetary theory would explain them (the movements in prices, interest rates and incomes affecting the demand for money and the movements in that part of the money supply attributable to domestic forces). The average percentage change in the money supply was decomposed in a merely arithmetical way (described in the footnote to the table) into a part reflecting how the money supply would have behaved if all gold flows into or out of the country had been allowed to affect it (by way of the multiple effects of reserves on the money supply) and a residual reflecting all other influences. Arithmetically speaking, the causes of changes in British and American money supplies differed sharply; virtually all the change in Britain was attributable to international flows of gold while virtually all the change in America was attributable to other, domestic sources of new money. Economically speaking, the differences are less sharp. Although over these three decades on average the rate of change of the money supply was far larger in America than in Britain, the difference is adequately explained in terms of the monetary theory by the faster growth of American income, given the similarity (in accord with the findings of the last section) in the behavior of prices and given the relative fall in American interest rates.

So much is apparent from the arithmetic of the British and American experience. To go further one needs a behavioral model explaining the annual balance of payments in terms of the monetary theory. The model is simplicity itself. It begins with a demand function for money, the only behavioral function in the model, asserting that the annual rate of change in the demand for money balances depends on the rates of change of the price level and of real income and on the absolute change

---

Table 10.2 *Sources* contd:

flows for the United States are given in US Bureau of the Census, *Historical Statistics of the United States* (Washington, DC, 1960), series U6.

Line 2 = Line 3 − Line 1.

Line 3. Source as in Line 1.

Line 4. US real gross national product is from Simon Kuznets' worksheets, reported in R. E. Lipsey, *Price and Quantity Trends in the Foreign Trade of the United States* (New York: National Bureau of Economic Research, 1963), p. 423; for years before 1889, the Kuznets figure Lipsey used was inferred from Lipsey's ratio of GNP to farm income and his estimate of farm income (pp. 423–4). UK real gross *domestic* product is from C. H. Feinstein, *National Income, Expenditure and Output of the United Kingdom, 1855–1965* (Cambridge: Cambridge University Press, 1971), Appendix Table 6, col. 4.

Line 5. For the US the figure is from Lipsey, as in Line 4. For the UK the figure is from Feinstein, Appendix Table 61, col. 7.

Line 6. The US interest rate is Macauley's unadjusted index number of yields of American railway bonds (*Historical Statistics of the U.S.*, as cited, series X332). The UK rate is the yield of consolidated government bonds (consols) in Mitchell, *Abstract of British Historical Statistics* (Cambridge: Cambridge University Press, 1962), p. 455.

in interest rates (asterisks signify rates of change):

$$M_d^{\star} = P^{\star} + f(y^{\star}, \triangle i)$$

And it ends with a domestic money supply function (literally, an identity using the observed money multiplier, as explained in the footnote to Table 10.2) and the statement that the money not supplied domestically was supplied through the balance of payments. It is evident that the monetary theory is simply a comparative statics theory of money's supply and demand, in which the balance of payments satisfies demands for money not satisfied by domestic sources.

By virtue of the unity of world markets and the assumed exogeneity of the growth of real income to the supply of money (which is itself a consequence of market unity and the availability of an elastic supply of money abroad), there is no simultaneous equation bias in estimating the demand for money by ordinary least squares. It is convenient to estimate the demand in real terms. The result for the United States 1884–1913 of regressing the rate of change of real balances on the rate of change in real income and the absolute change in the interest rate is (*t*-statistics in parentheses):

$$\underset{}{(M/P)^{\star}} = \underset{(4\cdot5)}{0\cdot030} + \underset{(4\cdot9)}{0\cdot61}\, y^{\star} - \underset{(2\cdot6)}{0\cdot10}\, \triangle i \qquad R^2 = 0\cdot59 \quad D.-W. = 2\cdot02$$

And for the United Kingdom:[34]

$$(M/P)^{\star} = \underset{(2\cdot4)}{0\cdot014} + \underset{(2\cdot2)}{0\cdot32}\, y^{\star} - \underset{(-1\cdot2)}{0\cdot005}\, \triangle i \qquad R^2 = 0\cdot27 \quad D.-W. = 1\cdot89$$

These appear to be reasonable demand equations, although the income elasticity in the equation for the United Kingdom is low, perhaps an artifact of errors in the series for income, which, given the low variability of British income, would reduce the fitted regression coefficient. Another explanation might be the substantial ownership of British money by foreigners, which would reduce the relevance of movements in British income to the 'British' money supply. Still, both demand equations accord reasonably well with other work on the demand for money.

The acid test of the model, of course, is its performance in predicting the balance of payments as a residual from the predicted demand for money and the actual domestically determined supply. Its performance is startlingly good. The good fit of the American demand equation offsets the relative unimportance of gold flows to the American supply, while the relative importance of gold flows to the British supply offsets the poor fit of the British demand equation. Figures 10.1 and 10.2

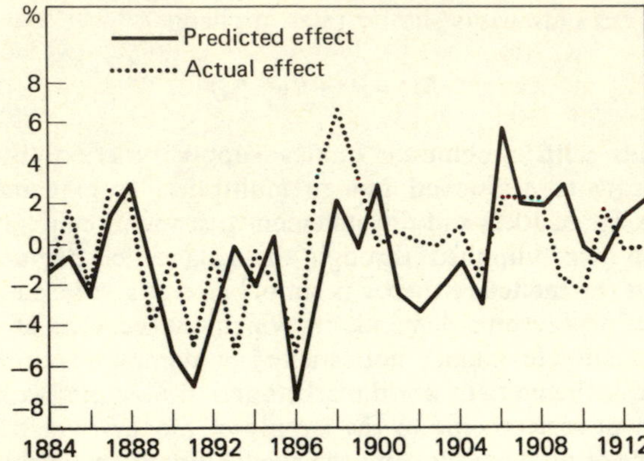

Figure 10.1 *Predicted (——) and actual (- - -) effects of gold flows on the US money stock, annual rates of change, 1884–1913*

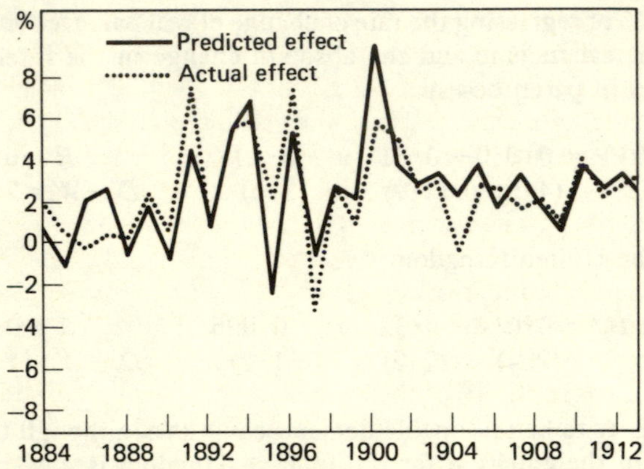

Figure 10.2 *Predicted (——) and actual (- - -) effects of gold flows on the UK money stock, annual rates of change, 1884–1913*

exhibit the results, comparing the actual effect of gold flows on the American and British money supplies with the predicted effect. The actual effect is calculated annually by applying the observed ratio of money to reserves (including gold) to the actual flow of gold, the predicted effect by subtracting the domestic sources of money from the demand for money predicted by the regressions. In other words, the predicted effect is the excess demand for money predicted by the regressions in conjunction with the actual changes in the money supply due to domestic sources. One could just as well make the comparison of predicted with actual flows of gold, translating the predicted excess demand for money in each country into an equivalent demand for gold imports. The result would be the same, namely, a close correspondence between the predictions of the theory and the observed behavior of the British and American stock of money and balance of payments.

No doubt the tests could be refined and more evidence could be examined. We believe, however, that we have established at least a prima facie case for viewing the world of the nineteenth-century gold standard as a world of unified markets, in which flows of gold represented the routine satisfaction of demands for money. We do not claim to have rejected decisively the view of the gold standard that depends on poor arbitrage between national markets or the view that predicts an inverse rather than a positive correlation between gold inflows and income or any of the other variants of the orthodox theories. Indeed, it is perfectly possible that these variants are partly true, perhaps true in the very short run, or under special circumstances, such as mass unemployment – the monetary theory is, in the sense described earlier, an equilibrium theory, which could be consistent with any number of theories about how the British and American economies behaved out of equilibrium. But a balance of payments surplus or deficit is not in itself, as has often been assumed, evidence that the economy in question is in fact out of equilibrium. The monetary theory's central message is that a growing, open economy, buffeted by external variations in prices and interest rates, will have a varying demand for money, which would only fortuitously be supplied exactly from domestic sources. A country's balance of payments, in other words, could be positive or negative over the course of a year even if all asset and commodity markets in the country were continuously in equilibrium, for the flow of money into the country during the year could exactly meet the year's change in the demand for money. The source of the simplicity of the monetary theory of the gold standard is clear: the monetary theory is an equilibrium model, whereas the alternative theories are to a greater or lesser extent dynamic, disequilibrium models. We believe (as must be evident by now) that the simpler model yields a persuasive interpretation of how the gold standard worked, 1880–1913.

NOTES

1 Many of these have been published in the Princeton Studies in International Finance. For example, Arthur I. Bloomfield, *Short-term Capital Movements under the Pre-1914 Gold Standard* (1963); the work cited below; and Peter H. Lindert, *Key Currencies and Gold, 1900–1913* (1969). Bloomfield's *Monetary Policy under the International Gold Standard* (New York: Federal Reserve Bank of New York, 1959) is seminal to this literature.

2 J. M. Keynes, *Treatise on Money* (London: Macmillan, 1930), Vol. II, pp. 306–7.

3 World official reserves at the end of 1913 of $7,100 million (16 percent of which was foreign exchange, a good part of it sterling) are estimated by Lindert, op. cit., pp. 10–12.

4 In 1964 Robert Triffin undertook to act as midwife, but as he concedes, the infant is still in poor health (see his *The Evolution of the International Monetary System: Historical Reappraisal and Future Perspectives*, Princeton Studies in International Finance, no. 12, Princeton: Department of Economics, 1964, appendix I).

5 Needless to say, these are crude estimates: to continue the metaphor above, the historical study of world income is barely into its adolescence. The estimate of $362 billion for 1913 world income in 1955 prices begins with Alfred Maizels' compilation of figures on gross *domestic* product at factor cost for twenty-one countries, given in his *Industrial Growth and World Trade* (Cambridge: Cambridge University Press, 1965), appendix E, p. 531. Czech and Hungarian income was estimated from Austrian income (post-1919 boundaries) on the basis of Colin Clark's ratios among the three (in *The Conditions of Economic Progress*, 2nd edn, London: Macmillan, 1951, p. 155). Russian income was estimated by extrapolating Simon Kuznets' estimate for 1958 back to 1913 on the basis of his figure for the decennial rate of growth, 1913–58 (in *Modern Economic Growth*, New Haven: Yale University Press, 1966, pp. 65 and 360), yielding a figure of $207 per capita in 1958 prices, which appears to be a reasonable order of magnitude. The Russian per capita figure was then applied to the population of Bulgaria, Greece, Poland, Romania and Spain, completing the coverage of Europe (boundary changes during the decade of war, 1910 to 1920, were especially important for these countries, except Spain; estimates of the relevant populations are given in R. R. Palmer, *Atlas of World History*, Chicago: Rand McNally, 1957, p. 193). Maizels gives estimates of national income for Canada, Australia, New Zealand, South Africa, Argentina and Japan in 1913. Income per head in 1955 dollars was taken to be $50 in Africa except South Africa, $100 in Latin America except Argentina, $50 in India, and $60 in Asia except India and Japan, all on the basis of Maizels' estimates for 1929 and an assumption of little growth. Population figures for these groups of countries around 1910 were taken from D. V. Glass and E. Grebenik, 'World population, 1800–1950', in H. J. Habakkuk and M. Postan, *Cambridge Economic History of Europe*, Vol. VI, pt 1 (Cambridge: Cambridge University Press, 1965), p. 58, with adjustments for the countries included in Maizels' estimates, from his population figures (op. cit., p. 540).

6 Skepticism on this point has long been widespread. Consider, for example, J. W. Angell, *The Theory of International Prices* (Cambridge: Harvard University Press, 1926), p. 400: 'It is perfectly obvious that neither the magnitudes nor the directions of the international flows of gold were adequate to explain those close and comparatively rapid adjustments of payments-disequilibria, and of price relationships, which were witnessed before the war.'

7 The American and British record is examined later in Table 10.2 below. Bruce Brittain of the Research Department, First National City Bank of New York, is currently engaged in examining the French experience in the light of the monetary theory.

8 P. Barrett Whale, 'The working of the pre-war gold standard', *Economica*, N.S., 4 (February 1937), pp. 18–32; reprinted in T. S. Ashton and R. S. Sayers (eds), *Papers in English Monetary History* (London: Oxford University Press, 1953), to which subsequent reference is made, p. 153. Compare R. H. I. Palgrave (ed.), *Dictionary of Political Economy* (London: Macmillan, 1901), article on Banks, France: 'The Bank of France endeavours to keep an even rate of discount. Thus for about five years, between 1883 and 1888, its rate of discount remained at 3%, while there were no fewer than 36 changes varying from 2% to 5% at the Bank of England during the same time.'

9 The sources for this calculation are given in Table 10.2 below.

10 Jacob Viner, *Studies in the Theory of International Trade* (1937; reprinted New York: A. M. Kelley, 1965), pp. 314–18.

11 Frank Taussig, 'Wages and prices in relation to international trade', *Quarterly*

Journal of Economics, 20 (August 1906), pp. 497–522, at p. 499.

12 William A. Brown, *The International Gold Standard Reinterpreted, 1914–1934* (New York: National Bureau of Economic Research, 1940), p. 775, italics added.

13 Robert Triffin, *The Evolution of the International Monetary System*, Princeton Studies in International Finance, no. 12 (Princeton: Department of Economics, 1964), p. 10 (his italics). P. B. Whale's article of 1937, cited above, is a startlingly complete anticipation of this and other elements in the monetary theory.

14 Alfred Marshall, *Money, Credit and Commerce* (London: Macmillan, 1923), p. 145 (italics added). Compare p. 228, where he argues that a duty placed on some of a country's imports will increase duty-free imports and that 'Gold and silver will *generally find a place* among these' (italics added).

15 Marshall, op. cit., pp. 152–4.

16 Triffin, op. cit., p. 4. He used export unit values. One could object that for many of the eleven countries he examined over the period 1870–1960 export unit values could be similar (namely, world wholesale prices for manufactures) without a corresponding similarity in the prices of domestic goods. Section 3 below overcomes this objection.

17 Milton Friedman and Anna J. Schwartz, *A Monetary History of the United States, 1867–1960* (Princeton: Princeton University Press, 1963), p. 99.

18 The price index is given in George F. Warren and Frank Pearson, *Prices* (New York: Wiley, 1933), pp. 11–13. The statistics on gold flows (silver flows do not disturb the pattern) are from the US Commerce Department, Census Bureau, *Monthly Summary of Foreign Commerce*, for January 1879 through December 1882. In 1882 the association between gold and prices reported in the text breaks down: prices rose in the first half of 1882 yet gold flowed out. This change, however, is consistent with the monetary theory, for in early 1882, according to the dating of the National Bureau of Economic Research, the business expansion that had begun in early 1879 came to an end. As the next few paragraphs in the text will emphasise, a fall in income reduces the demand for money and, other things equal, releases money for export.

19 W. M. Scammel, 'The working of the gold standard', *Yorkshire Bulletin of Economic and Social Research*, 17 (May 1965), pp. 32–45.

20 The incorrect predictions of the orthodox theory on this point arise in part from a confusion between the balance of *trade* and the balance of *payments*. The working model is that the balance of payments is equal to the balance of trade plus a random error term (the balance on capital account). See, for example, Viner, *Studies*, cited above, and J. E. Meade, *The Balance of Payments* (London: Oxford University Press, 1951), p. 80. George Macesich used just such a model to explain the behavior of the American economy in an early period of the gold standard ('Sources of monetary disturbances in the United States, 1834–1845', *Journal of Economic History*, 20, September 1960, pp. 407–34). He asserted (p. 414) that 'The heavy and varied capital flows thus had implications for the required behavior of exchange rates, specie flows, money supply, relative prices and the balance of trade.' The exogeneity and randomness of the capital account in the American experience during the nineteenth century was asserted still more explicitly by J. Ernest Tanner and Vittorio Bonomo, in a criticism of the book by Williamson cited below (Tanner and Bonomo, 'Gold, capital flows and long swings in American business activity', *Journal of Political Economy*, 76, Jan./Feb. 1968, pp. 44–52). Williamson, however, in an attack on Macesich's argument (J. G. Williamson, 'International trade and United States economic development, 1827–1843', *Journal of Economic History*, 21, September 1961, pp. 372–83) made the decisive point (p. 377): 'concomitant with real growth, there is a tendency to generate excess demands for real money balances, reflected, under a gold standard system, by an increasing inflow of gold. The solution is a general equilibrium one . . . demands for money (gold), goods and securities must be solved simultaneously in a general equilibrium context.' This is a clear anticipation of the foundations of the monetary theory.

21 A. P. Andrew, 'The Treasury and the banks under Secretary Shaw', *Quarterly Journal of Economics*, 21 (August 1907), pp. 519–68. W. E. Beach, *British International Gold Movements and Banking Policy, 1881–1913* (Cambridge: Harvard University Press, 1935; see especially Charts xvii, xviii and xix, and p. 77: 'In general gold imports became important during the latter stages of the periods of business expansion, and at the same time the volume of currency in the hands of the public was expanding. In recession the flows were reversed'). A. G. Ford, *The Gold Standard 1880–1914, Britain and Argentina* (Oxford: Clarendon Press, 1962); see especially p. 36: 'international gold movements, instead of being the determinants of the supply of money in Britain in this period, were probably determined by domestic monetary needs to some extent'.

22 J. G. Williamson, *American Growth and the Balance of Payments* (Chapel Hill: University of North Carolina Press, 1964), especially ch. V; Williamson, 'Real growth, monetary disturbances and the transfer process: the United States, 1879–1900', *Southern Economic Journal*, 29 (January 1963), pp. 167–80; and his article cited in the note above. It is testimony to the staying power of the tradition that Williamson is attacking that most of his work concerns the influences on the commodity and capital account separately. As was noted above, this procedure is otiose if it is indeed the balance of payments that is at issue. Williamson himself makes this point, in the chapter of his book (V) that presents the germ of the monetary theory: 'in previous chapters we have exaggerated the independence of the movements in net capital flows and the trade balance . . . the main point seems to be that gold flows cannot be treated simply as residuals' from the trade and capital accounts together (pp. 163–4).

23 Whale, op. cit., pp. 158–9.

24 Whale, op. cit., p. 156. He was referring to K. F. Maier, *Goldwanderungen: ein Beitrag zur Theorie des Geldes* [*Migration of Gold: A Contribution to the Theory of Money*], 1935.

25 The sample is described in the appendix of the longer paper, available from the authors on request.

26 From 1880–2 to 1889–91 the ratio of the Berlin to the British price of wheat increased 30 percent and remained at the higher ratio thereafter.

27 This and all subsequent regressions were subjected to the Cochrane–Orcutt iterative technique, removing in all cases understatement of the standard errors of the coefficients resulting from any autocorrelation of the residuals.

28 We have received a good deal of enlightenment on this point from H. Gregg Lewis of the University of Chicago and Hugh Rockoff of Rutgers University. The issue is as follows. Suppose, to simplify at the outset, that one chooses the same set of weights ($w_1, w_2, \ldots, w_N$) to form the two indexes of prices (I_A and I_B) in the two countries (A and B). What is the relationship between the weighted average of the individual correlations,

$$w_1(\text{corr } P_1^A, P_1^B) + w_2(\text{corr } P_2^A, P_2^B) + \ldots + w_N(\text{corr } P_N^A, P_N^B),$$

and the correlation of the weighted averages, corr (I_A, I_B) (where $I_A = w_1P_1^A + w_2P_2^A + \ldots + w_NP_N^A$)? For the case of two prices we have written out both correlations in terms of the relevant covariances (expressing the prices in standardised form, thereby eliminating variances of the individual prices and making the corresponding covariances identical to correlation coefficients), with no very illuminating results. If no restrictions are placed on the covariances we can generate counterexamples to the proposition that the two are equal. But we suspect that we are neglecting true restrictions among the covariances (one set implying values for another set) and, further, that the case of large N would give more useful results.

29 For the calculation for the UK in 1913, see D. N. McCloskey, *Markets Abroad and British Economic Growth, 1820–1913*, ch. 1 (MS. available on request), p. 18.

30 J. W. Angell, *The Theory of International Prices* (Cambridge: Harvard University Press, 1926), p. 381. Later Angell conceded in part the point made below, although he believed (p. 392) that 'it cannot be adequate to explain the comparatively quick adjustments [of domestic to international prices] that actually take place'.

31 Bertil Ohlin, *Interregional and International Trade*, rev. edn (Cambridge: Harvard University Press, 1967), p. 104. His italics, question mark added; first edn, 1933. Contrast Jacob Viner's *Canada's Balance of International Indebtedness 1900–1913* (Cambridge: Harvard University Press, 1924), p. 210: 'The prices of services and what may be termed "domestic commodities", commodities which are too perishable or too bulky to enter regularly and substantially into foreign trade, are wholly or largely independent of *direct* relationship with foreign prices. World price-factors influence them only through their influence on the prices of international commodities, with which the prices of domestic commodities, as part of a common price-system, must retain a somewhat flexible relationship' (his italics). Although this is an improvement on the earlier formulation by Cairnes (quoted by Viner on the next page) that 'with regard to these, there is nothing to prevent the widest divergence in their gold prices', it falls short of a full analysis of what is meant by 'direct' and 'somewhat flexible', an analysis provided by Ohlin. In long-run equilibrium the distinction between direct and indirect is beside the point and the relationship of domestic to international prices is not even somewhat flexible. Viner's work, incidentally, is one of a series of books on the balance of payments published in the Harvard Economic Studies in the 1920s and 1930s under the influence, direct or indirect, of Taussig: J. H. Williams, *Argentine International Trade under Inconvertible Paper Money: 1880–1900* (1920); Viner (1924); Angell (1926); Ohlin (1933); Harry D. White, *The French International Accounts, 1880–1913* (1933); and Beach (1935). Students of the history of economic thought will find it significant that of these Ohlin, who acknowledges explicitly his debt to the Stockholm School (among them Cassel, Heckscher and Wicksell, all of whom emphasized the intimate relationship between domestic and international prices), broke most sharply with Taussig on this issue.

32 The notion of an 'Atlantic economy', incidentally, receives support from these figures: the average correlation of French with other retail price indexes, a crude measure of the appropriateness of including a country in the Atlantic economy, is 0·36, while the same statistic for the United States is 0·37; on this reading, it would be as appropriate to exclude France from the economy of Western Europe as to exclude the United States.

33 We have passed by, for example, the issue of how unified were the markets for assets. The correlation between the annual changes in the British and American long-term interest rates 1882 to 1913 used in the model fitted below was 0·36, and could no doubt be improved by a closer attention to gathering homogeneous data than we have thought necessary for now. Michael Edelstein, for example, reports in his 'The determinants of U.K. investment abroad: the U.S. case' (unpublished MS., p. 10n.) a correlation coefficent of 0·77 between annual changes in the levels of yields on first-class American railway bonds offered in London and in New York from 1871 to 1913, a period including years before the refixing of the sterling–dollar exchange rate in 1879. The discount rates of central banks may be taken as a rough measure of the short-term interest rate. The recent revisionist literature on the gold standard has emphasized the close correlations between these rates in different countries. Triffin (op. cit., p. 9), for example, quotes Bloomfield, approvingly, to the effect that 'the annual averages of the discount rates of twelve [European] central banks reveal the . . . interesting fact that, in their larger movements at least, the discount rates of virtually all the banks tended to rise and fall together' (A. I. Bloomfield, *Monetary Policy under the International Gold Standard*, as cited, p. 35). Bloomfield and Triffin attribute the parallelism to a corresponding parallelism in the business cycles of the nations involved, but the

finding can also be interpreted as evidence of direct or indirect arbitrage in the international capital market. Lance E. Davis' finding that the internal American capital market was poorly arbitraged in this period, suggests that for America at least arbitrage was little better within than between countries (Davis' work is summarised in his contribution to R. W. Fogel and S. L. Engerman, *The Reinterpretation of American Economic History*, New York: Harper & Row, 1971, 'Capital mobility and American economic growth', pp. 285–300). The widely believed assertion that domestic British industry was starved of funds in favor of British investment in Argentine railways and Indian government bonds can be given a similar interpretation.

34 The evidence is described in the footnote to Table 10.2. The interest rate on three-month bankers' bills (Mitchell, *Abstract of British Historical Statistics*, Cambridge University Press, 1962, p. 460) performed better than the consol rate, and was used here.

Index